DRAMATIS PERSONAE

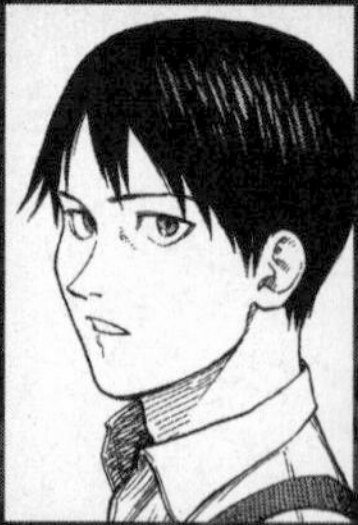
KEI NAGAI

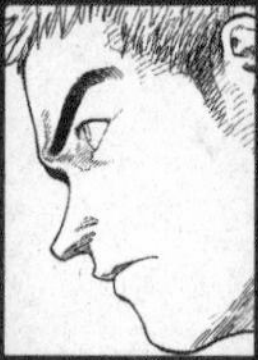
KO NAKANO

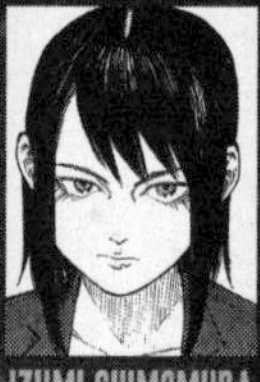
IZUMI SHIMOMURA

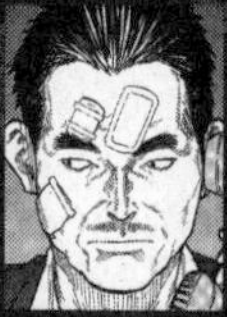
MANABE

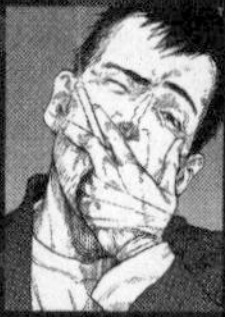
DR. IKUYA OGURA

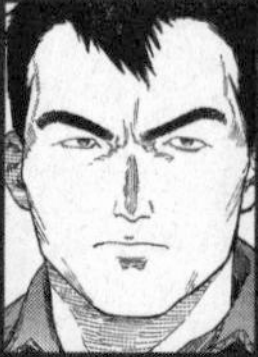
AKIYAMA

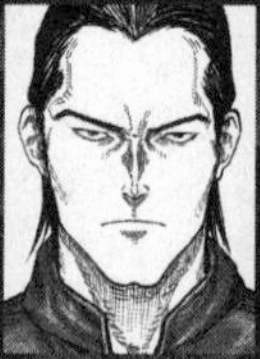
TANAKA

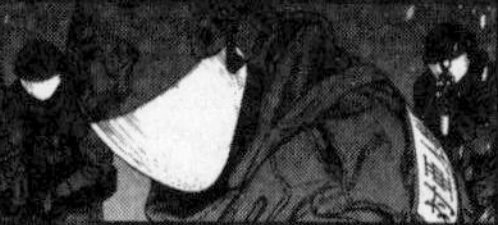
ANTI-DEMI SPECIAL FORCES

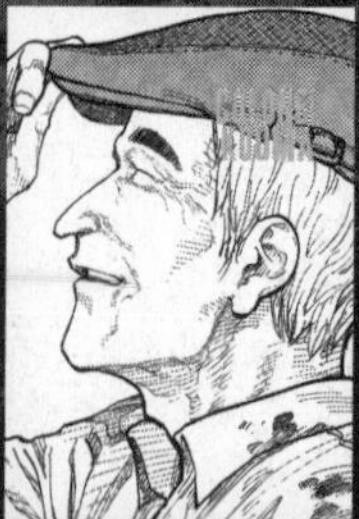
SATO

File: 74

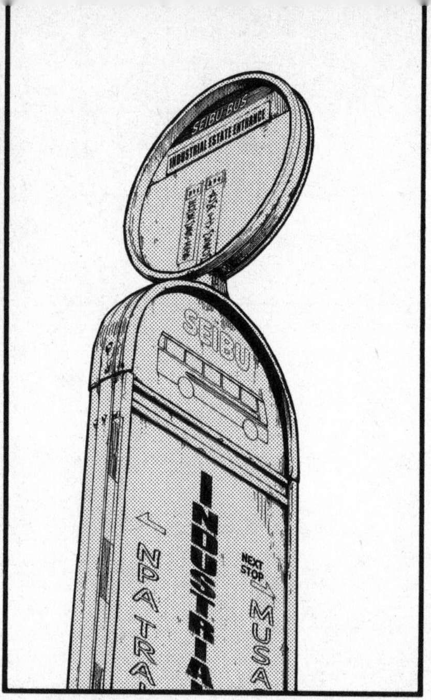
SEIBU BUS
INDUSTRIAL ESTATE ENTRANCE
SEIBU
NEXT STOP

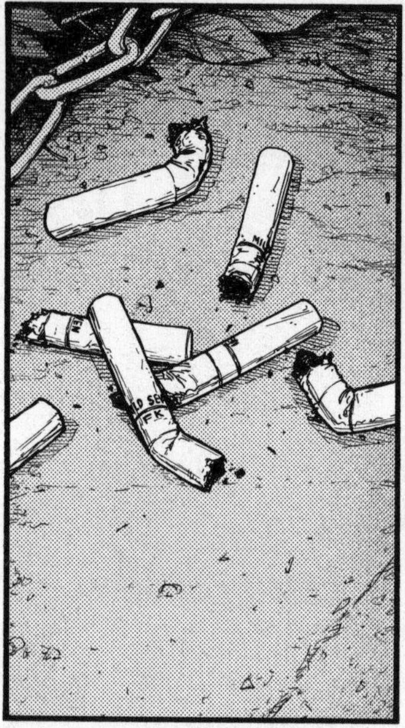

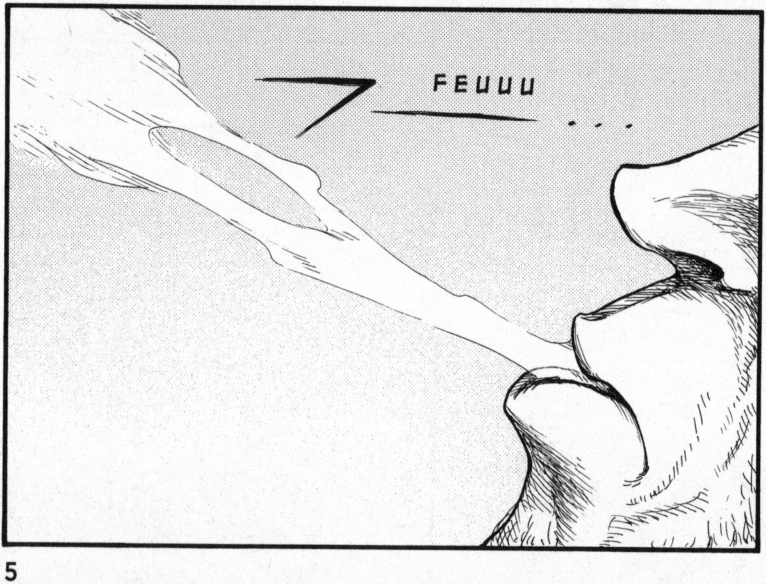
FEUUU...

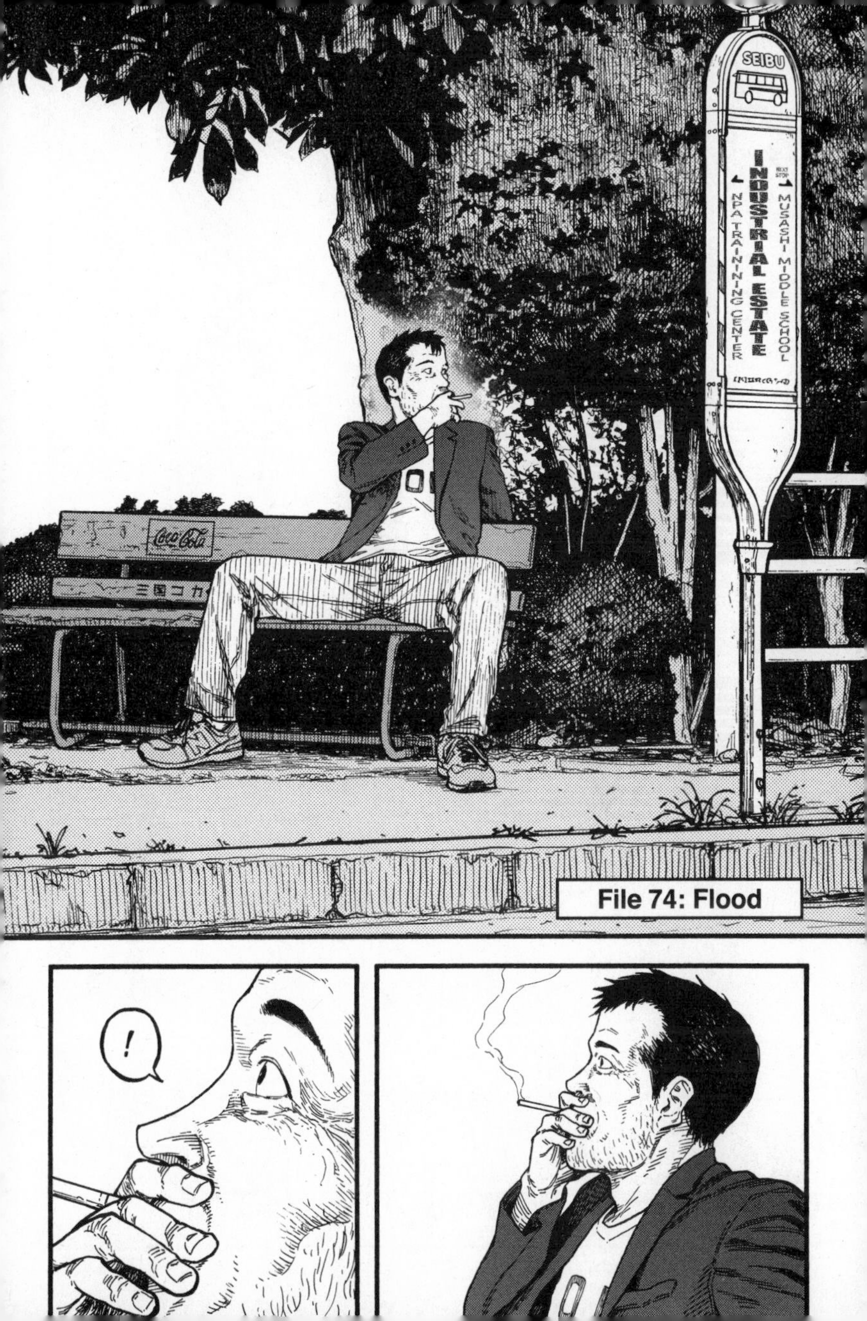
SEIBU
INDUSTRIAL ESTATE
NEXT STOP
MUSASHI MIDDLE SCHOOL
NPA TRAINING CENTER
Coca-Cola
三国コカ
File 74: Flood
!

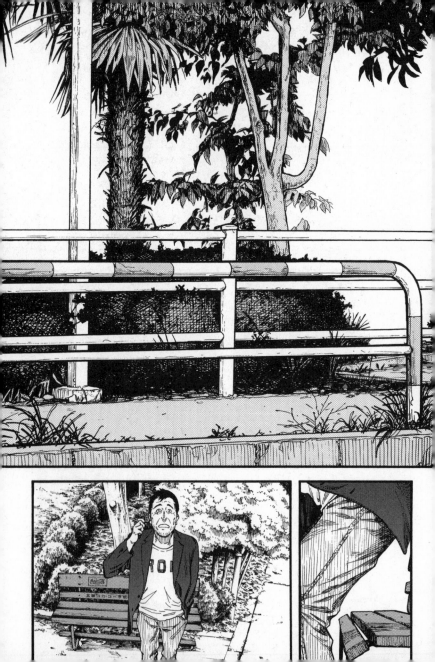

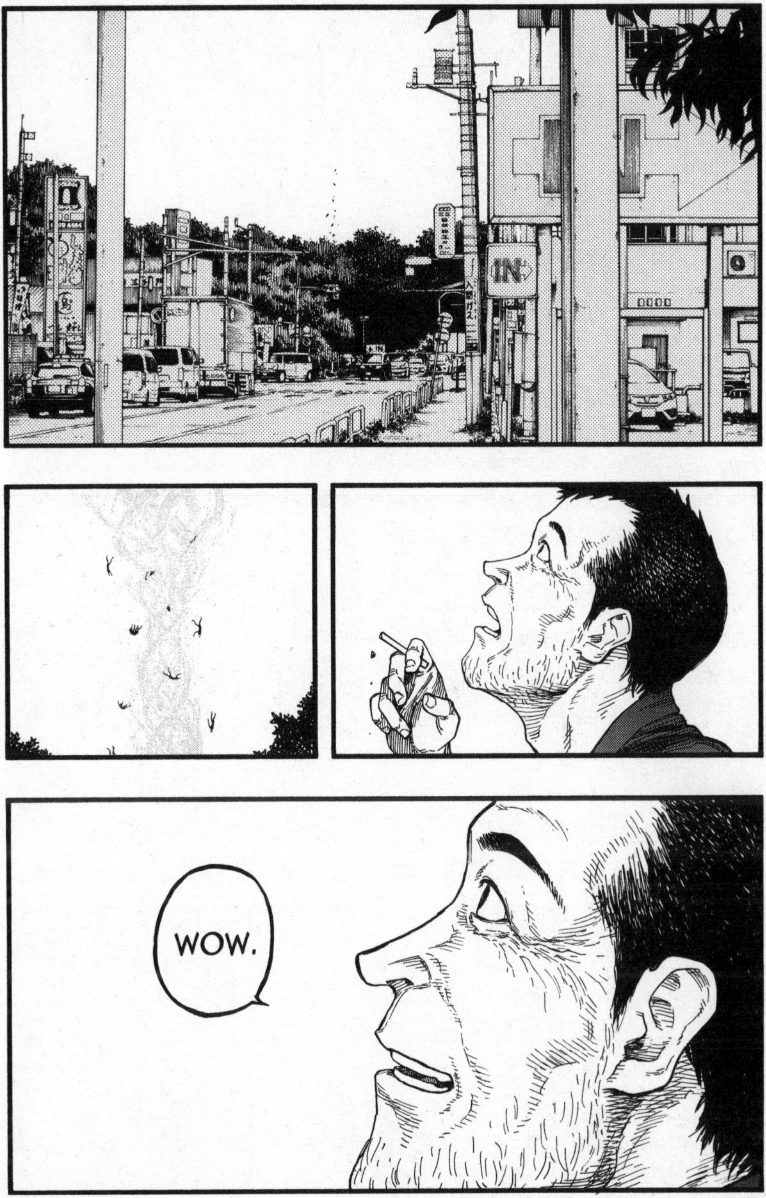
IN
WOW.

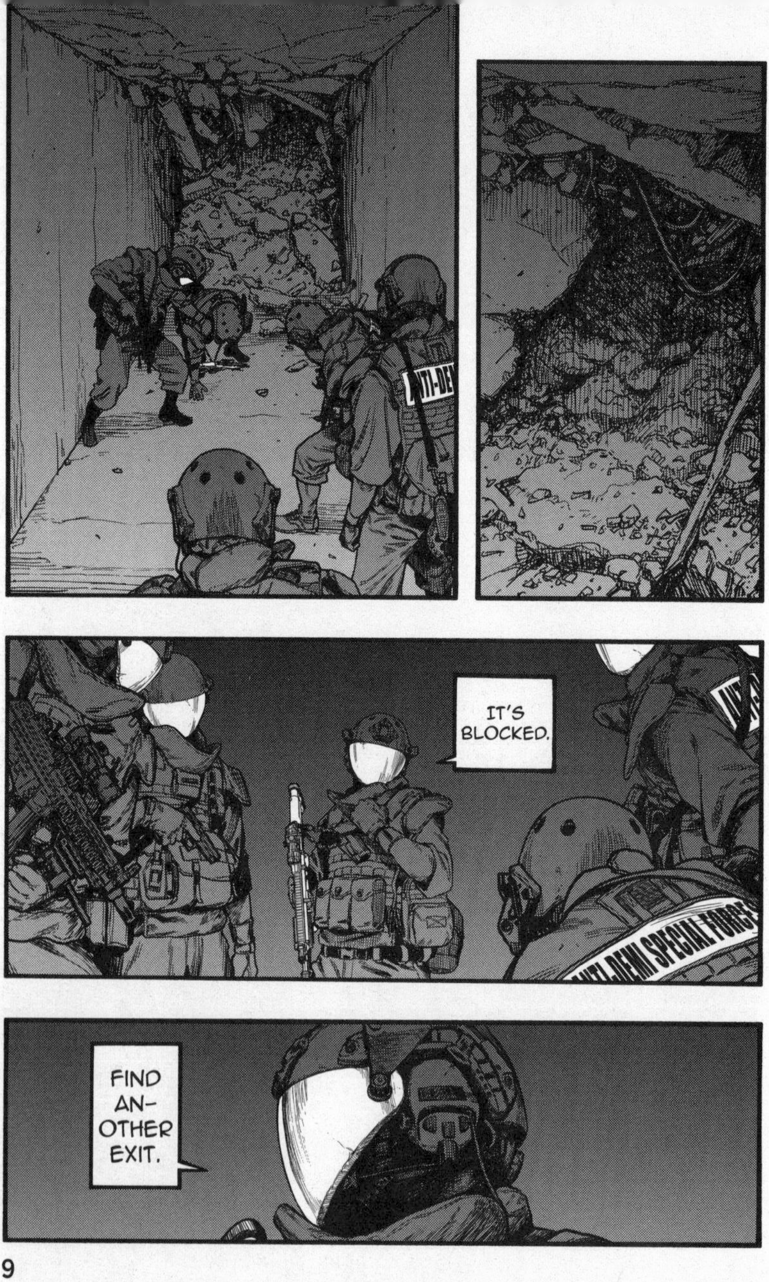
IT'S BLOCKED.
FIND AN-OTHER EXIT.

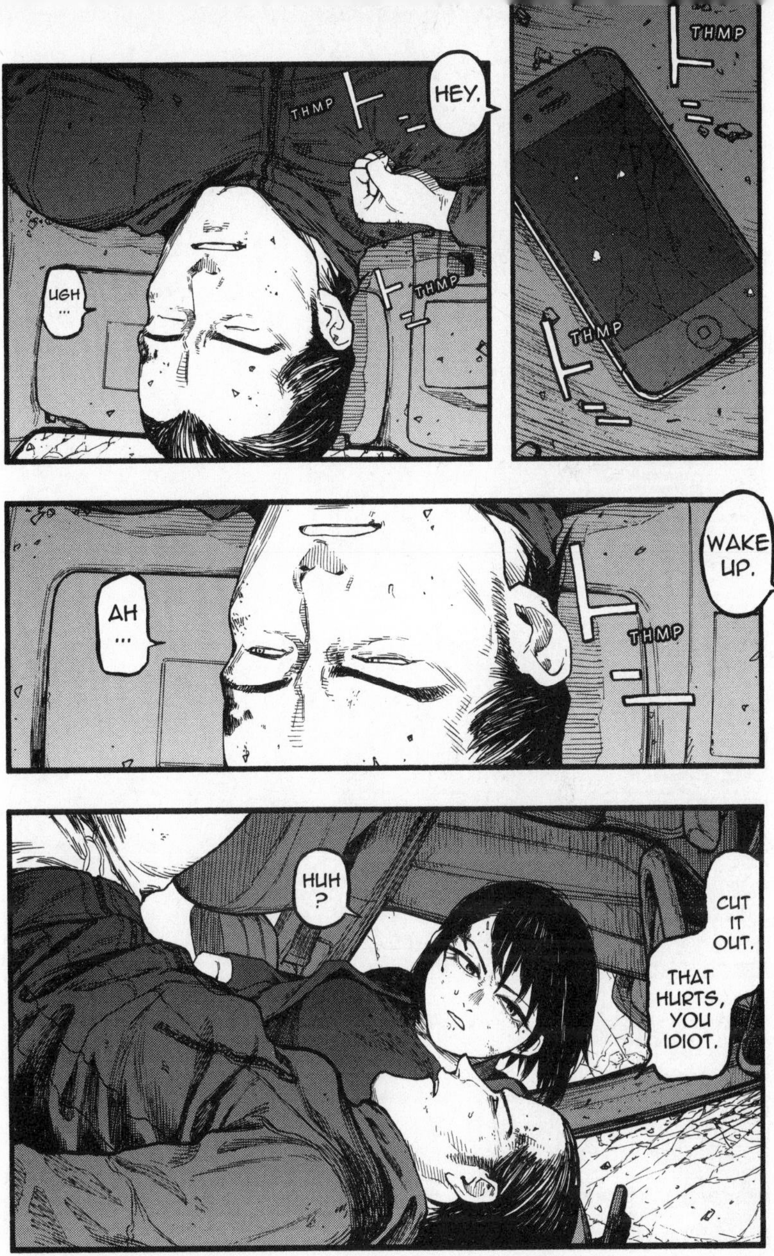
THMP
THMP
HEY.
THMP
THMP
UGH ...
WAKE UP.
THMP
AH ...
CUT IT OUT.
THAT HURTS, YOU IDIOT.
HUH?

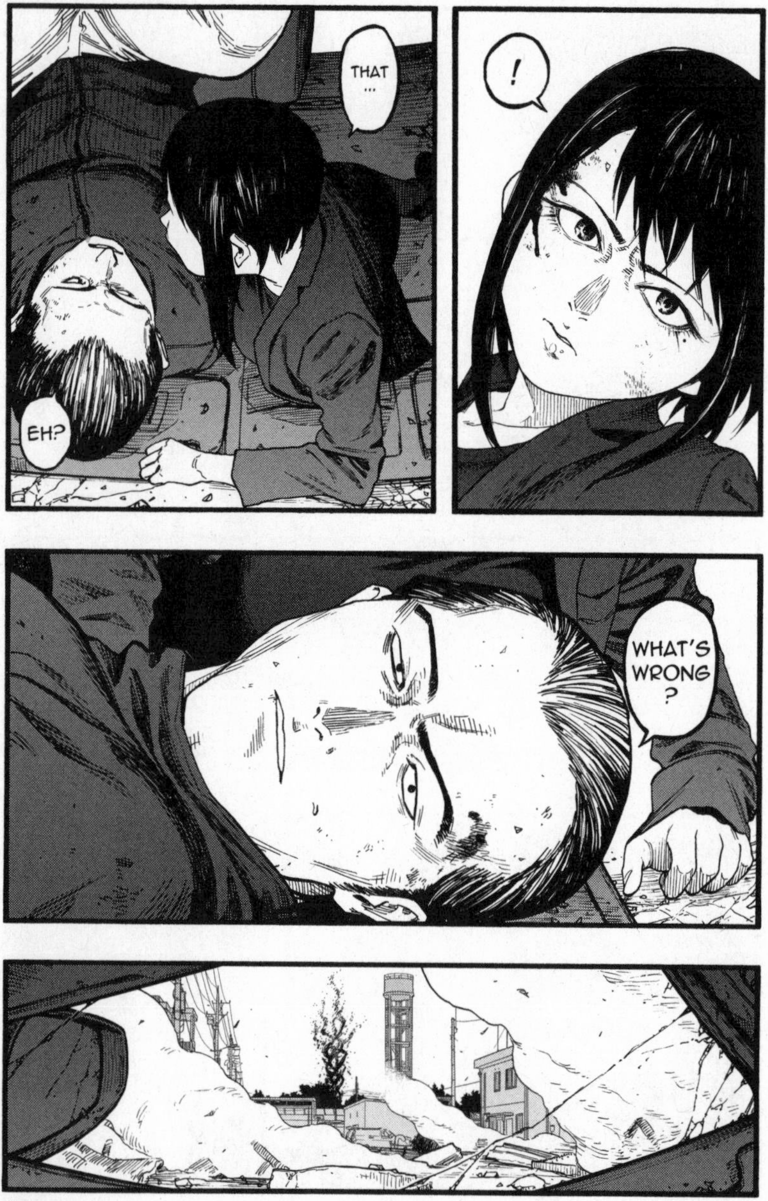
!
THAT ...
EH?
WHAT'S WRONG ?

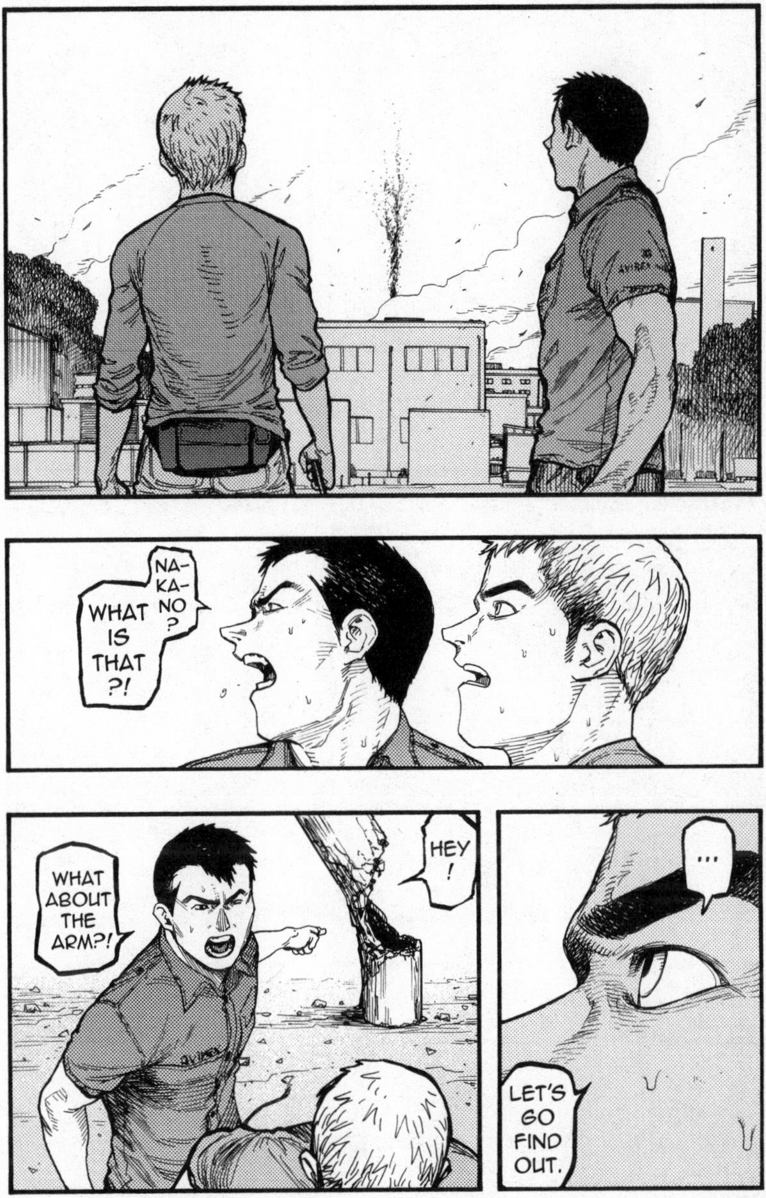
NA-KA-NO?
WHAT IS THAT?!
...
LET'S GO FIND OUT.
HEY!
WHAT ABOUT THE ARM?!

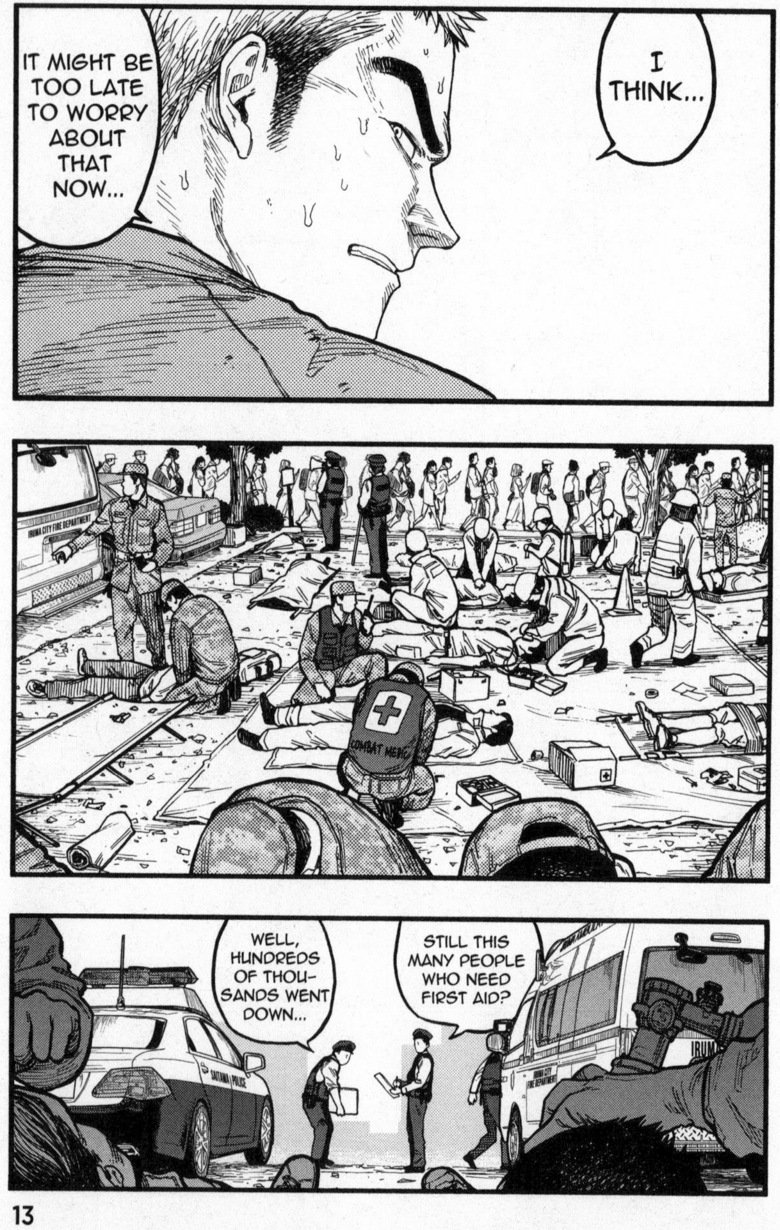
I THINK...
IT MIGHT BE TOO LATE TO WORRY ABOUT THAT NOW...
IRUMA CITY FIRE DEPARTMENT
COMBAT MEDIC
STILL THIS MANY PEOPLE WHO NEED FIRST AID?
WELL, HUNDREDS OF THOU-SANDS WENT DOWN...

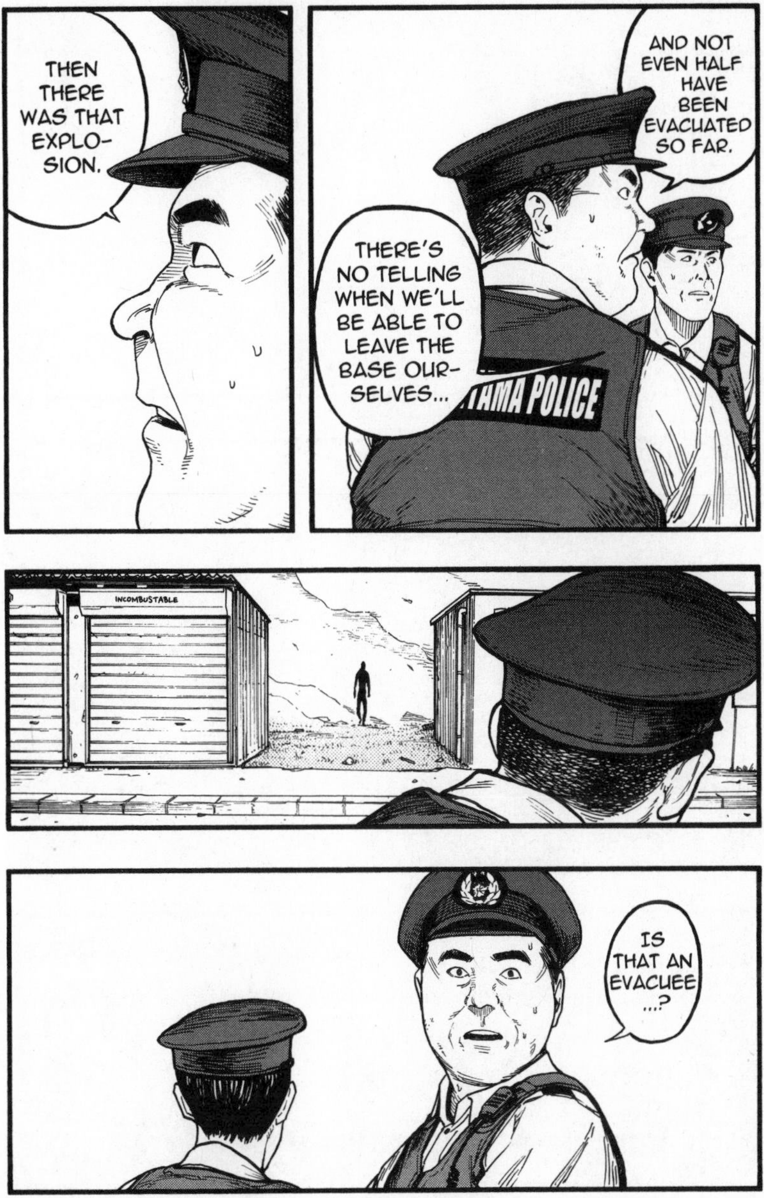
AND NOT EVEN HALF HAVE BEEN EVACUATED SO FAR.
THERE'S NO TELLING WHEN WE'LL BE ABLE TO LEAVE THE BASE OUR-SELVES...
TAMA POLICE
THEN THERE WAS THAT EXPLO-SION.
INCOMBUSTABLE
IS THAT AN EVACUEE ...?

ZAKK
LOOK BOTH WAYS
ZAKK
ZAKK
ZAKK
ZAKK

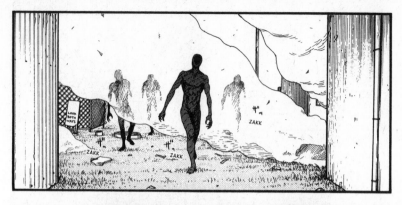

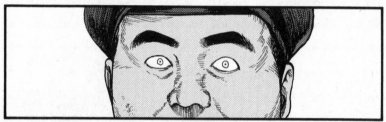

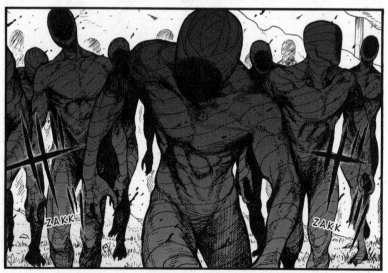

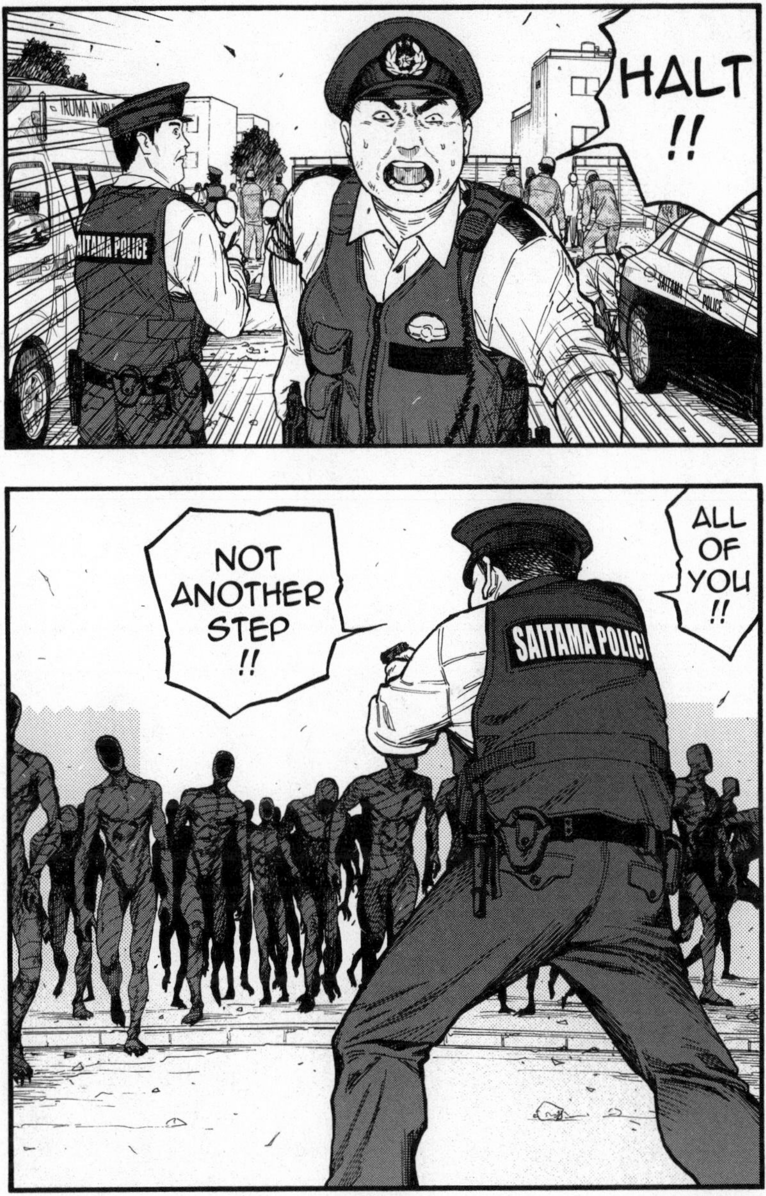
HALT !!
SAITAMA POLICE
ALL OF YOU !!
NOT ANOTHER STEP !!

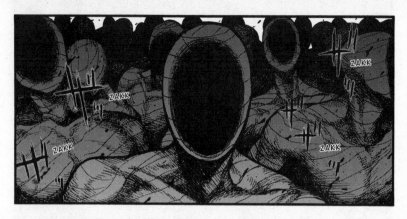

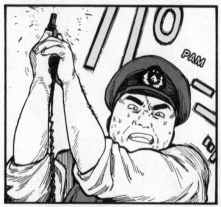

PAM

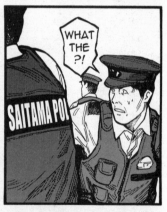

WHAT THE ?!

SAITAMA POL

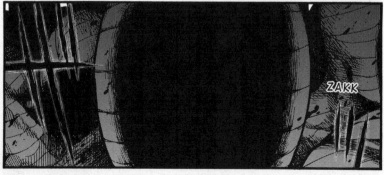

ZAKK

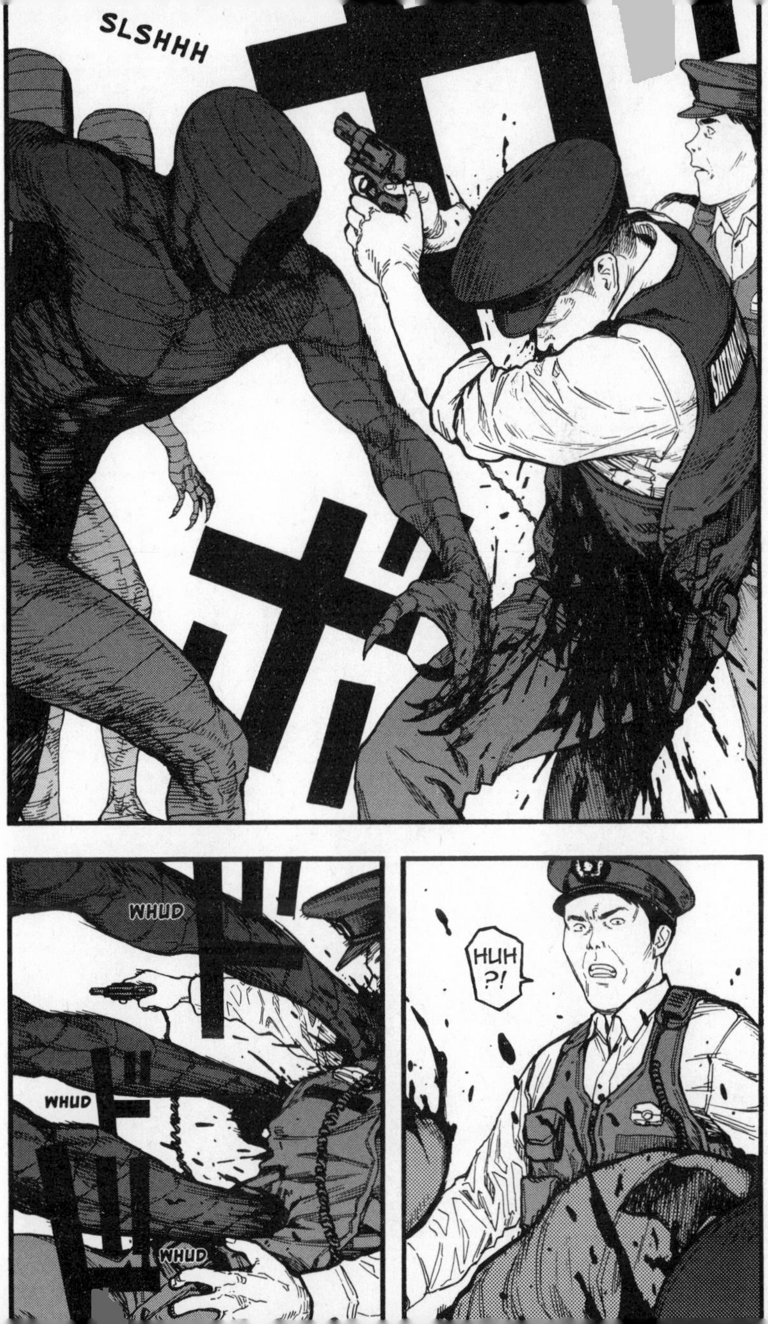
SLSHHH
HUH ?!
WHUD
WHUD
WHUD

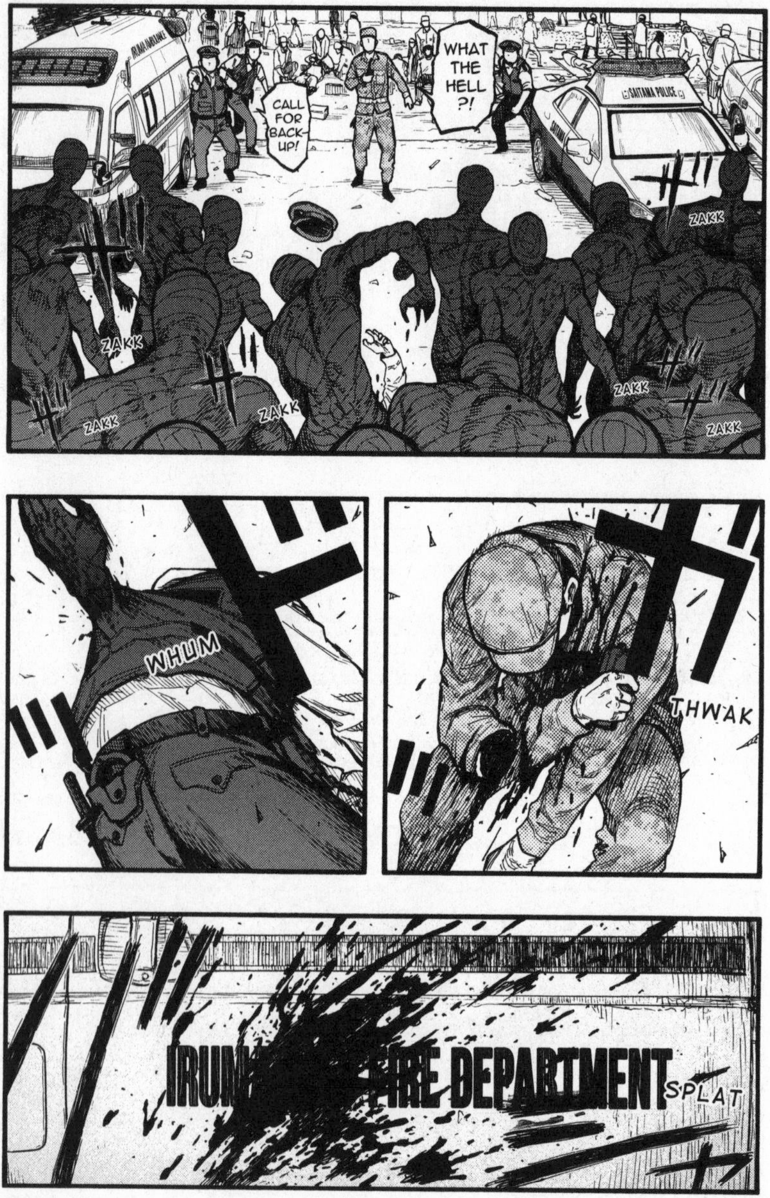
WHAT THE HELL ?!
CALL FOR BACK-UP!
ZAKK
ZAKK
ZAKK
ZAKK
ZAKK
ZAKK
THWAK
WHUM
FIRE DEPARTMENT
SPLAT

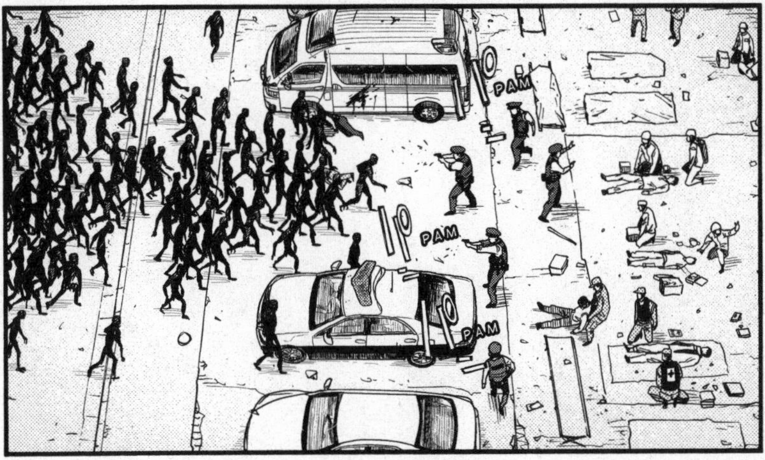
PAM
PAM
PAM

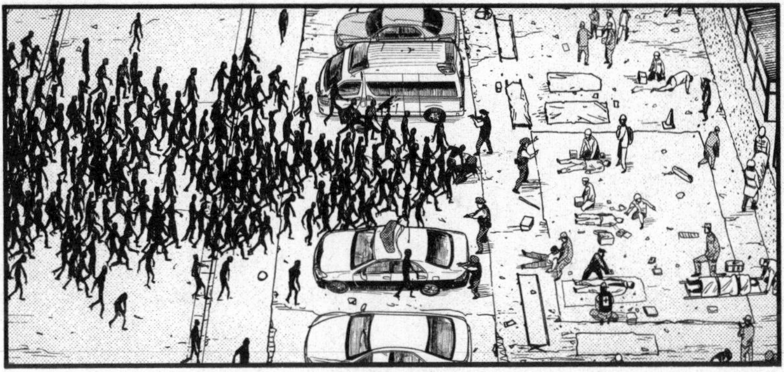

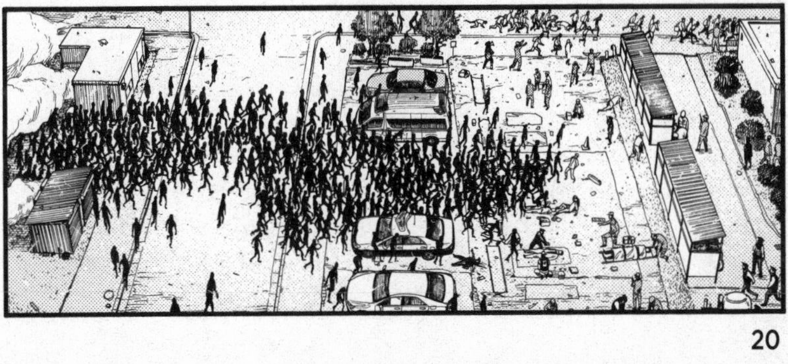

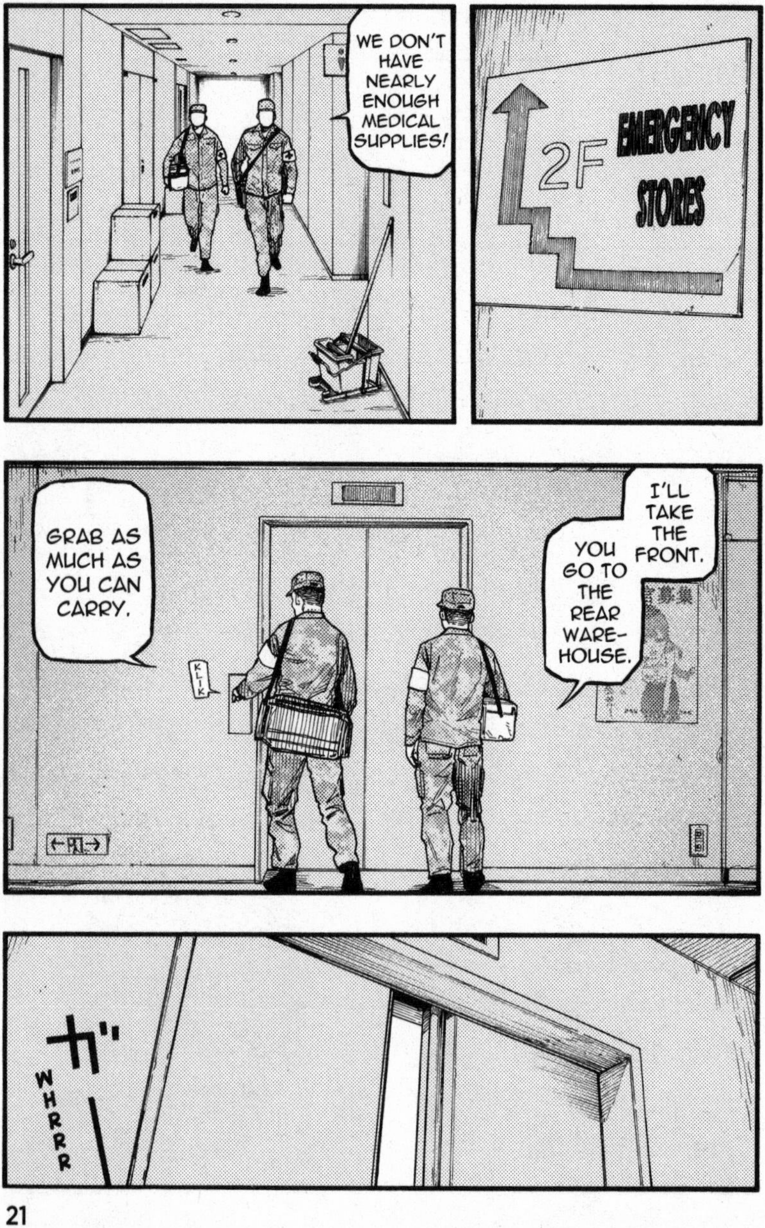
2F
EMERGENCY STORES
WE DON'T HAVE NEARLY ENOUGH MEDICAL SUPPLIES!
I'LL TAKE THE FRONT.
YOU GO TO THE REAR WARE-HOUSE.
KLIK
GRAB AS MUCH AS YOU CAN CARRY.
ガ
WHRRR

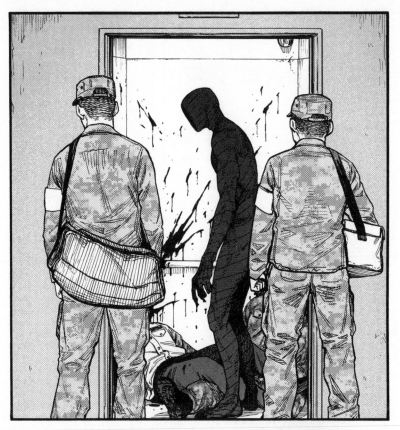

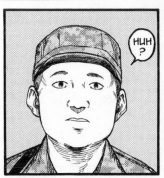

НИН
？

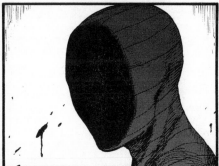

22

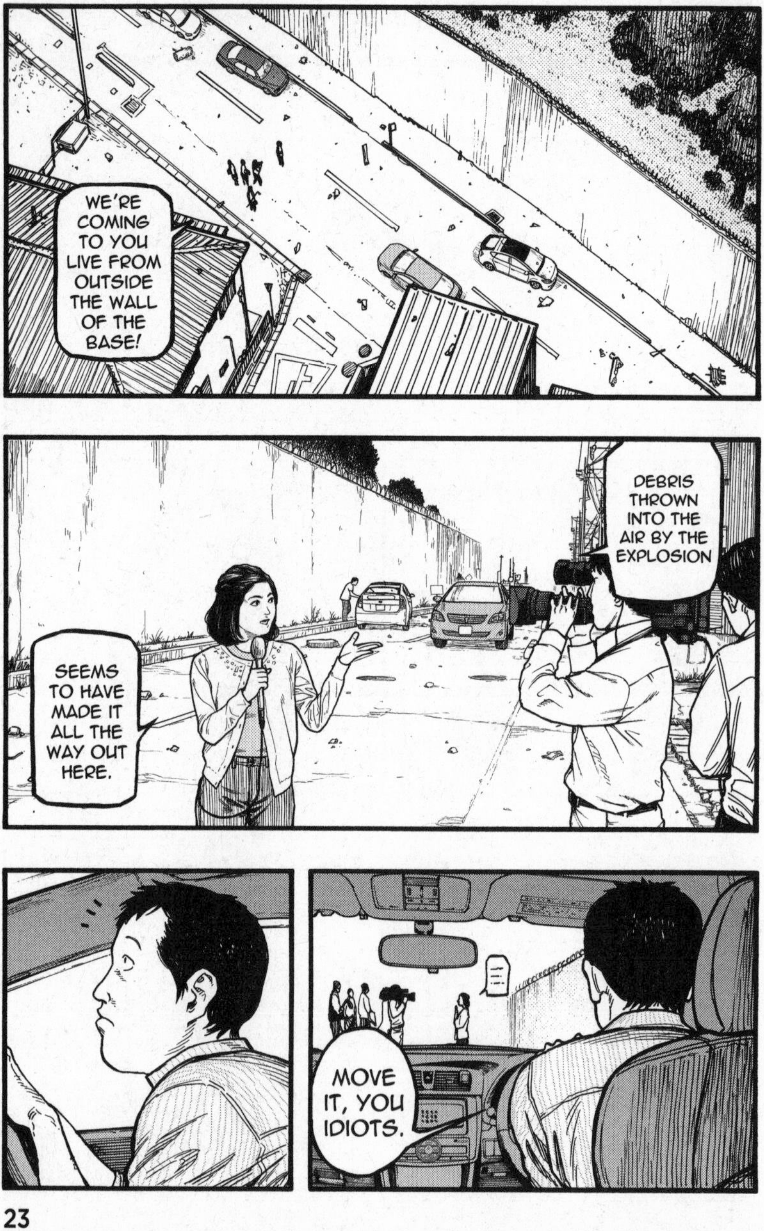
WE'RE COMING TO YOU LIVE FROM OUTSIDE THE WALL OF THE BASE!
DEBRIS THROWN INTO THE AIR BY THE EXPLOSION
SEEMS TO HAVE MADE IT ALL THE WAY OUT HERE.
MOVE IT, YOU IDIOTS.

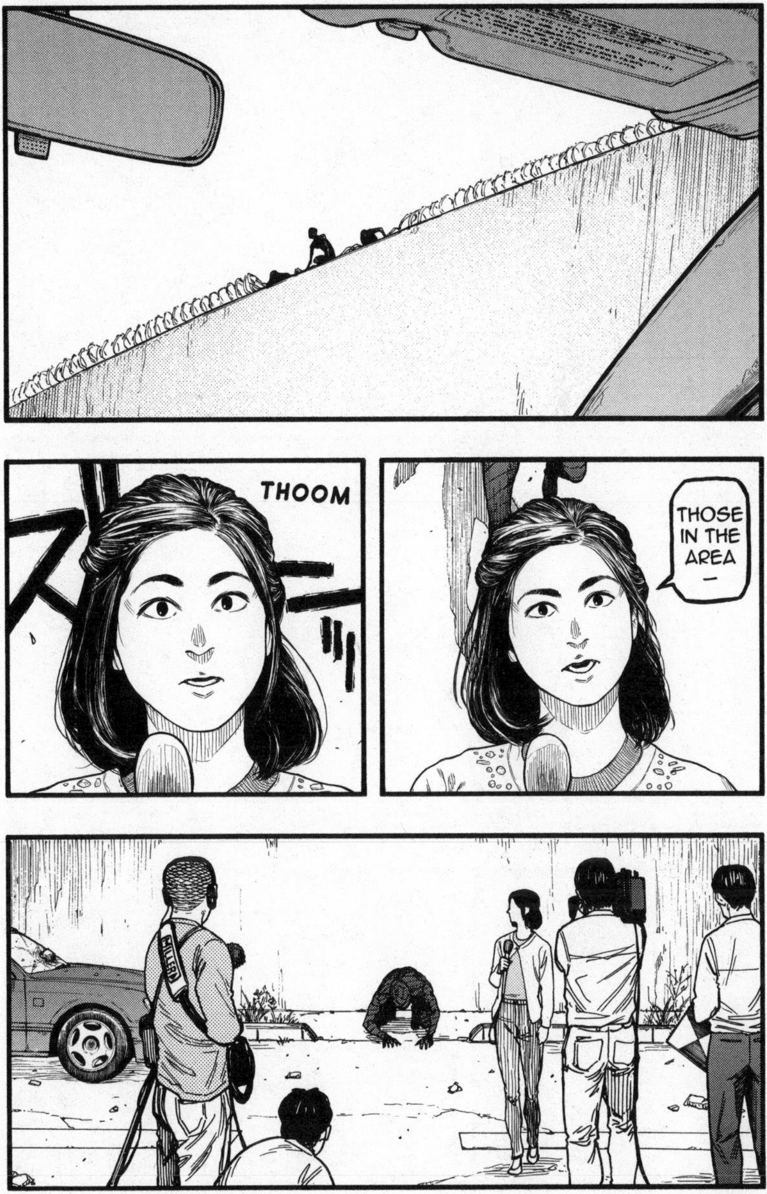
THOSE IN THE AREA —
THOOM

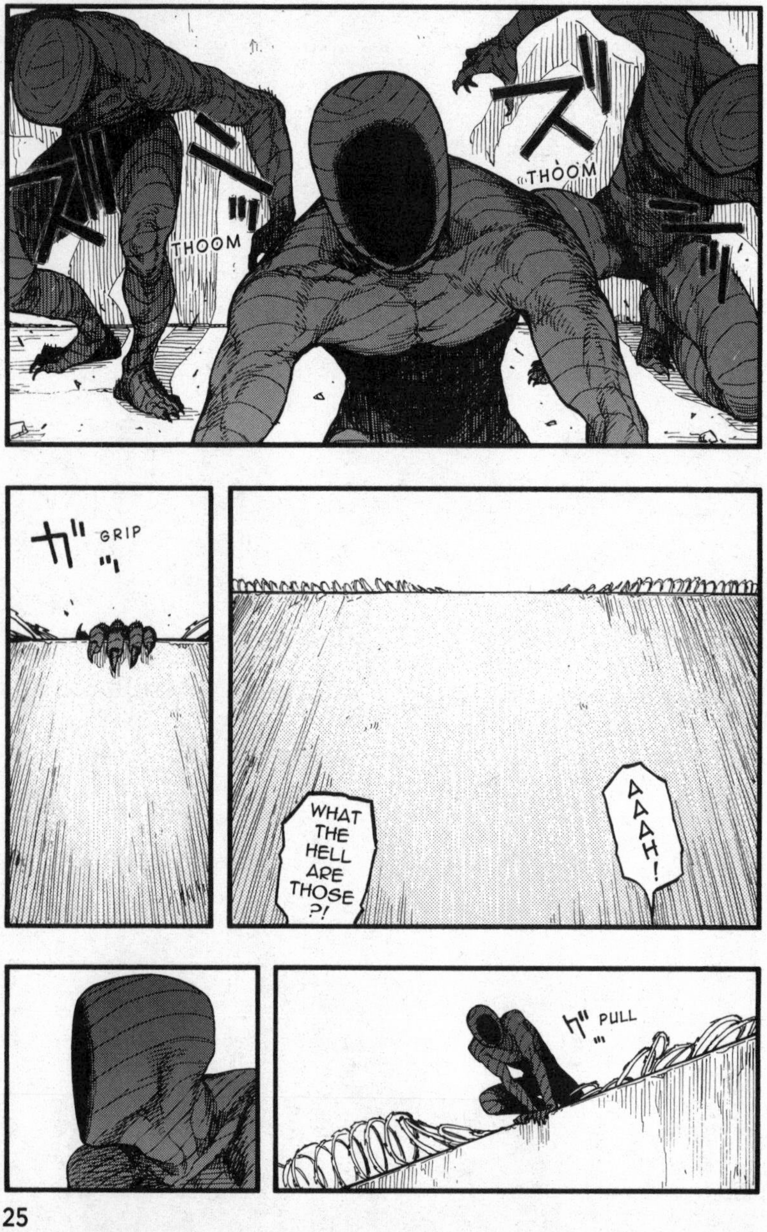
THOOM
THOOM
AAAH!
WHAT THE HELL ARE THOSE ?!
GRIP
PULL

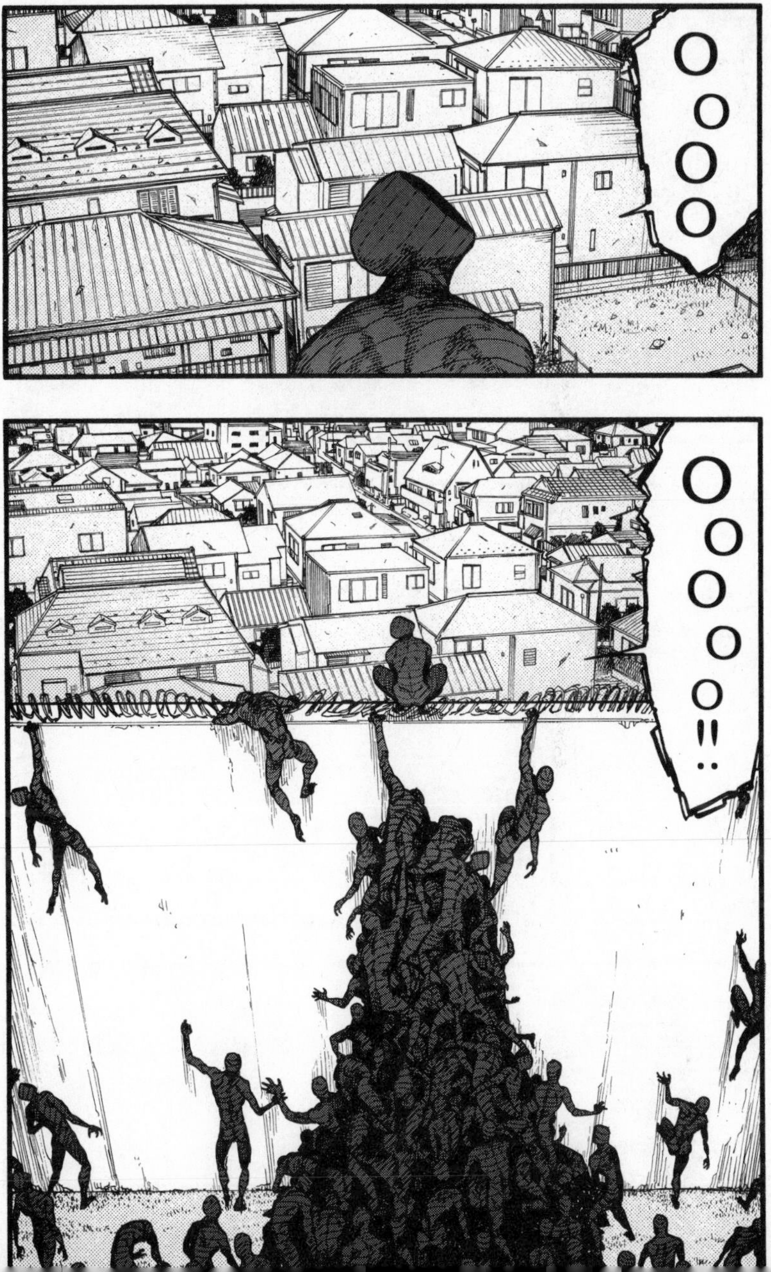
OOOO
OOOOO!!

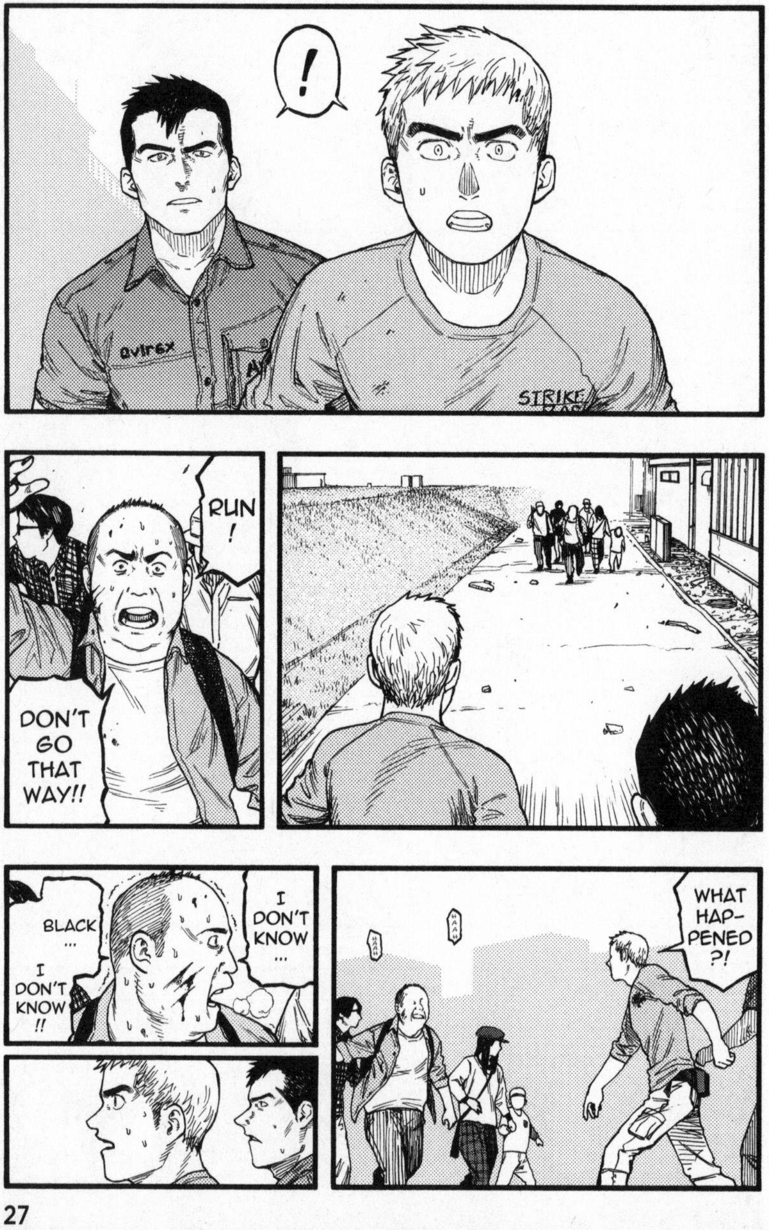
!
avirex
STRIKE
DON'T GO THAT WAY!!
RUN!
WHAT HAP-PENED?!
HAAH
HAAH
I DON'T KNOW...
BLACK...
I DON'T KNOW!!

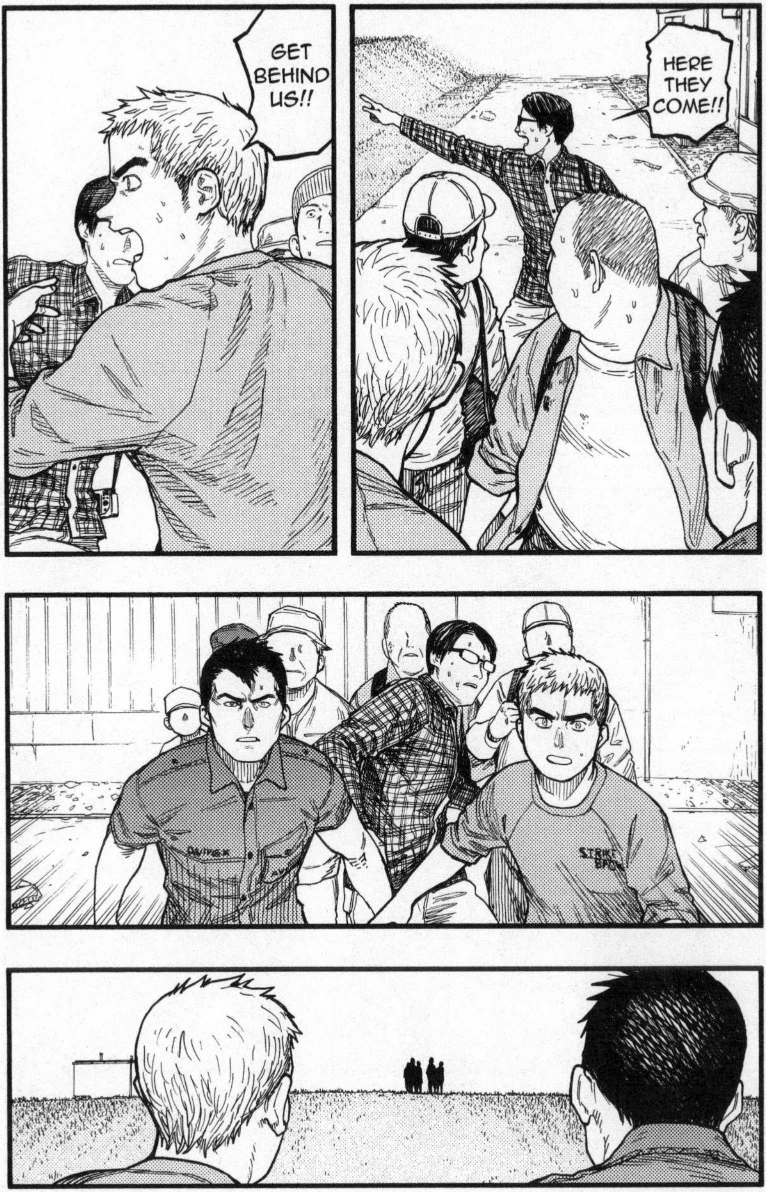
HERE THEY COME!!
GET BEHIND US!!

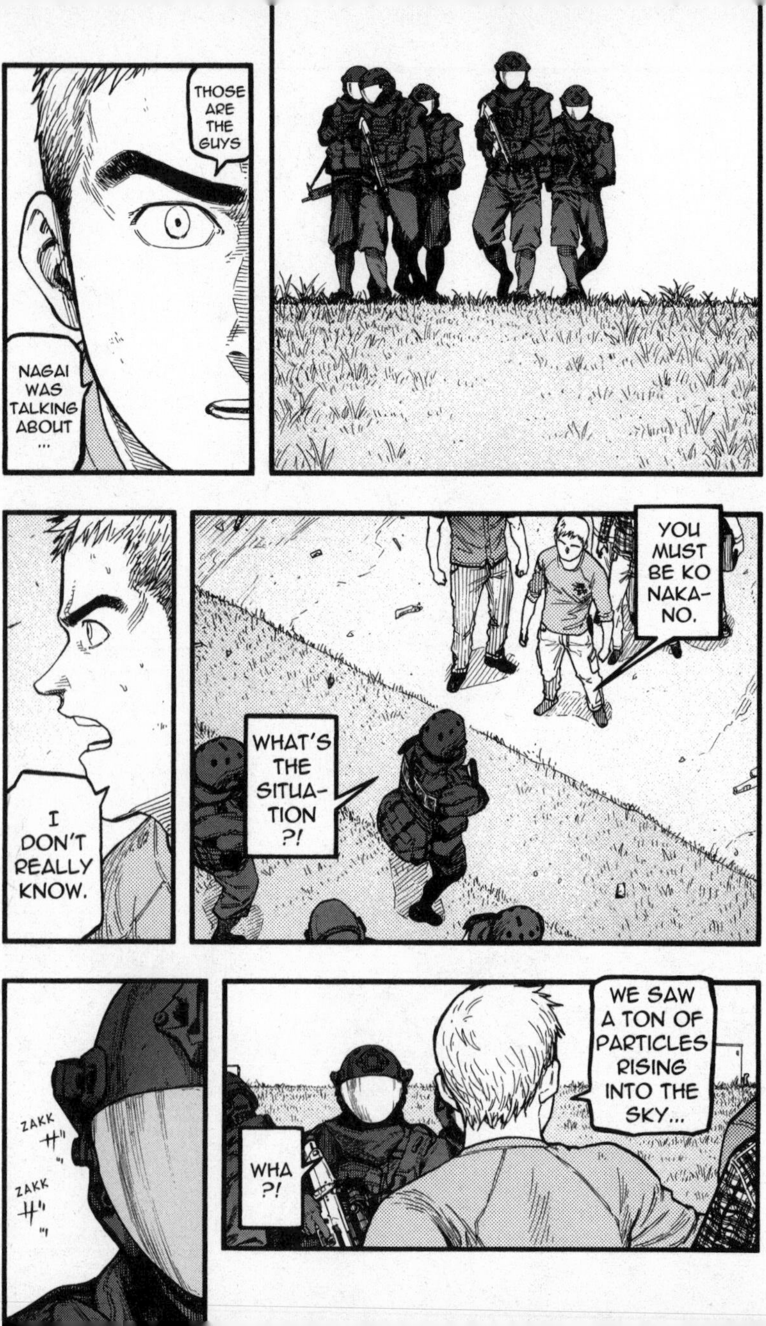
THOSE ARE THE GUYS
NAGAI WAS TALKING ABOUT ...
YOU MUST BE KO NAKA-NO.
WHAT'S THE SITUA-TION ?!
I DON'T REALLY KNOW.
WE SAW A TON OF PARTICLES RISING INTO THE SKY...
WHA ?!
ZAKK
ZAKK

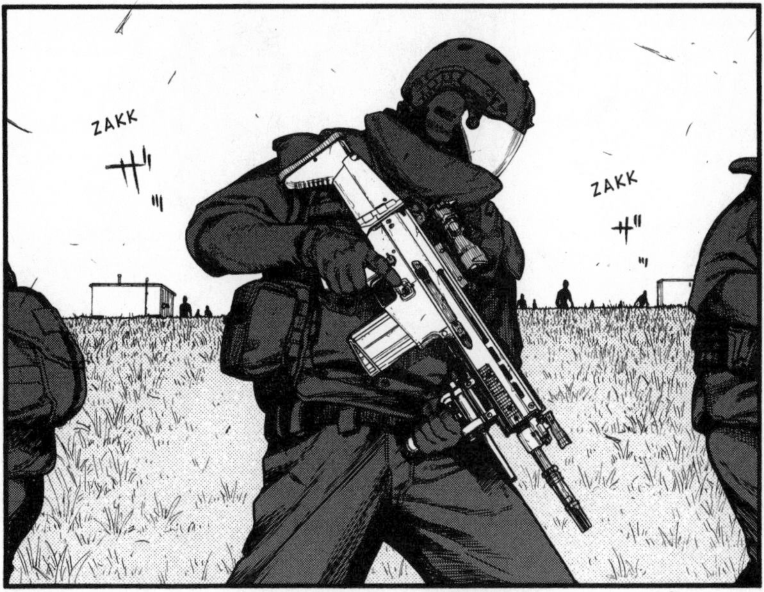
ZAKK
ZAKK
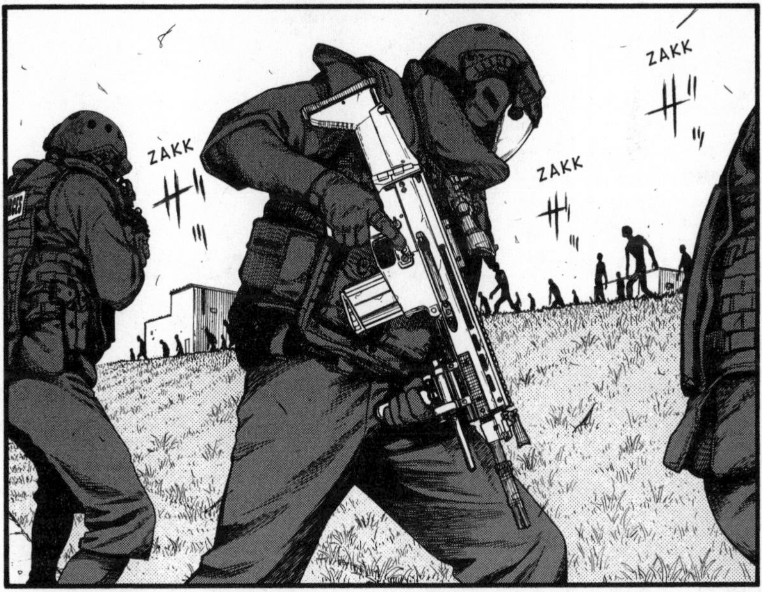
ZAKK
ZAKK
ZAKK

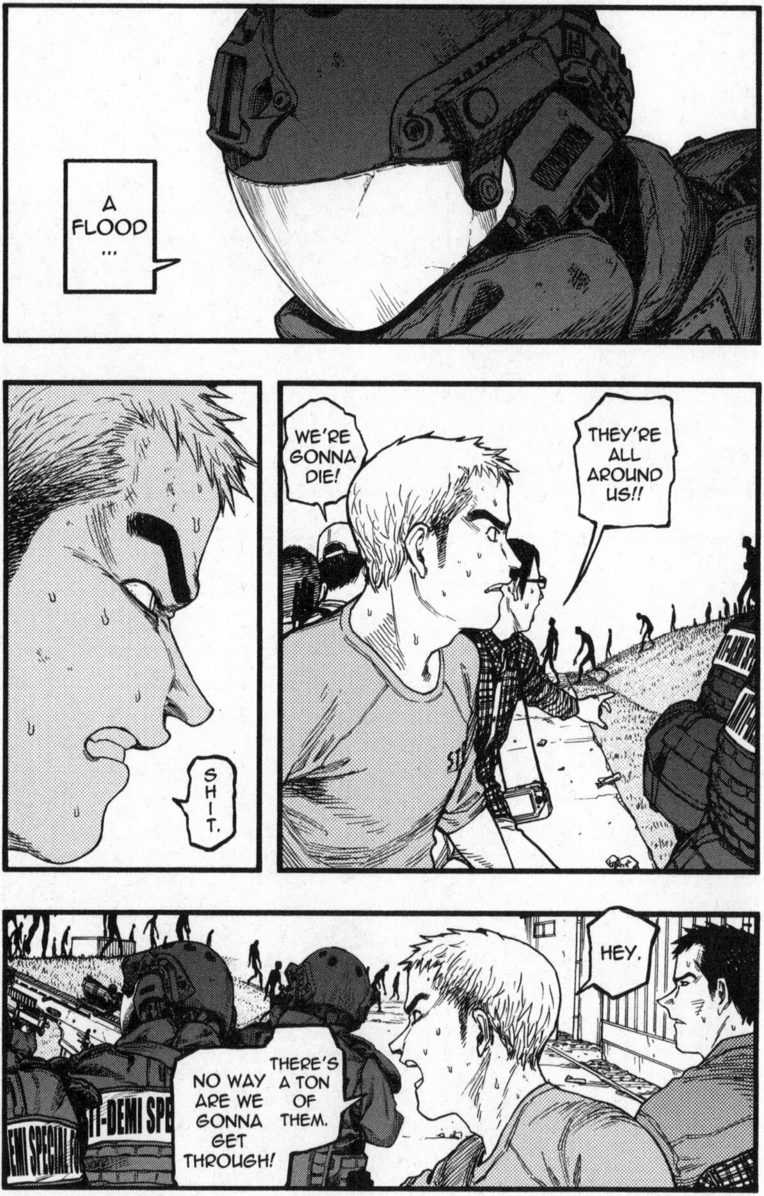
A FLOOD ...
THEY'RE ALL AROUND US!!
WE'RE GONNA DIE!
SHIT.
HEY.
THERE'S A TON OF THEM.
NO WAY ARE WE GONNA GET THROUGH!

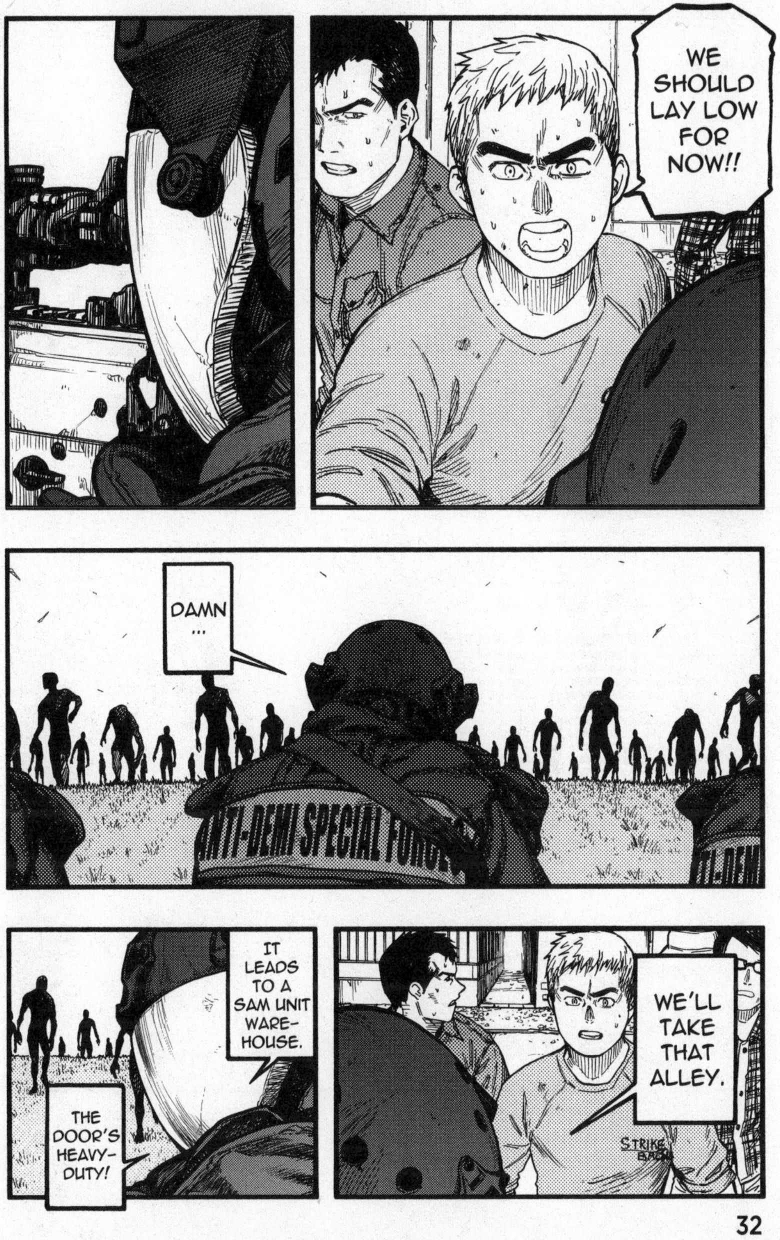
WE SHOULD LAY LOW FOR NOW!!
DAMN ...
ANTI-DEMI SPECIAL FORCE
WE'LL TAKE THAT ALLEY.
IT LEADS TO A SAM UNIT WARE-HOUSE.
THE DOOR'S HEAVY-DUTY!

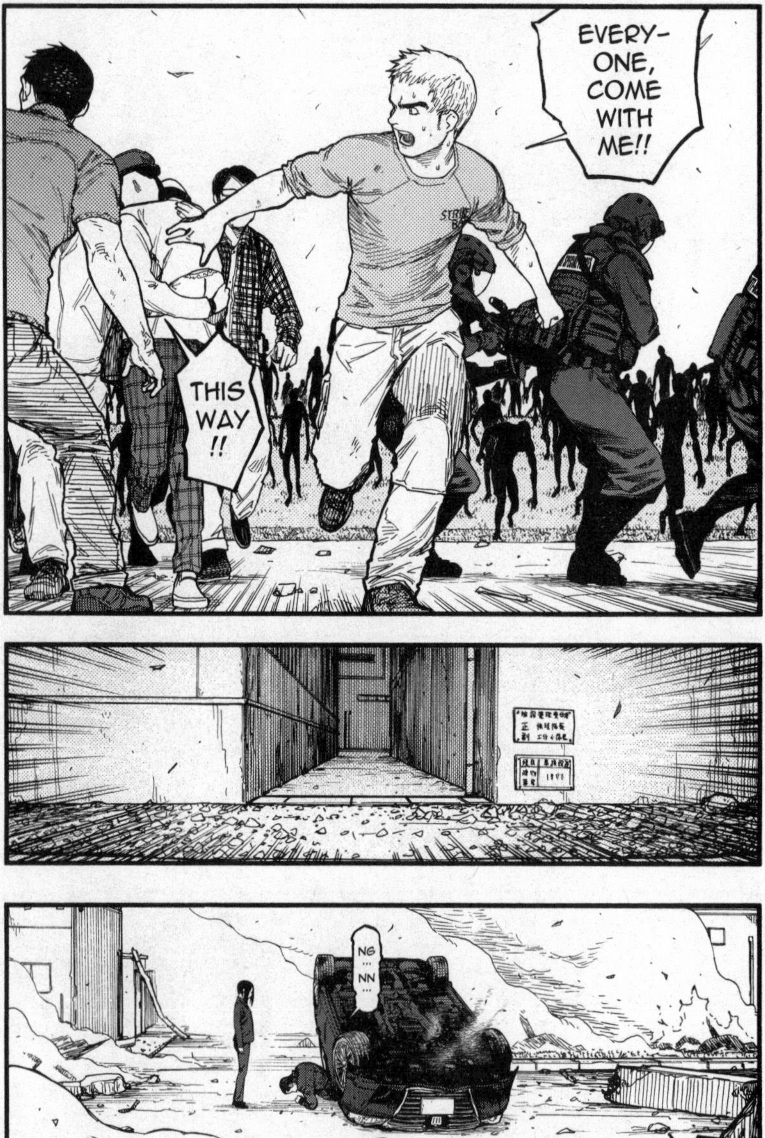
EVERY-ONE, COME WITH ME!!
THIS WAY !!
NG... NN...

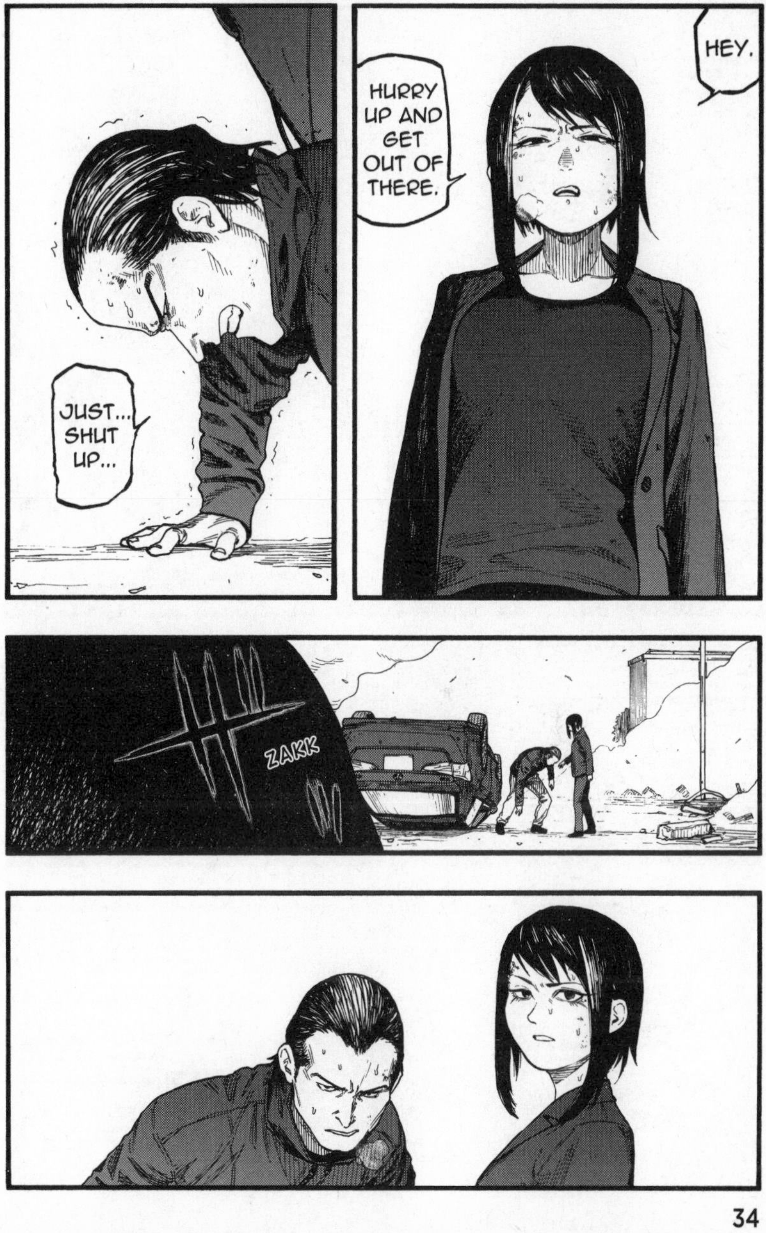
HEY.
HURRY UP AND GET OUT OF THERE.
JUST... SHUT UP...
ZAKK

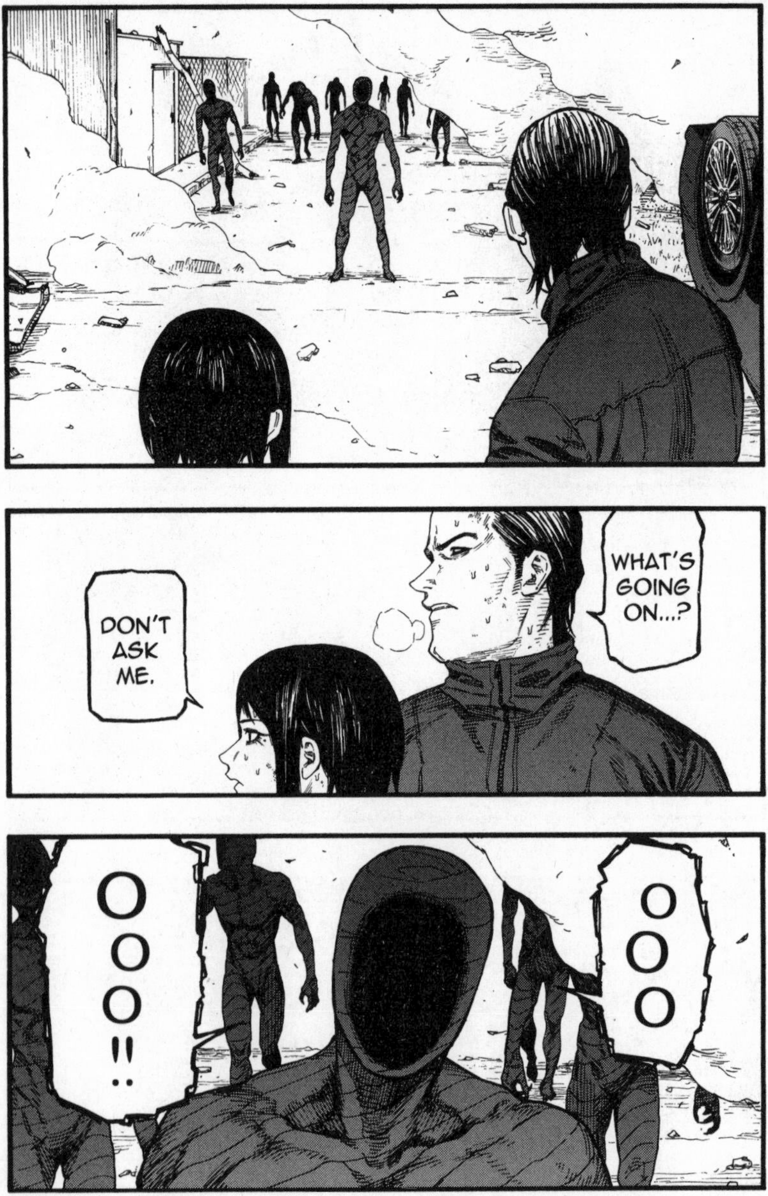
WHAT'S GOING ON...?
DON'T ASK ME.
OOO
OOO!!

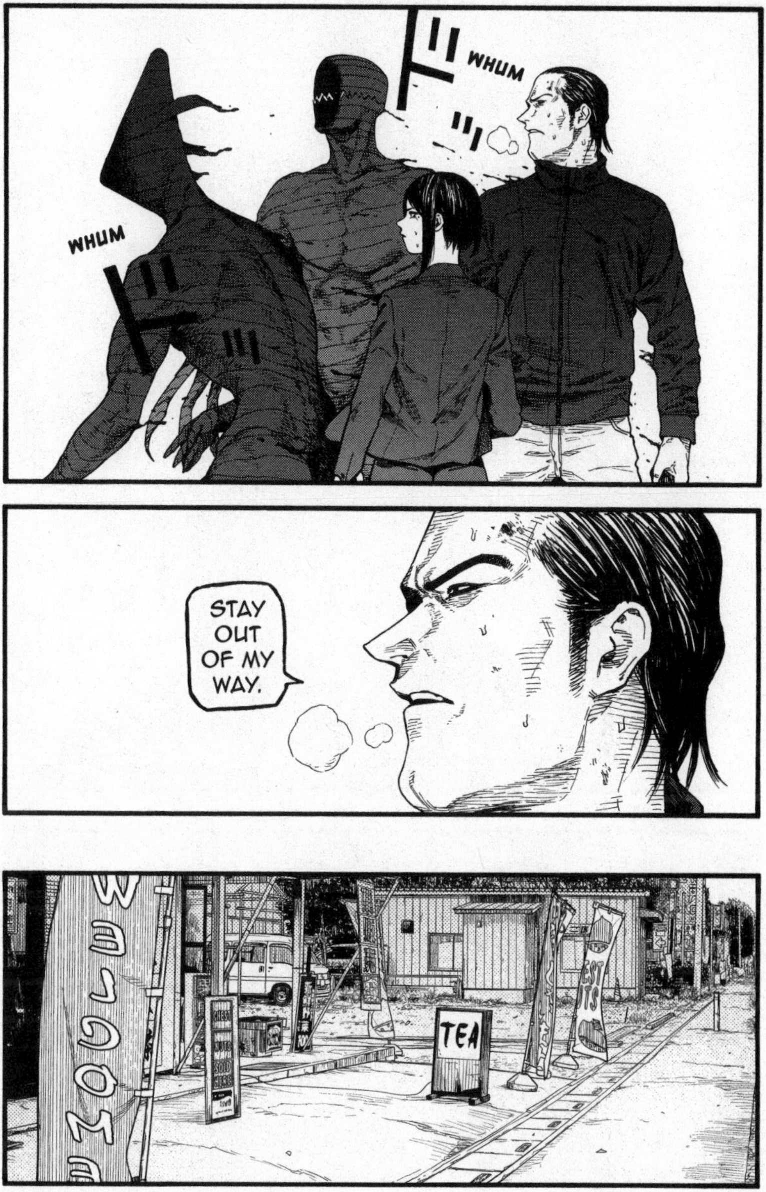
WHUM
WHUM
STAY OUT OF MY WAY.
WELCOME
TEA

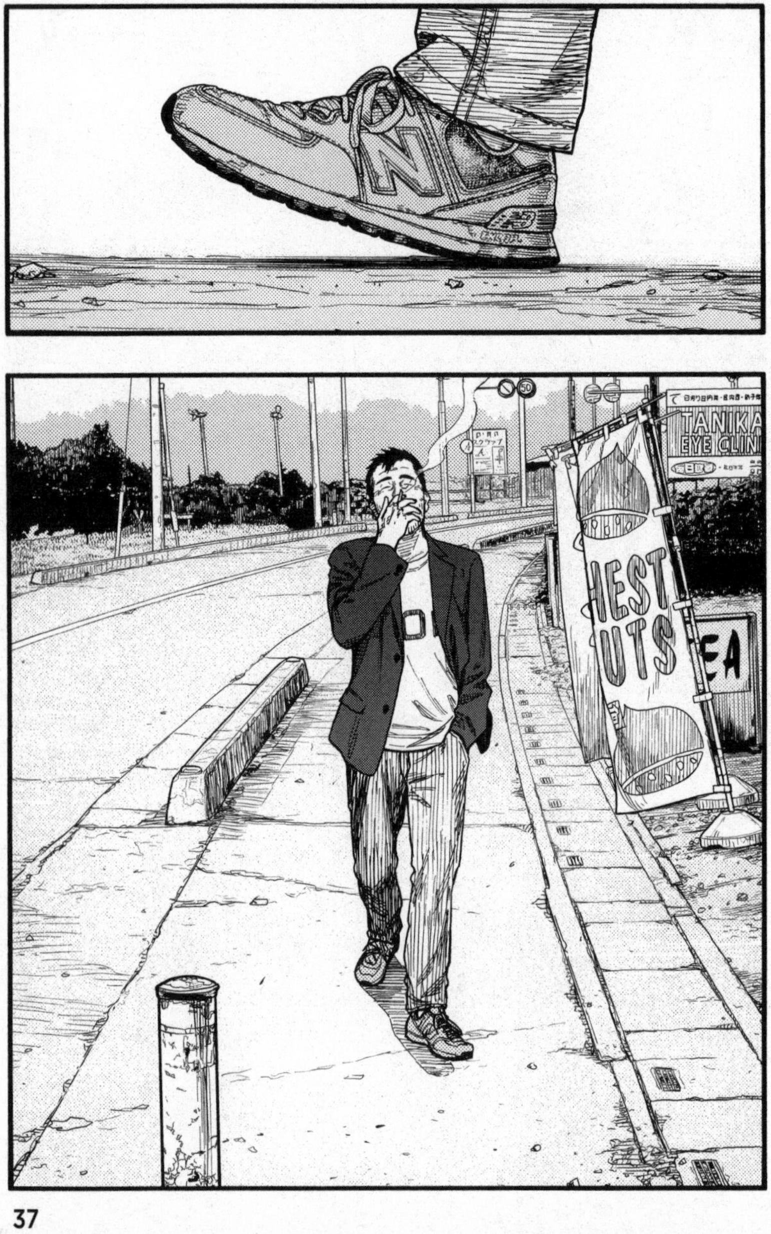
50
TANIKA
EYE CLINI
HEST
UTS
EA

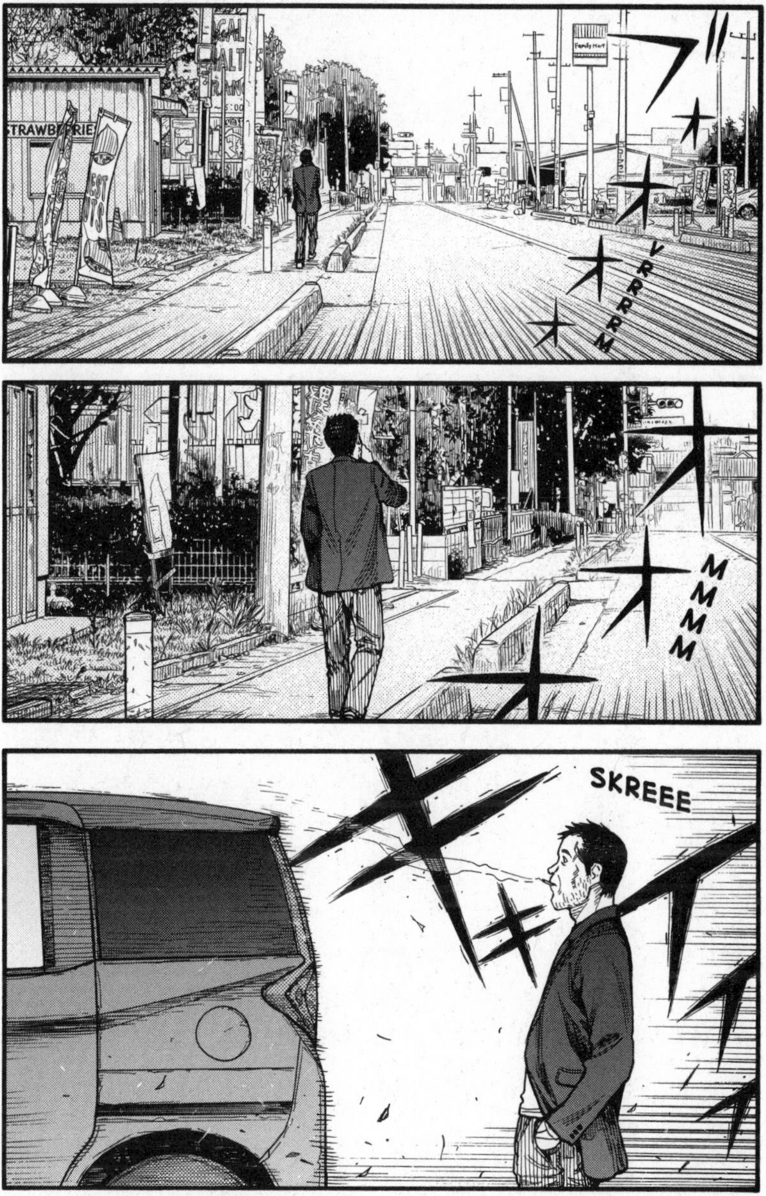
VRRRRM
MMMM
SKREEE

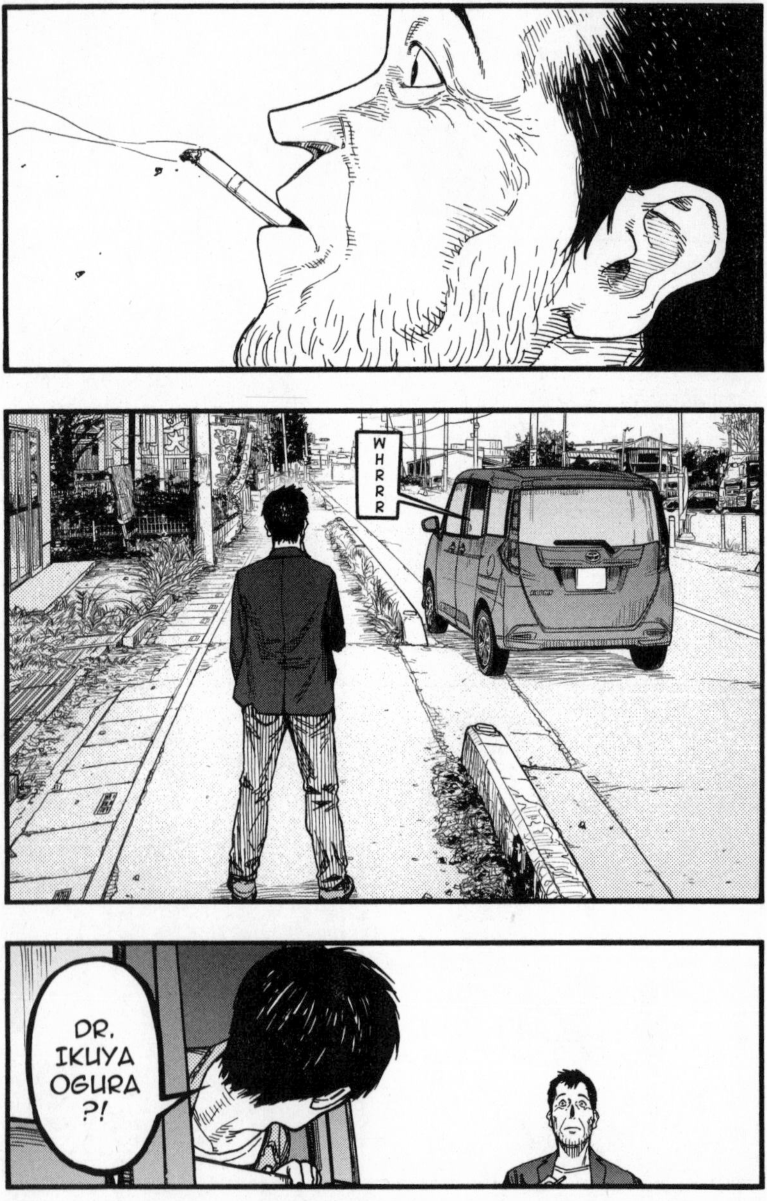
WHRRR
DR. IKUYA OGURA ?!

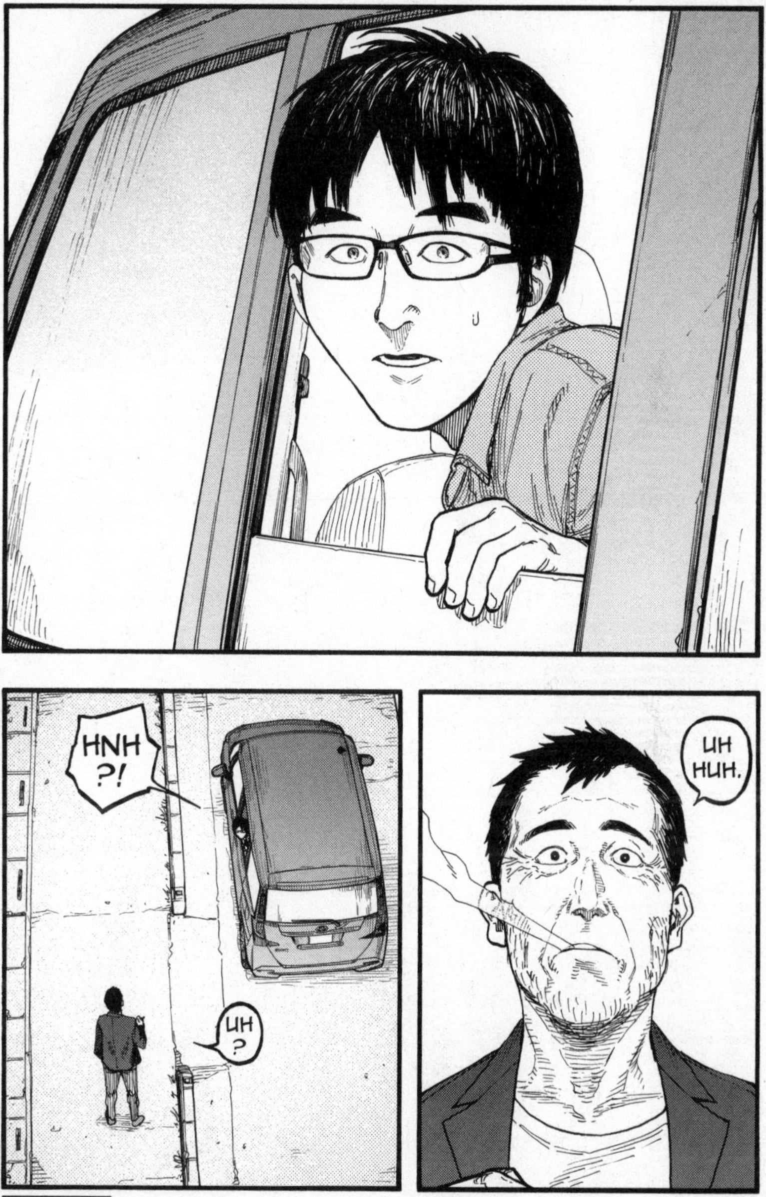
UH HUH.
HNH ?!
UH ?

File:74 End

File: 75

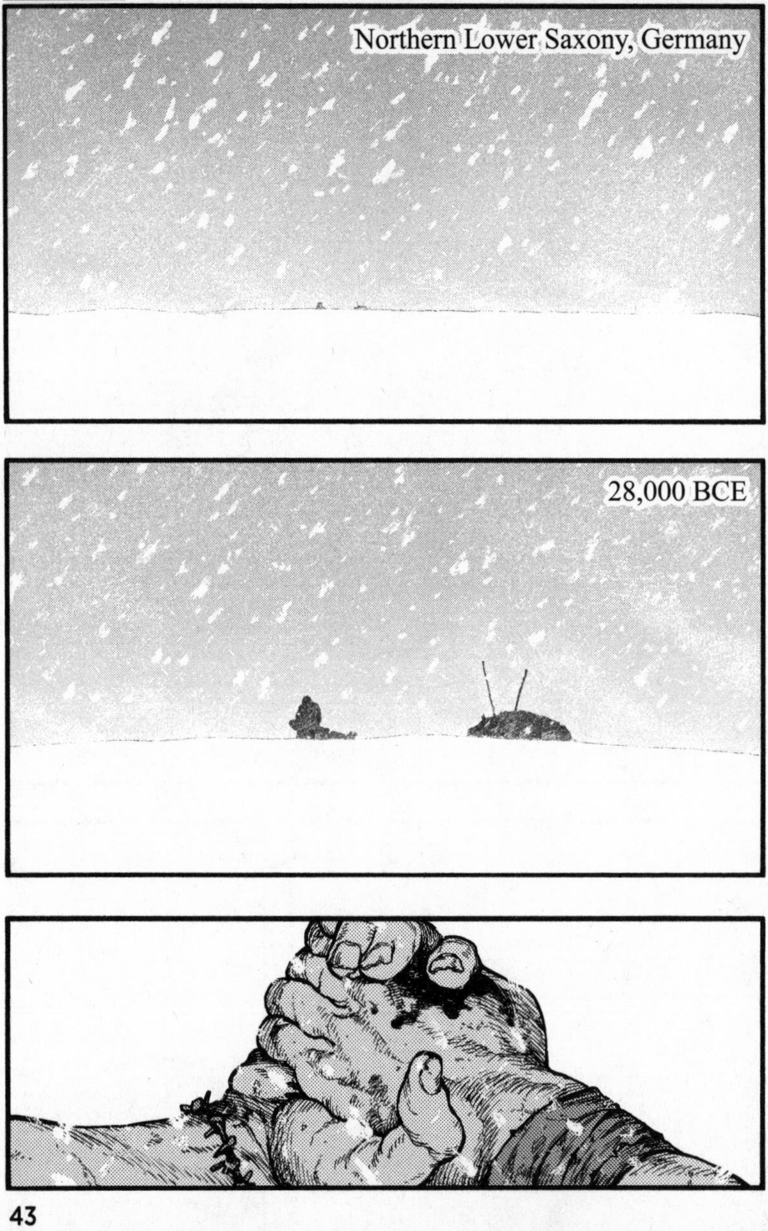
Northern Lower Saxony, Germany
28,000 BCE

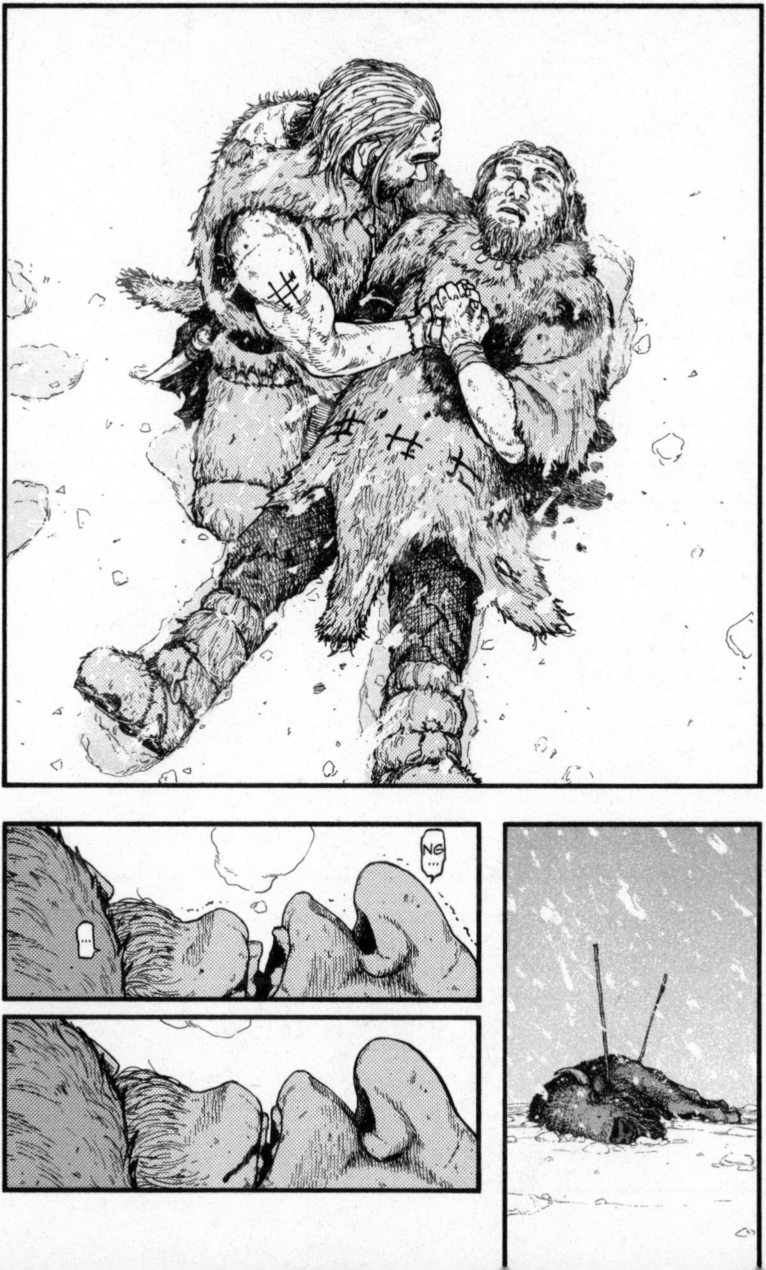
NG...
...

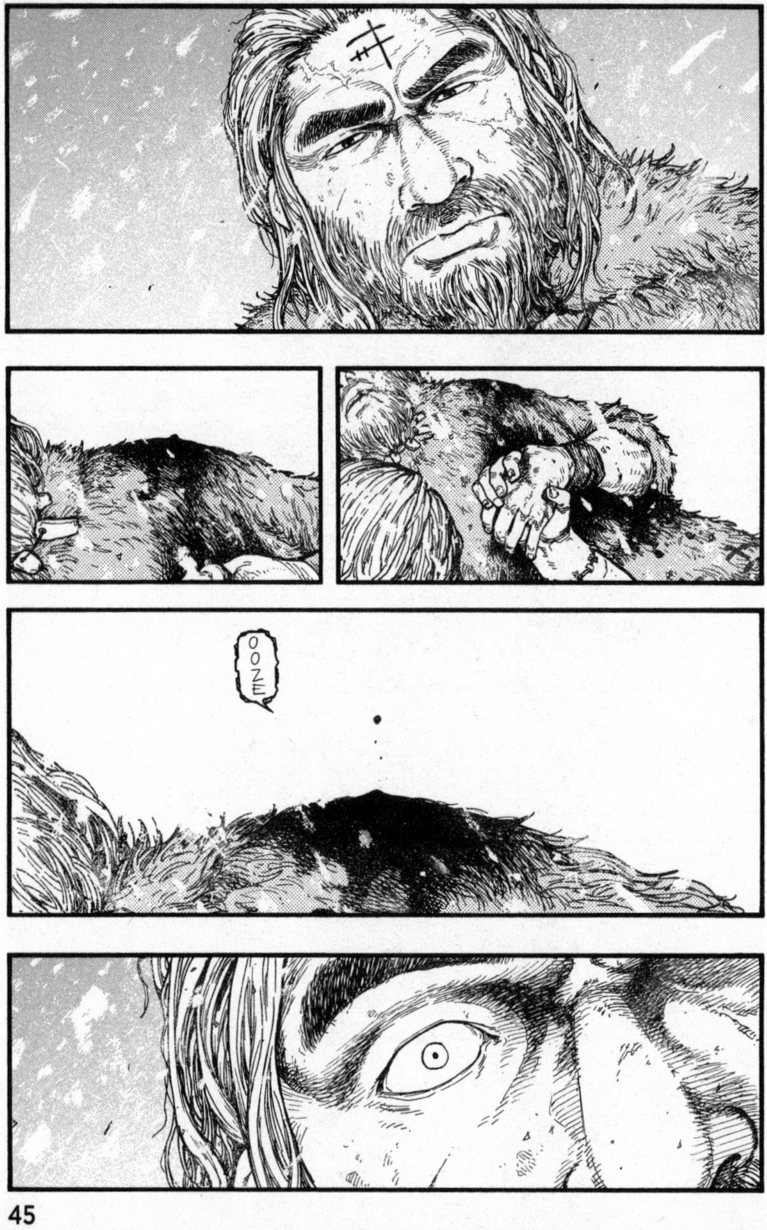
OOZE

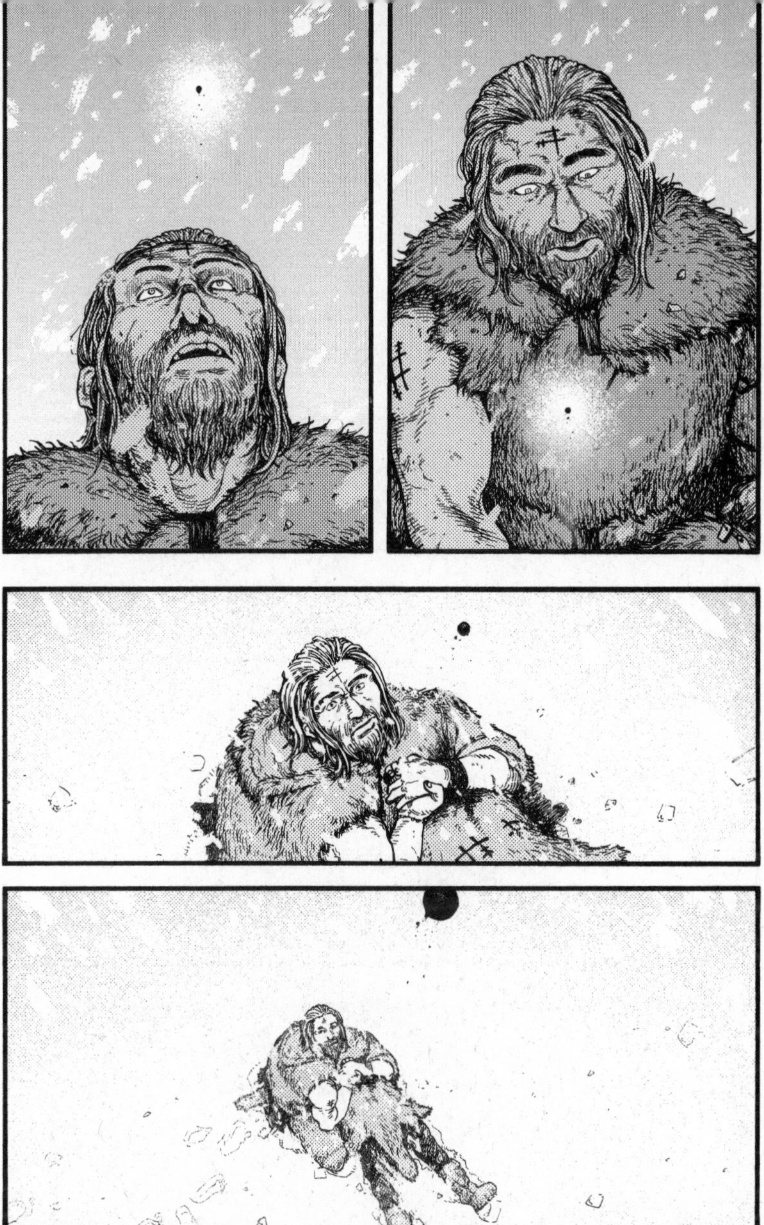

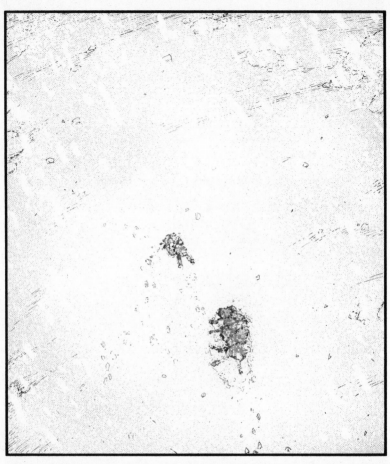

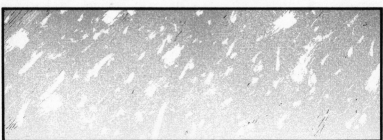

File 75: Leap into the Unknown

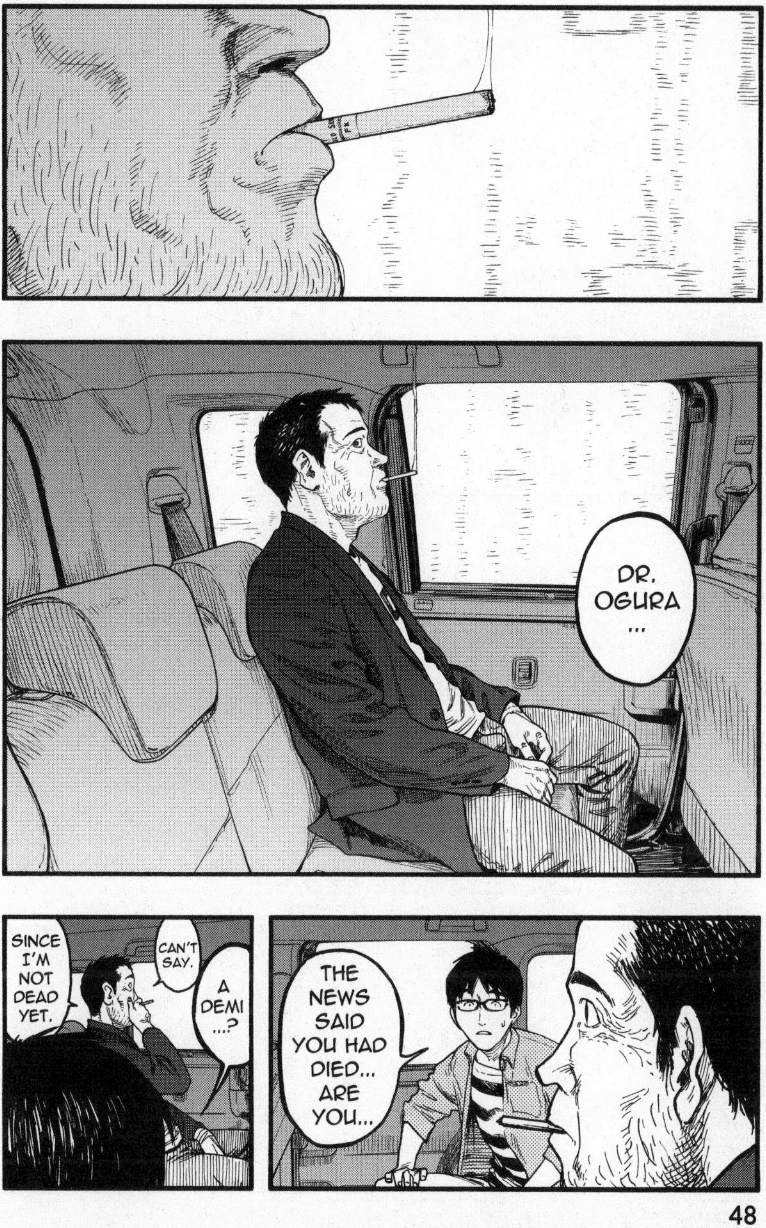
DR. OGURA ...
THE NEWS SAID YOU HAD DIED... ARE YOU...
A DEMI ...?
CAN'T SAY.
SINCE I'M NOT DEAD YET.

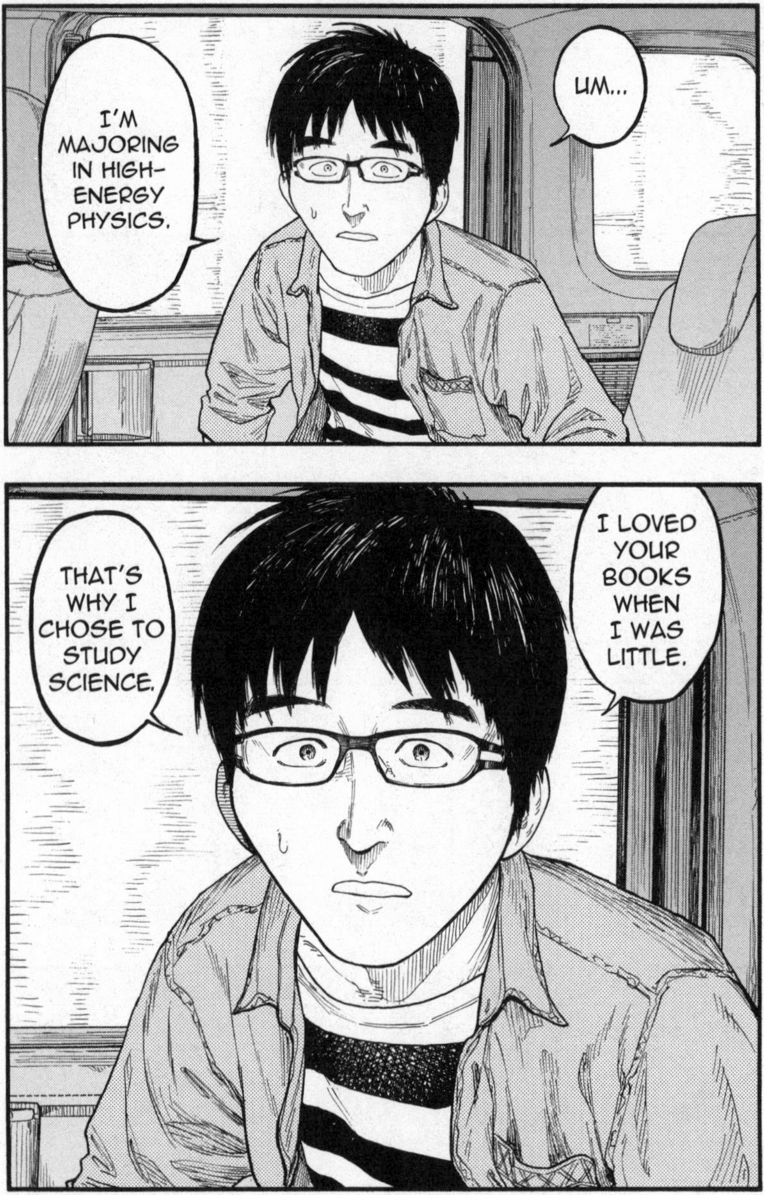
UM...
I'M MAJORING IN HIGH-ENERGY PHYSICS.
I LOVED YOUR BOOKS WHEN I WAS LITTLE.
THAT'S WHY I CHOSE TO STUDY SCIENCE.

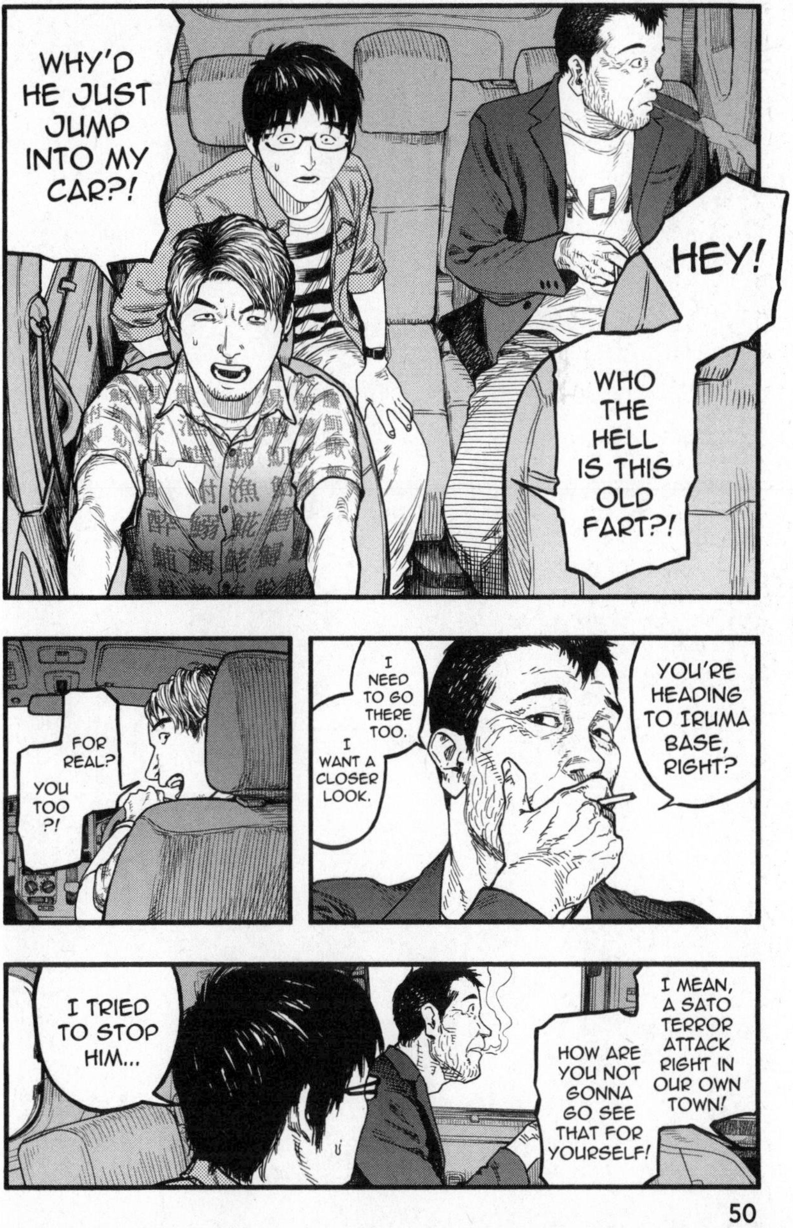
HEY!
WHO THE HELL IS THIS OLD FART?!
WHY'D HE JUST JUMP INTO MY CAR?!
YOU'RE HEADING TO IRUMA BASE, RIGHT?
I NEED TO GO THERE TOO.
I WANT A CLOSER LOOK.
FOR REAL?
YOU TOO?!
I MEAN, A SATO TERROR ATTACK RIGHT IN OUR OWN TOWN!
HOW ARE YOU NOT GONNA GO SEE THAT FOR YOURSELF!
I TRIED TO STOP HIM...

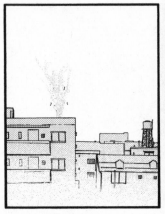

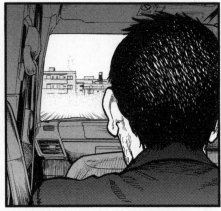

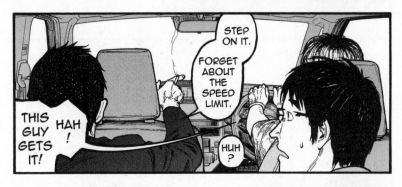

STEP ON IT.

FORGET ABOUT THE SPEED LIMIT.

THIS GUY GETS IT!

HAH!

HUH?

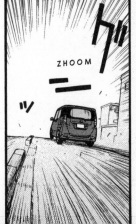

ZHOOM

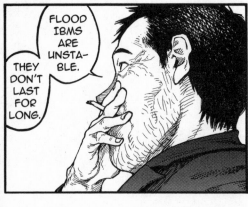

FLOOD IBMS ARE UNSTA-BLE.

THEY DON'T LAST FOR LONG.

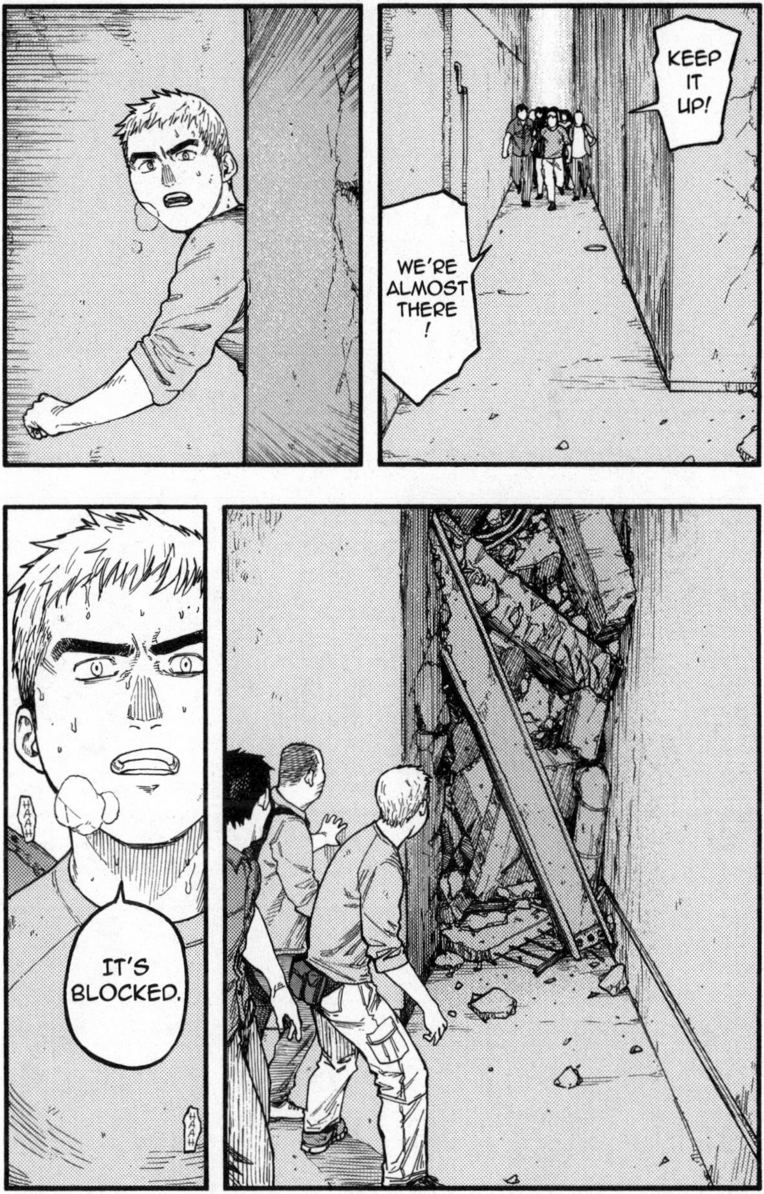
KEEP IT UP!
WE'RE ALMOST THERE!
HAAH
IT'S BLOCKED.
HAAH

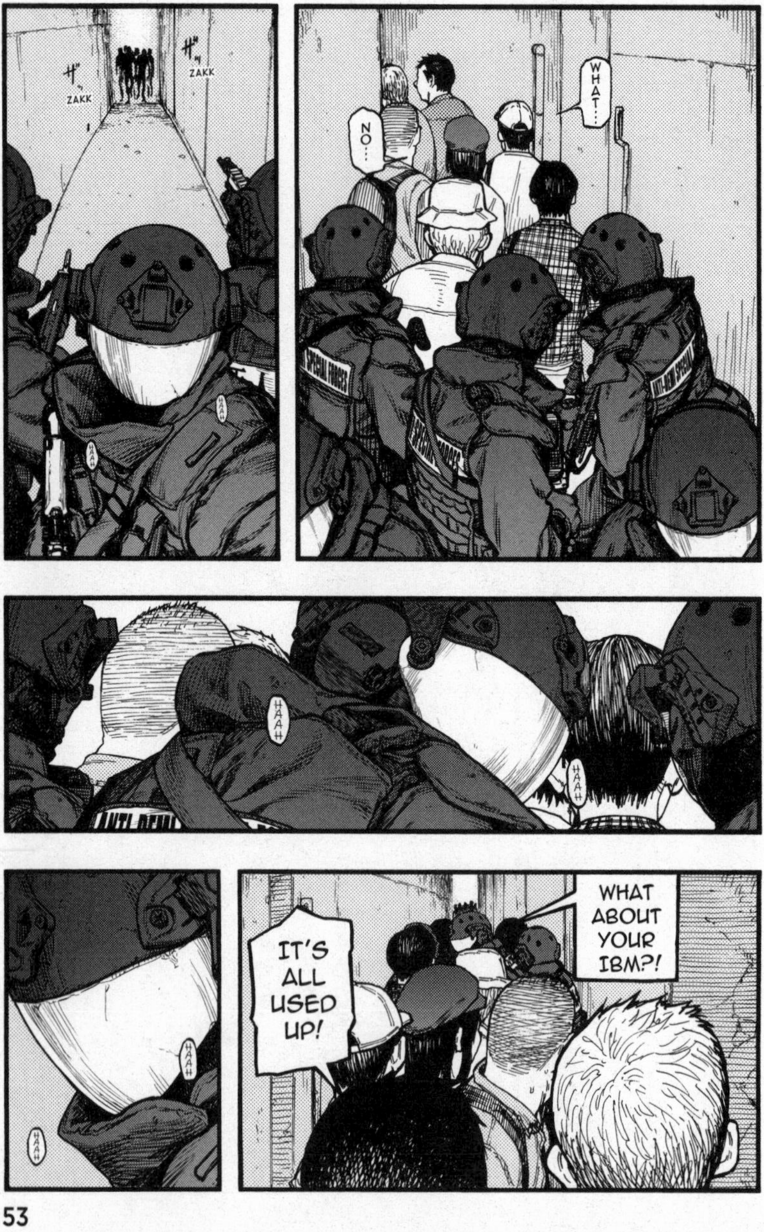
WHAT...
NO...
ZAKK
ZAKK
HAAH
HAAH
HAAH
HAAH
WHAT ABOUT YOUR IBM?!
IT'S ALL USED UP!
HAAH
HAAH

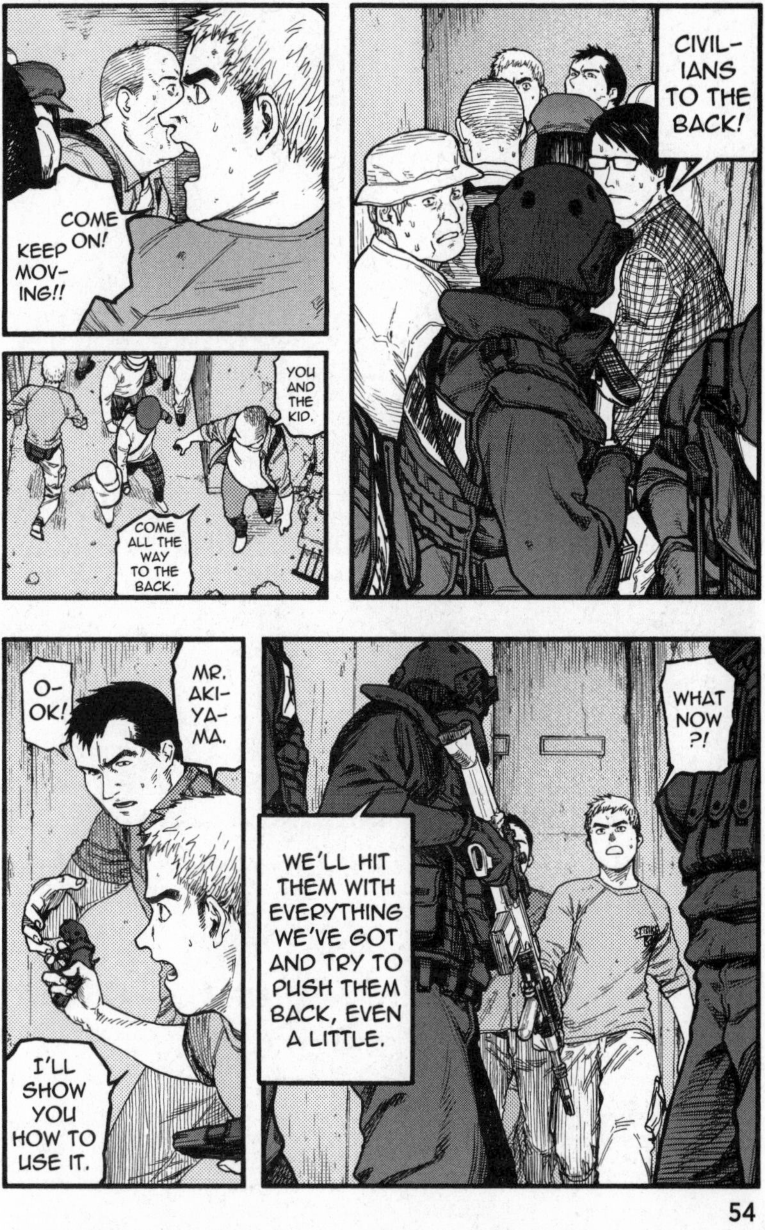
CIVILIANS TO THE BACK!
COME ON!
KEEP MOVING!!
YOU AND THE KID.
COME ALL THE WAY TO THE BACK.
WHAT NOW?!
WE'LL HIT THEM WITH EVERYTHING WE'VE GOT AND TRY TO PUSH THEM BACK, EVEN A LITTLE.
MR. AKIYAMA.
O-OK!
I'LL SHOW YOU HOW TO USE IT.

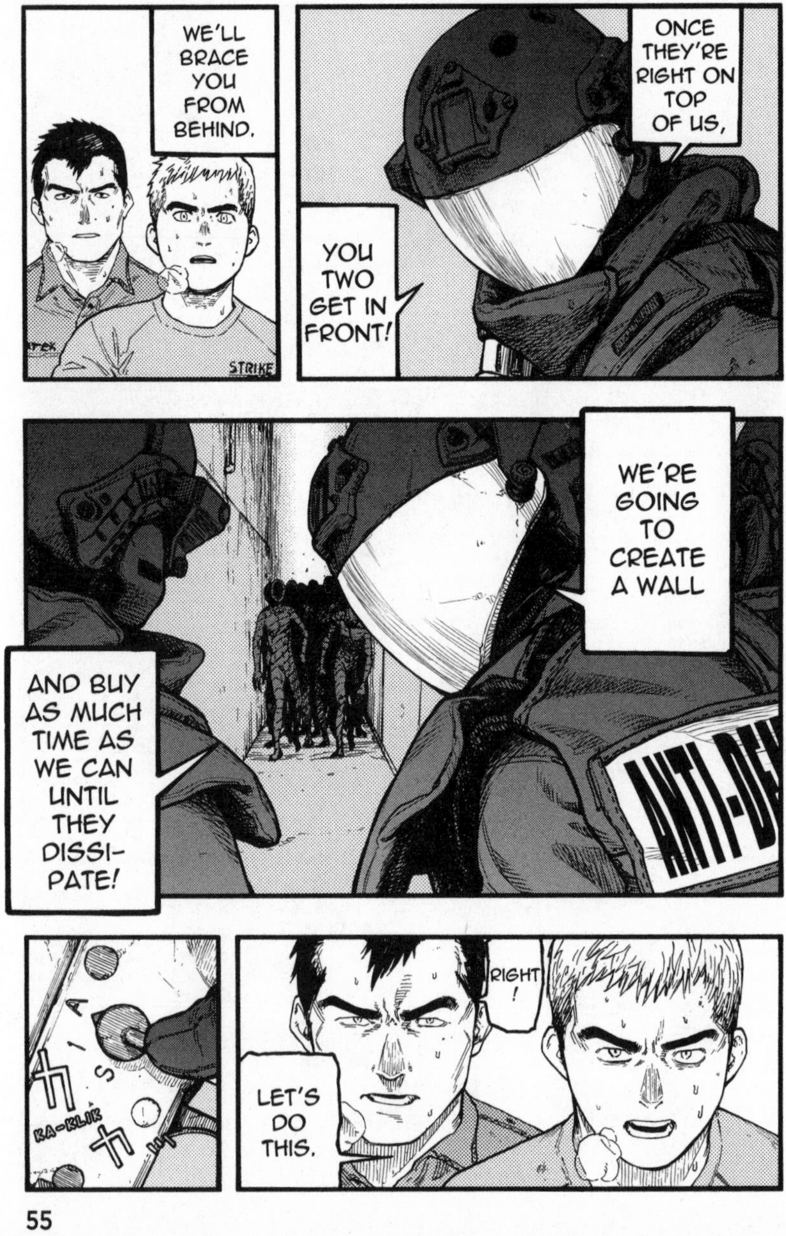
ONCE THEY'RE RIGHT ON TOP OF US,
YOU TWO GET IN FRONT!
WE'LL BRACE YOU FROM BEHIND.
STRIKE
WE'RE GOING TO CREATE A WALL
AND BUY AS MUCH TIME AS WE CAN UNTIL THEY DISSIPATE!
RIGHT!
LET'S DO THIS.
KA-KLIK

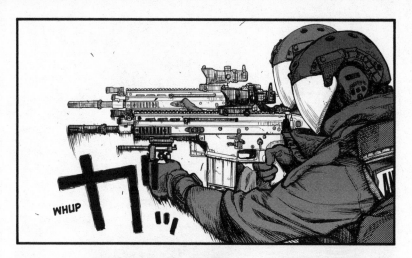

WHUP

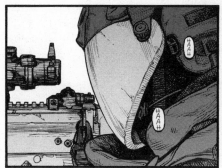

HAAH

HAAH

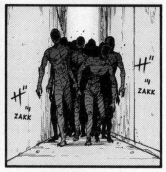

#" ZAKK

#" ZAKK

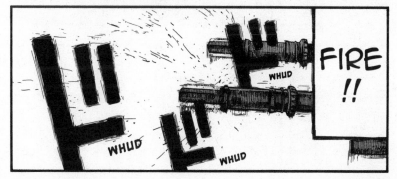

WHUD

WHUD

WHUD

FIRE !!

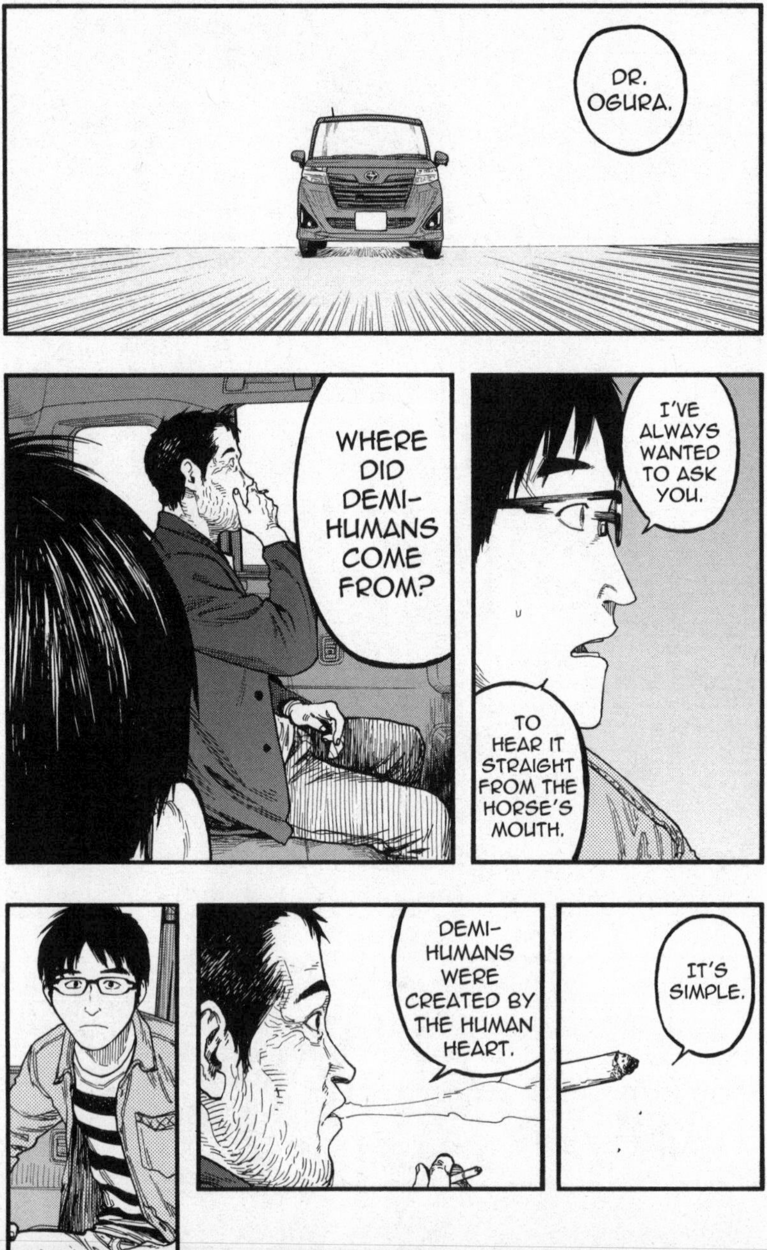
DR. OGURA.
I'VE ALWAYS WANTED TO ASK YOU.
TO HEAR IT STRAIGHT FROM THE HORSE'S MOUTH.
WHERE DID DEMI-HUMANS COME FROM?
IT'S SIMPLE.
DEMI-HUMANS WERE CREATED BY THE HUMAN HEART.

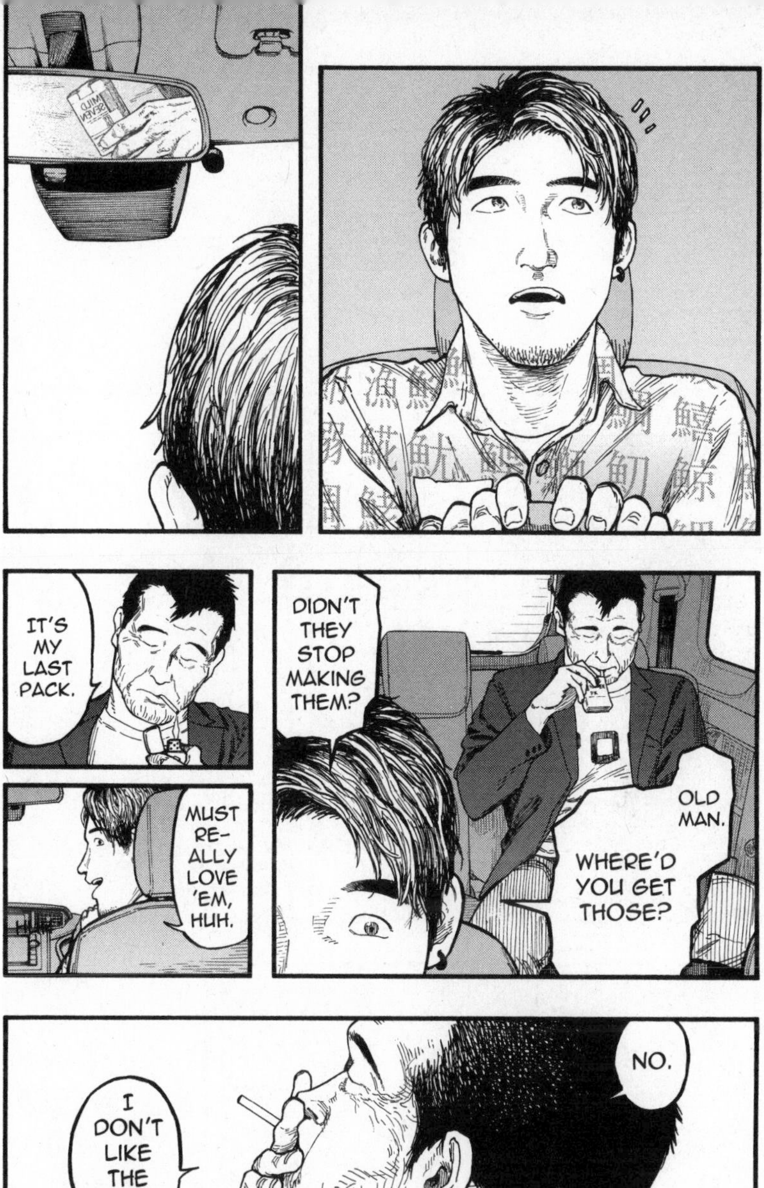
OLD MAN.
WHERE'D YOU GET THOSE?
DIDN'T THEY STOP MAKING THEM?
IT'S MY LAST PACK.
MUST RE-ALLY LOVE 'EM, HUH.
NO.
I DON'T LIKE THE TASTE.

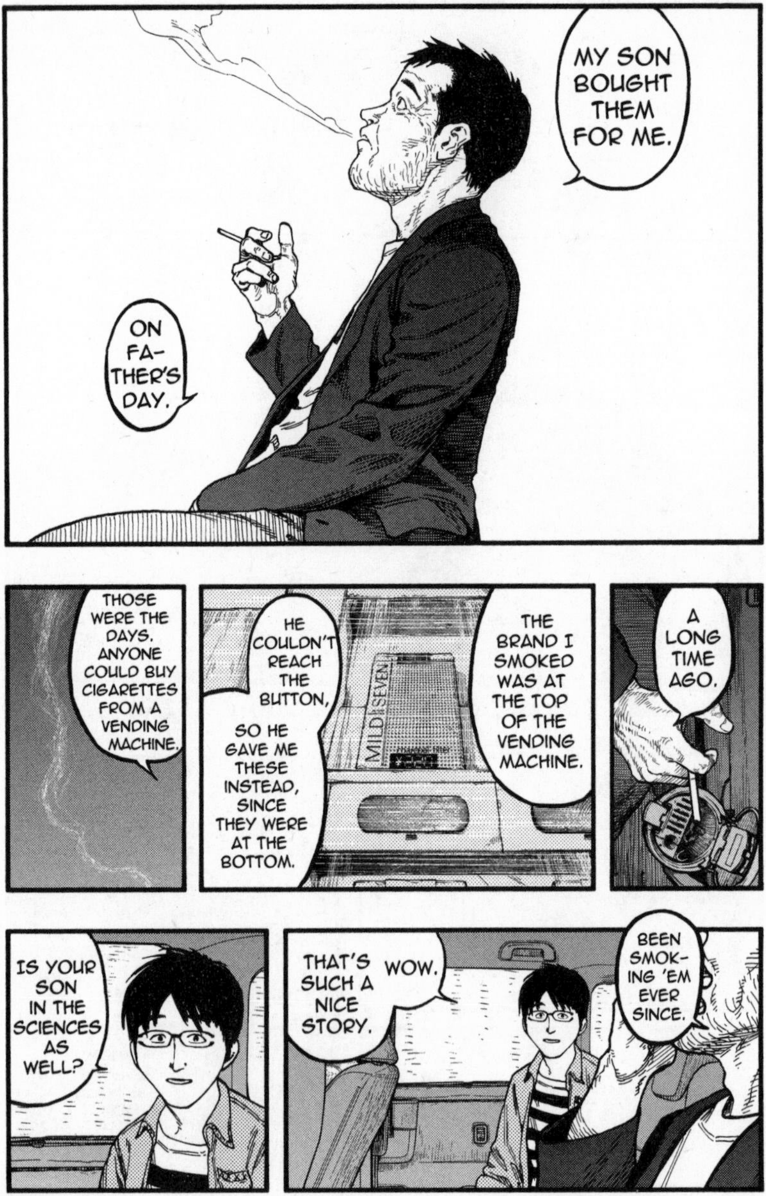
MY SON BOUGHT THEM FOR ME.
ON FA-THER'S DAY.
A LONG TIME AGO.
THE BRAND I SMOKED WAS AT THE TOP OF THE VENDING MACHINE.
MILD SEVEN
HE COULDN'T REACH THE BUTTON,
SO HE GAVE ME THESE INSTEAD, SINCE THEY WERE AT THE BOTTOM.
THOSE WERE THE DAYS. ANYONE COULD BUY CIGARETTES FROM A VENDING MACHINE.
BEEN SMOK-ING 'EM EVER SINCE.
WOW.
THAT'S SUCH A NICE STORY.
IS YOUR SON IN THE SCIENCES AS WELL?

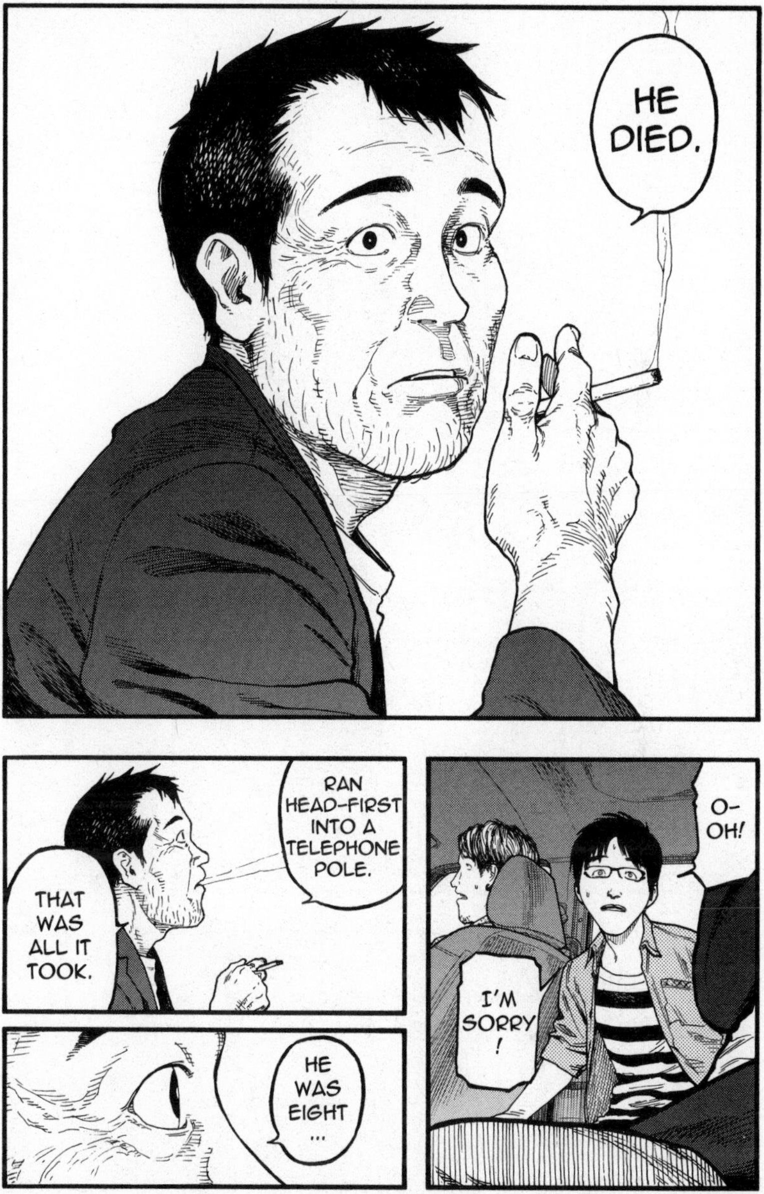
HE DIED.
O-OH!
I'M SORRY!
RAN HEAD-FIRST INTO A TELEPHONE POLE.
THAT WAS ALL IT TOOK.
HE WAS EIGHT ...

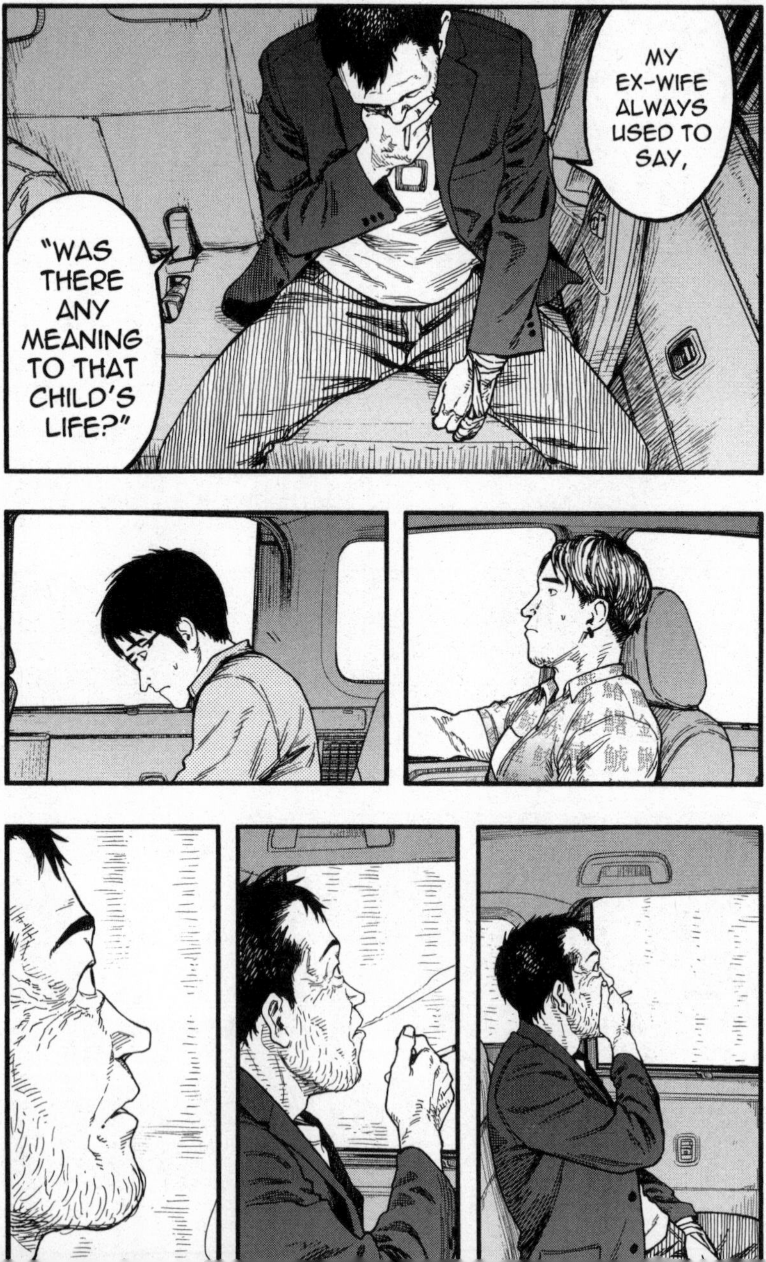
MY EX-WIFE ALWAYS USED TO SAY,
"WAS THERE ANY MEANING TO THAT CHILD'S LIFE?"

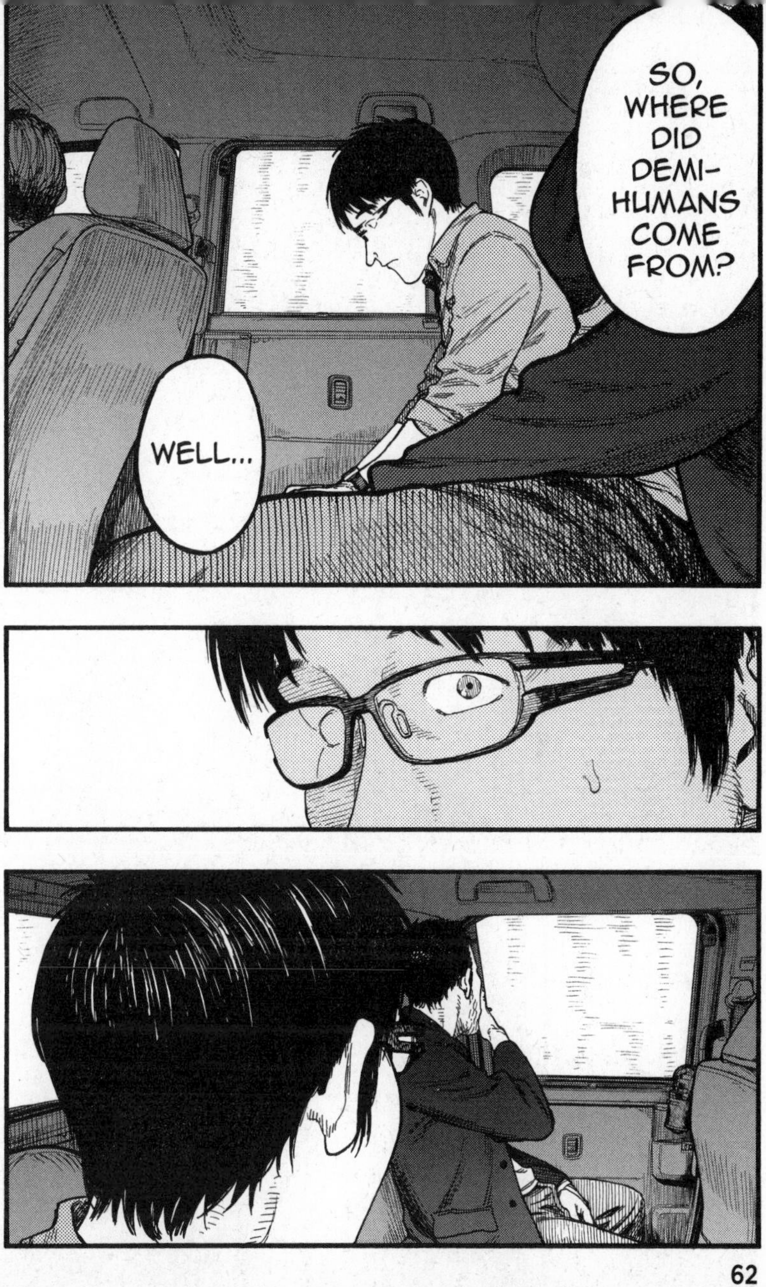
SO, WHERE DID DEMI-HUMANS COME FROM?
WELL...

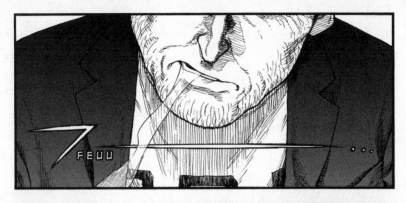

FEUU

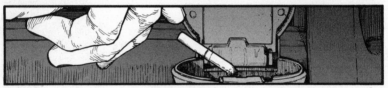

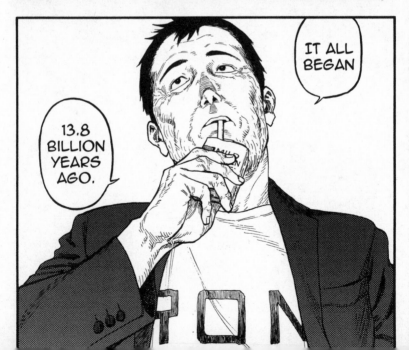

IT ALL BEGAN

13.8 BILLION YEARS AGO.

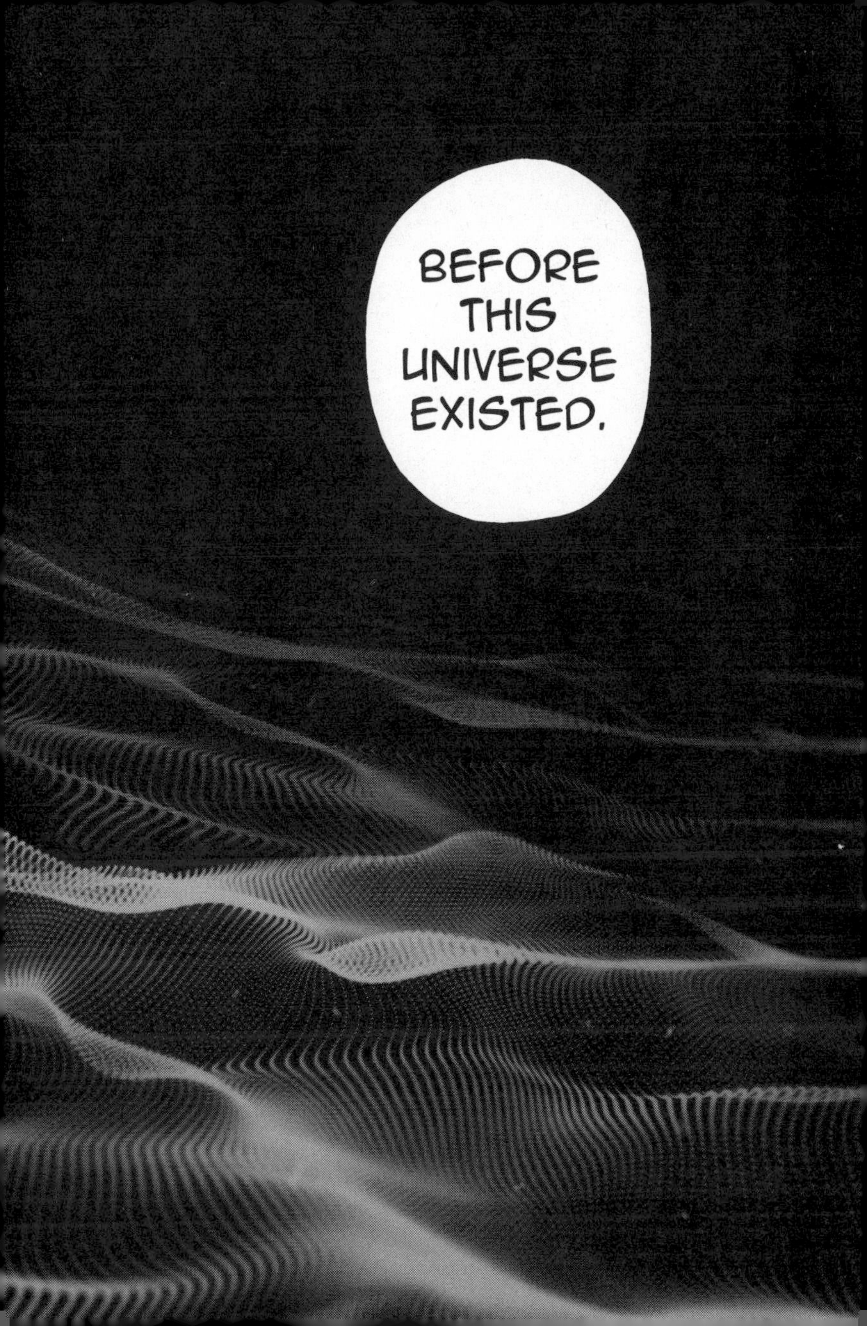
BEFORE THIS UNIVERSE EXISTED.

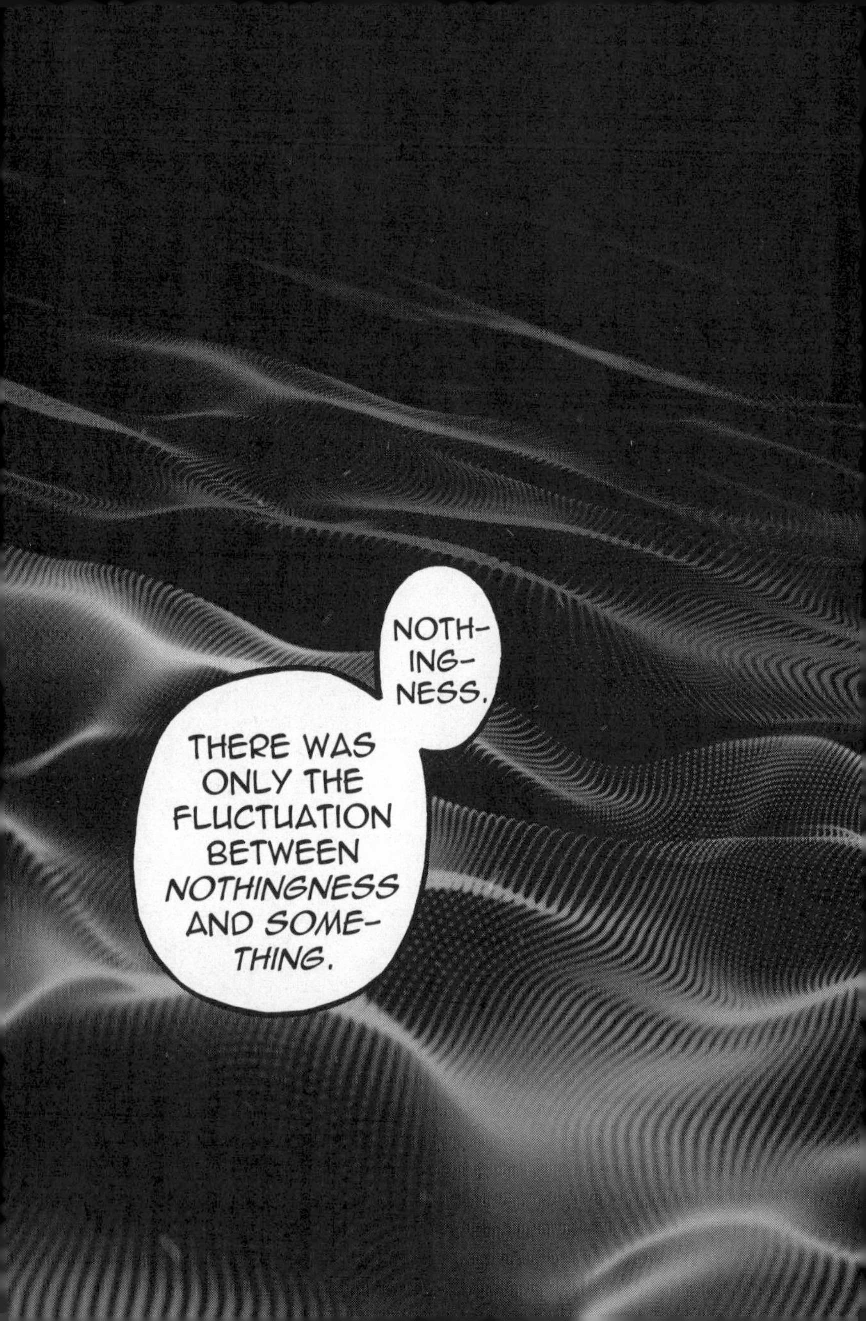
NOTH-ING-NESS.
THERE WAS ONLY THE FLUCTUATION BETWEEN *NOTHINGNESS* AND *SOME-THING*.

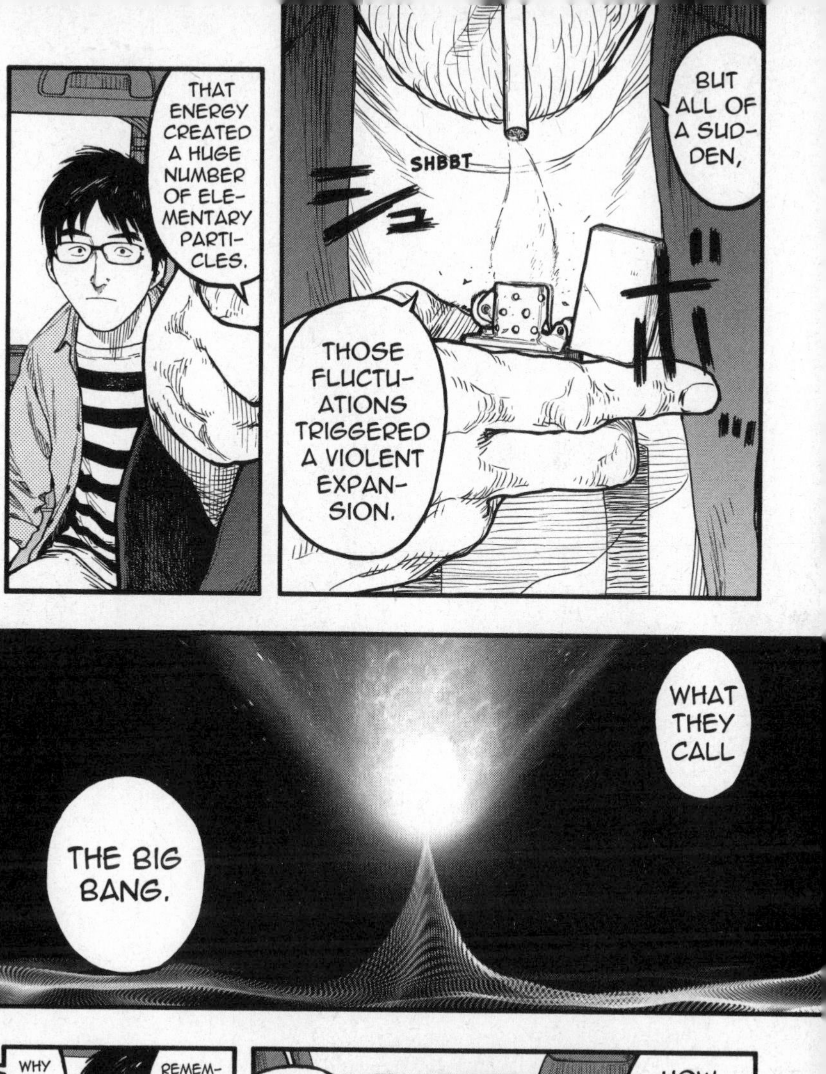
BUT ALL OF A SUD-DEN,
SHBBT
THOSE FLUCTU-ATIONS TRIGGERED A VIOLENT EXPAN-SION.
THAT ENERGY CREATED A HUGE NUMBER OF ELE-MENTARY PARTI-CLES.
WHAT THEY CALL
THE BIG BANG.
HOW DOES ENERGY TURN INTO MATTER ?
IT'S THE BASIS OF PHYS-ICS.
ENERGY CAN BE CON-VERTED INTO MATTER.
REMEM-BER WHAT THE GUIDE SAID
WHEN WE VISITED HIROSHIMA IN MIDDLE SCHOOL?
WHY THE HELL WOULD I?

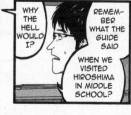

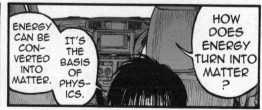

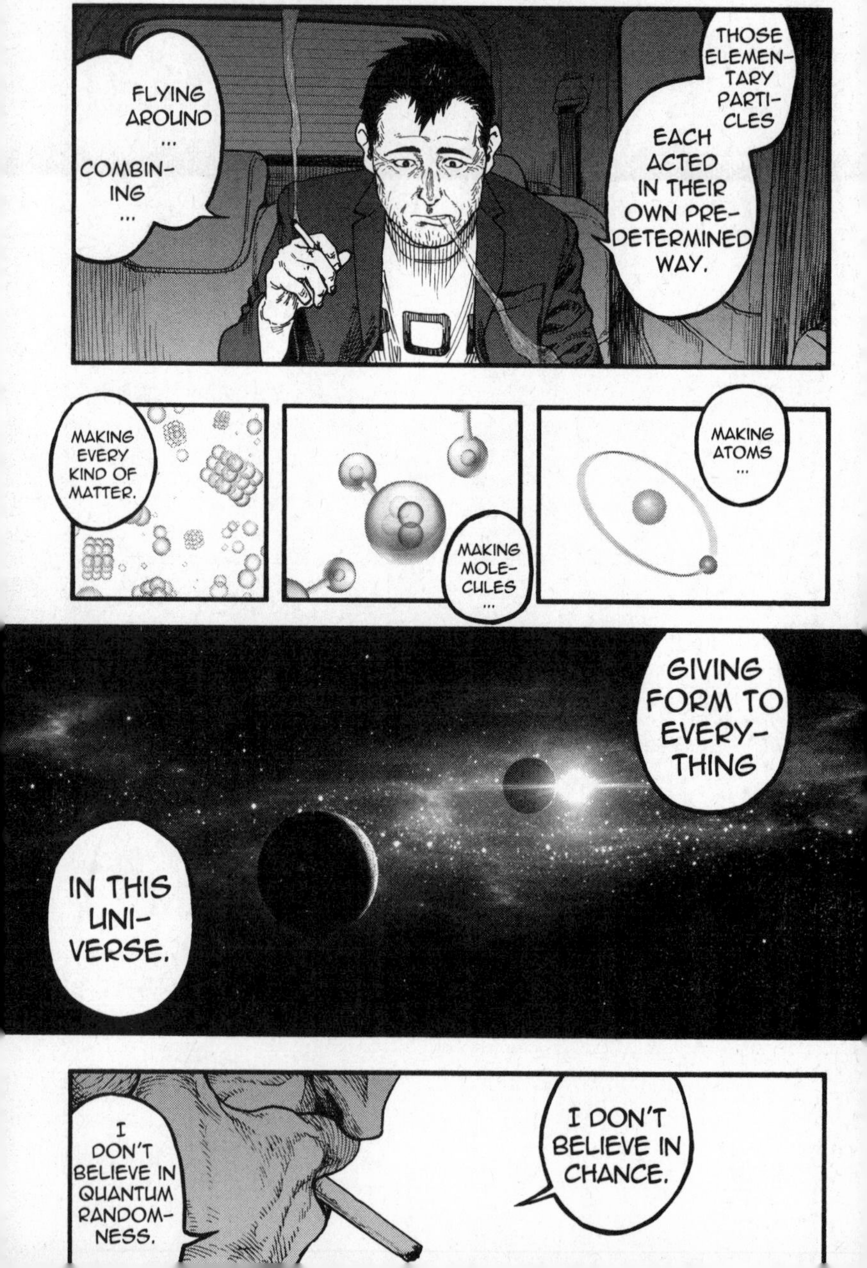
THOSE ELEMEN-TARY PARTI-CLES
EACH ACTED IN THEIR OWN PRE-DETERMINED WAY.
FLYING AROUND ... COMBIN-ING ...
MAKING ATOMS ...
MAKING MOLE-CULES ...
MAKING EVERY KIND OF MATTER.
GIVING FORM TO EVERY-THING
IN THIS UNI-VERSE.
I DON'T BELIEVE IN CHANCE.
I DON'T BELIEVE IN QUANTUM RANDOM-NESS.

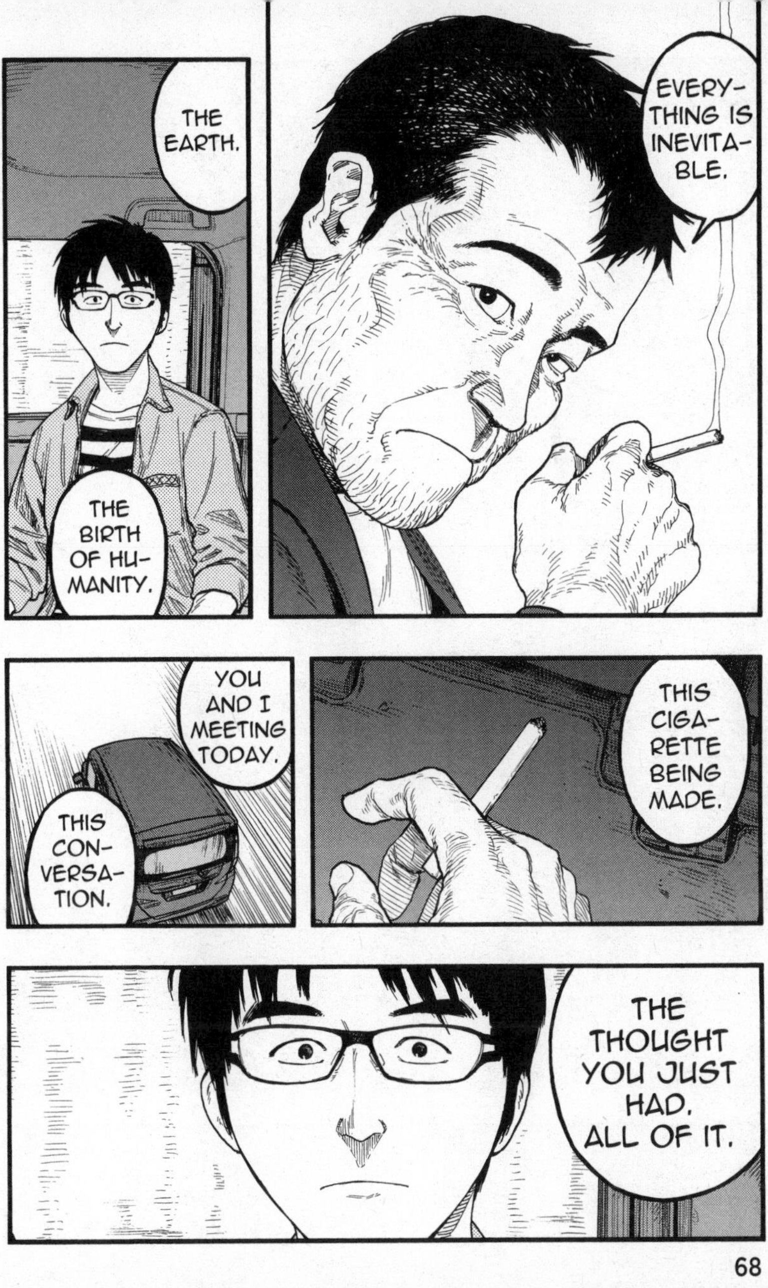
EVERYTHING IS INEVITABLE.
THE EARTH.
THE BIRTH OF HUMANITY.
THIS CIGARETTE BEING MADE.
YOU AND I MEETING TODAY.
THIS CONVERSATION.
THE THOUGHT YOU JUST HAD. ALL OF IT.

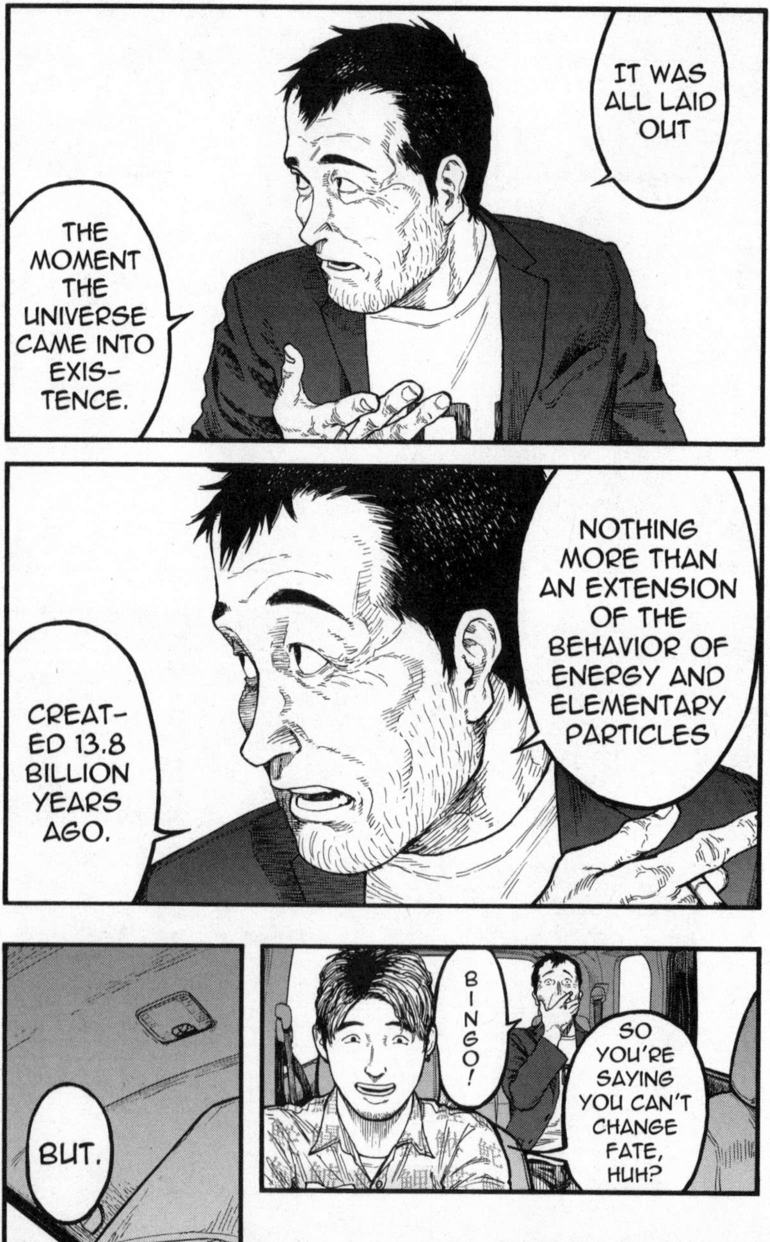
IT WAS ALL LAID OUT
THE MOMENT THE UNIVERSE CAME INTO EXISTENCE.
NOTHING MORE THAN AN EXTENSION OF THE BEHAVIOR OF ENERGY AND ELEMENTARY PARTICLES
CREATED 13.8 BILLION YEARS AGO.
SO YOU'RE SAYING YOU CAN'T CHANGE FATE, HUH?
BINGO!
BUT.

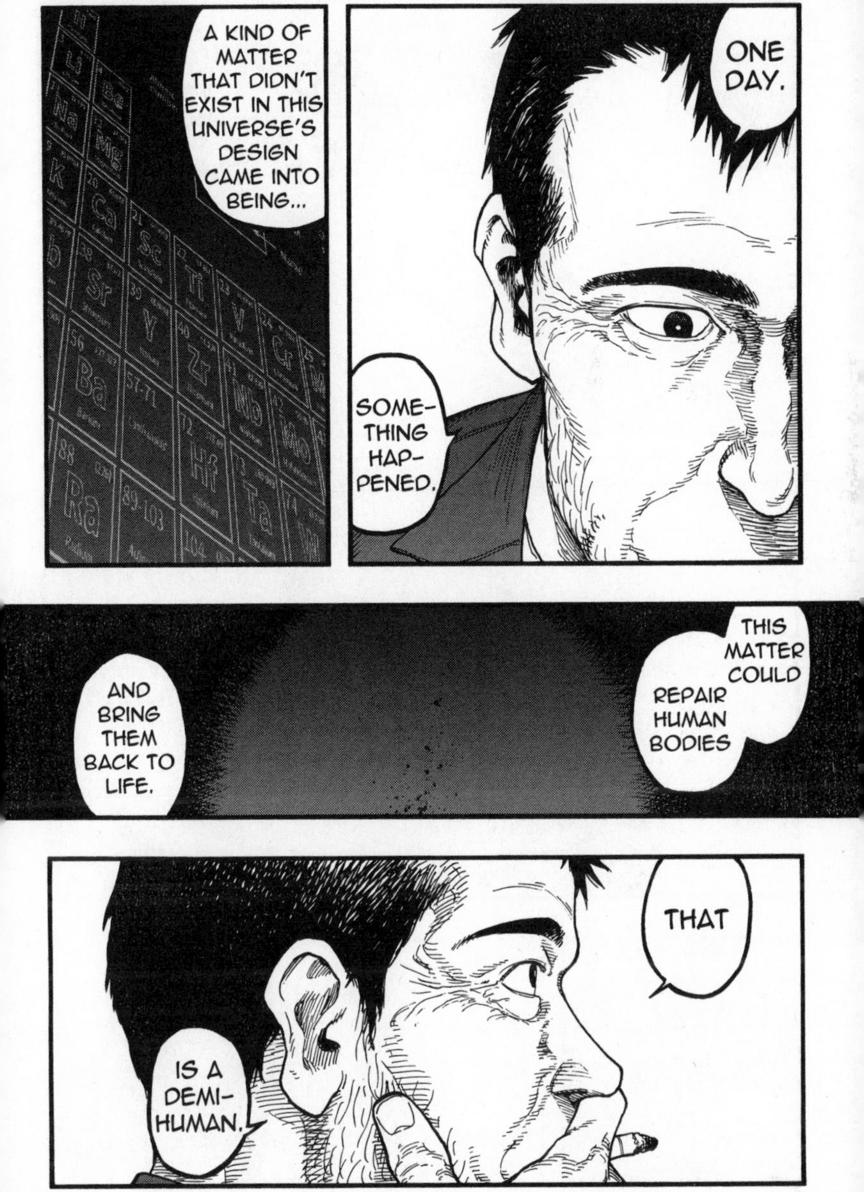
ONE DAY.
SOME-THING HAP-PENED.
A KIND OF MATTER THAT DIDN'T EXIST IN THIS UNIVERSE'S DESIGN CAME INTO BEING...
THIS MATTER COULD REPAIR HUMAN BODIES
AND BRING THEM BACK TO LIFE.
THAT
IS A DEMI-HUMAN.

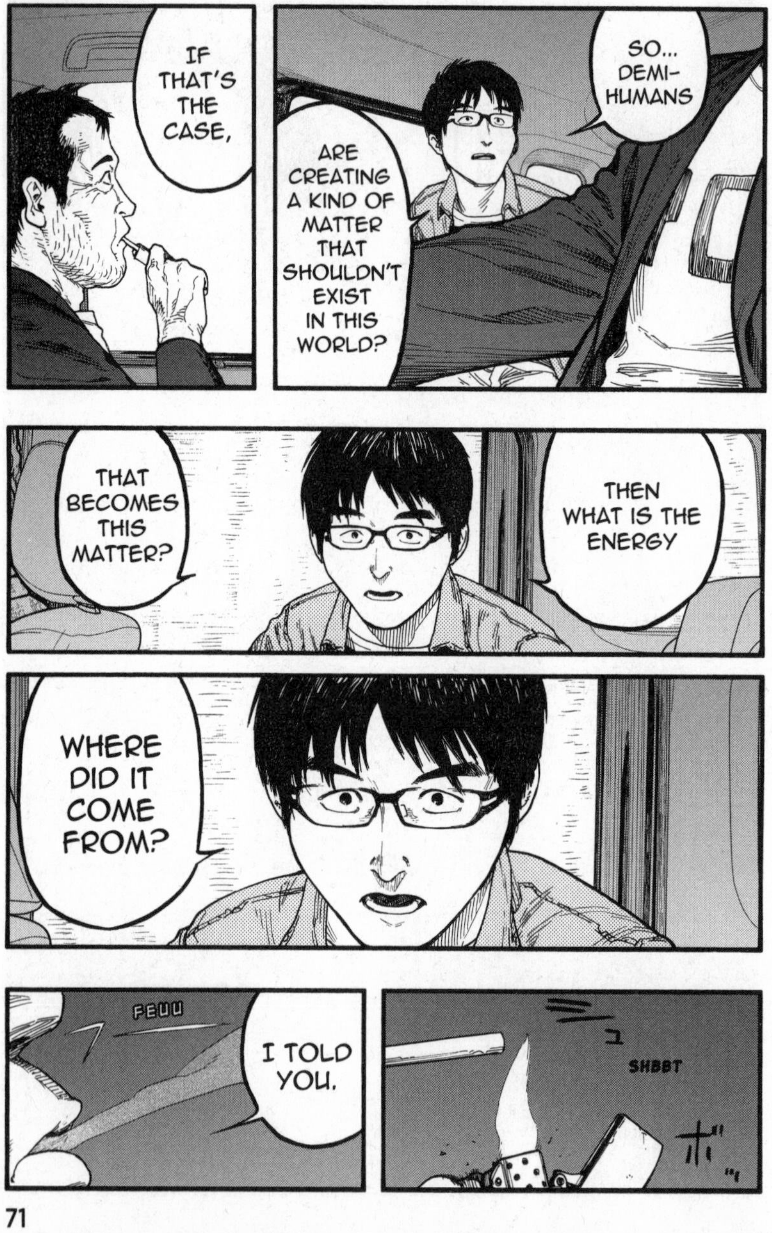
SO... DEMI-HUMANS
ARE CREATING A KIND OF MATTER THAT SHOULDN'T EXIST IN THIS WORLD?
IF THAT'S THE CASE,
THEN WHAT IS THE ENERGY
THAT BECOMES THIS MATTER?
WHERE DID IT COME FROM?
SHBBT
ボ
FEUU
I TOLD YOU.

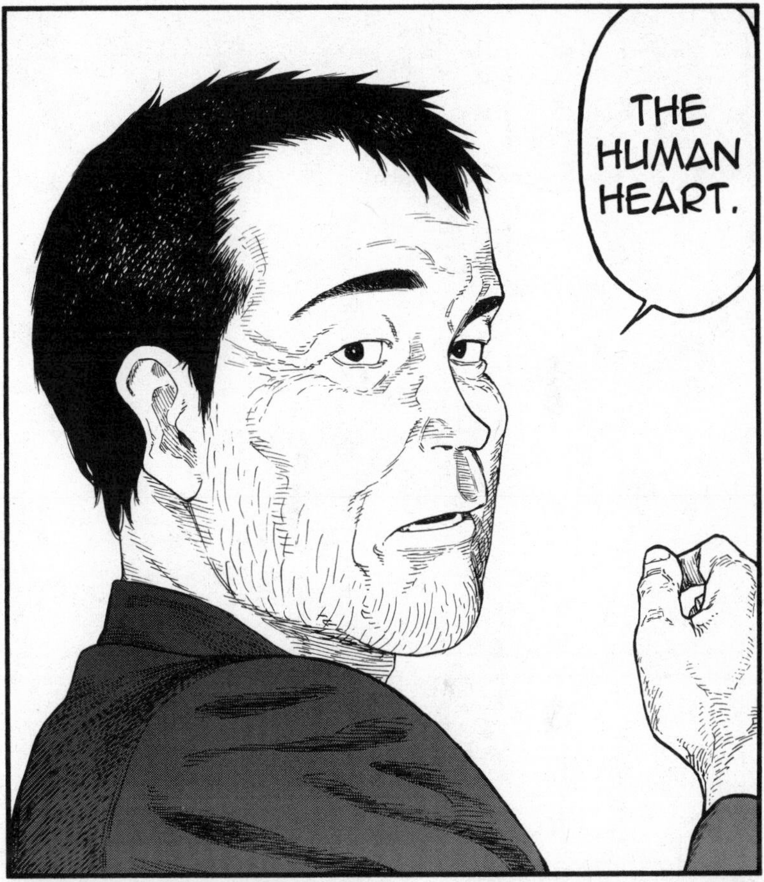
THE HUMAN HEART.
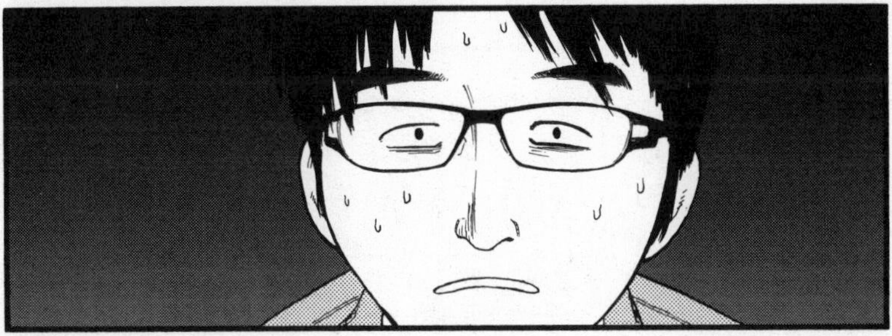

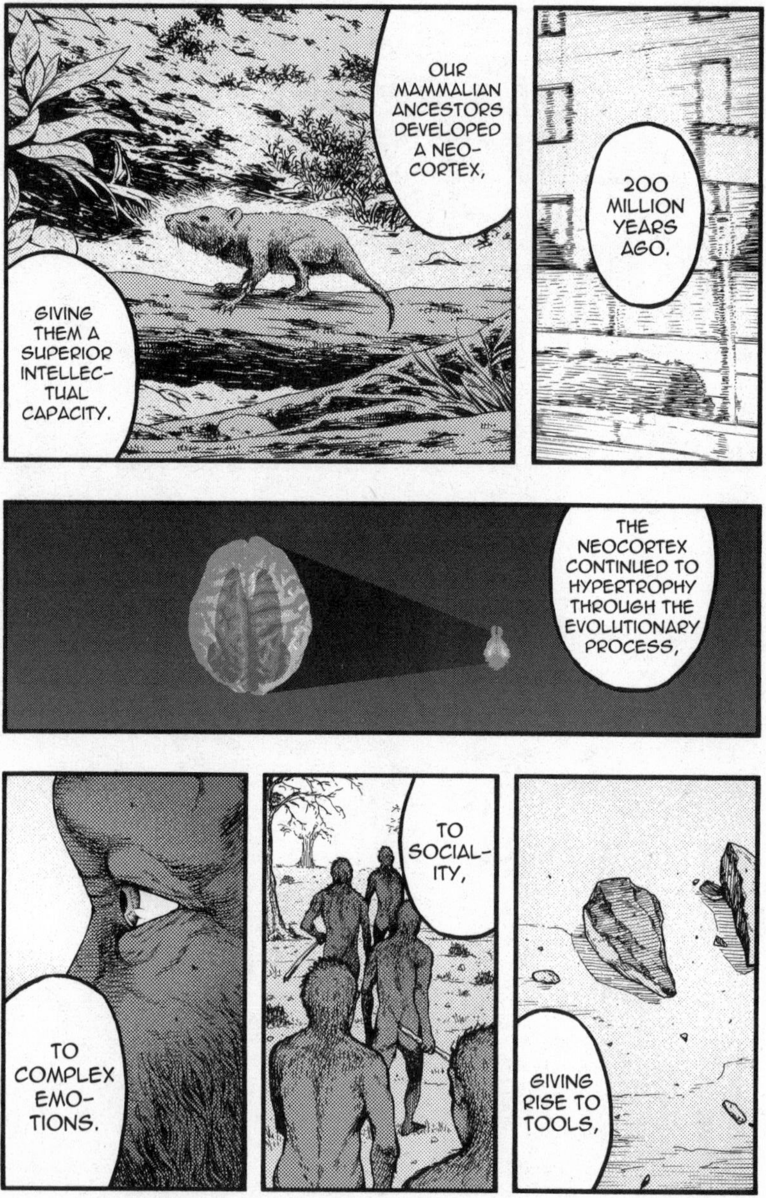
200 MILLION YEARS AGO.
OUR MAMMALIAN ANCESTORS DEVELOPED A NEO-CORTEX,
GIVING THEM A SUPERIOR INTELLEC-TUAL CAPACITY.
THE NEOCORTEX CONTINUED TO HYPERTROPHY THROUGH THE EVOLUTIONARY PROCESS,
GIVING RISE TO TOOLS,
TO SOCIAL-ITY,
TO COMPLEX EMO-TIONS.

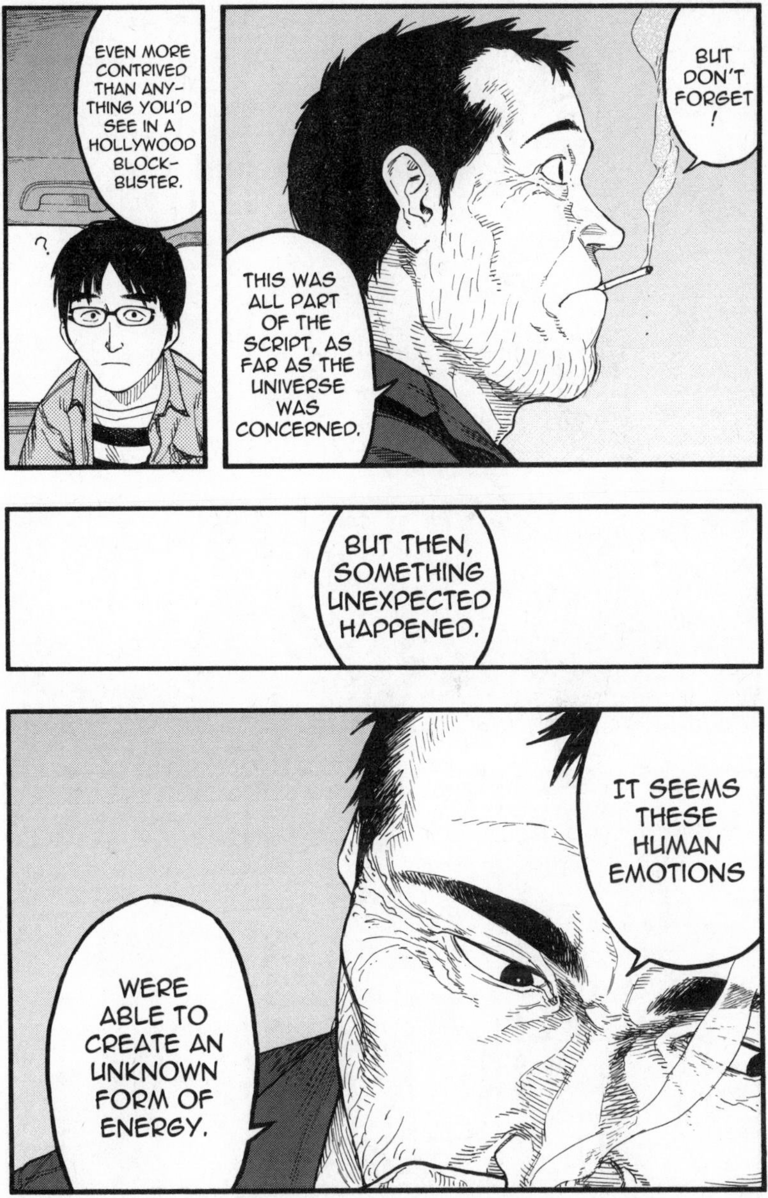
BUT DON'T FORGET!
THIS WAS ALL PART OF THE SCRIPT, AS FAR AS THE UNIVERSE WAS CONCERNED.
EVEN MORE CONTRIVED THAN ANYTHING YOU'D SEE IN A HOLLYWOOD BLOCKBUSTER.
?
BUT THEN, SOMETHING UNEXPECTED HAPPENED.
IT SEEMS THESE HUMAN EMOTIONS
WERE ABLE TO CREATE AN UNKNOWN FORM OF ENERGY.

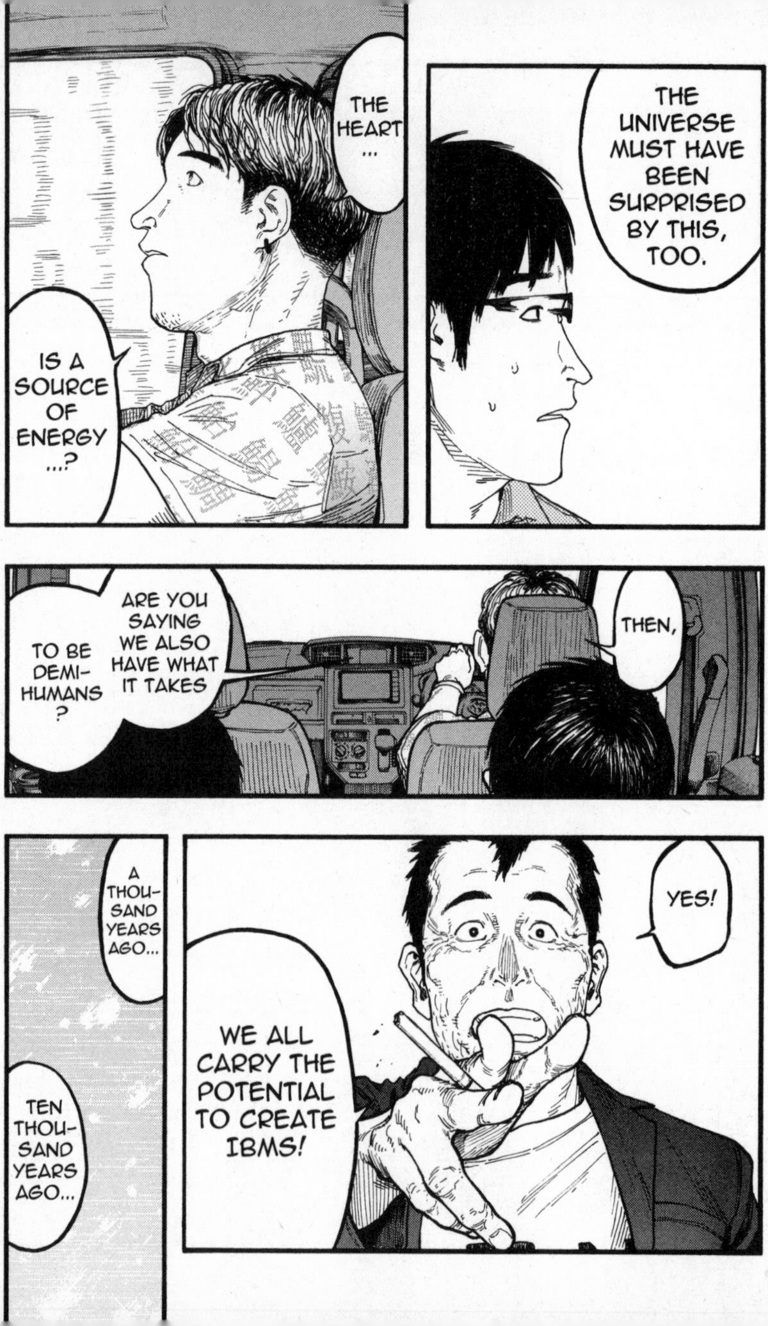
THE UNIVERSE MUST HAVE BEEN SURPRISED BY THIS, TOO.
THE HEART...
IS A SOURCE OF ENERGY...?
THEN,
ARE YOU SAYING WE ALSO HAVE WHAT IT TAKES
TO BE DEMI-HUMANS?
YES!
WE ALL CARRY THE POTENTIAL TO CREATE IBMS!
A THOUSAND YEARS AGO...
TEN THOUSAND YEARS AGO...

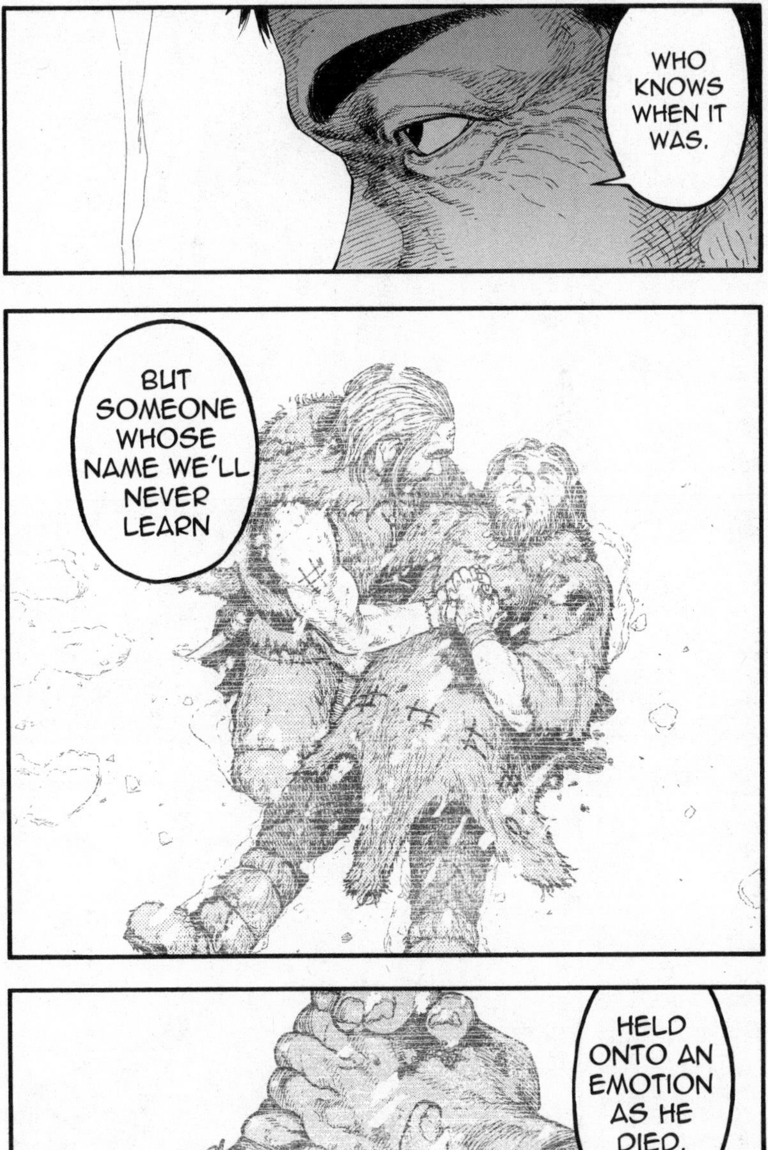
WHO KNOWS WHEN IT WAS.
BUT SOMEONE WHOSE NAME WE'LL NEVER LEARN
HELD ONTO AN EMOTION AS HE DIED.

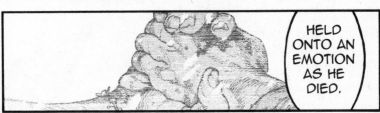

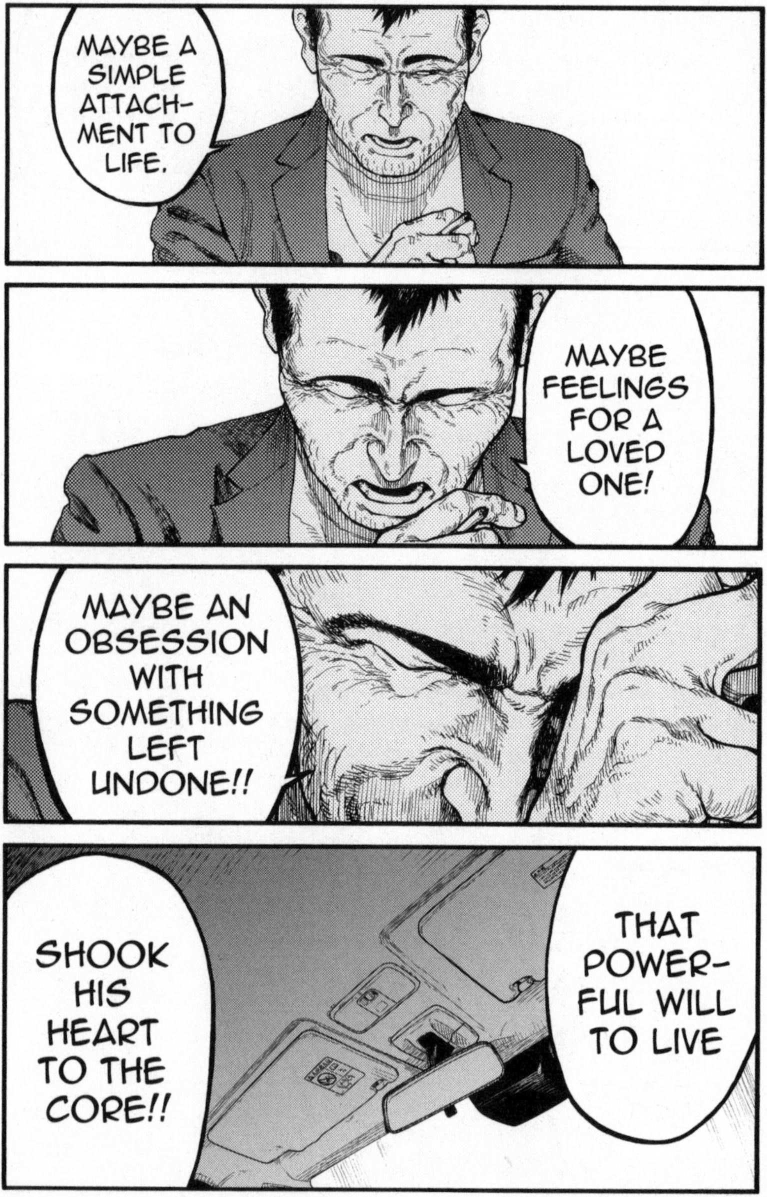
MAYBE A SIMPLE ATTACHMENT TO LIFE.
MAYBE FEELINGS FOR A LOVED ONE!
MAYBE AN OBSESSION WITH SOMETHING LEFT UNDONE!!
THAT POWERFUL WILL TO LIVE
SHOOK HIS HEART TO THE CORE!!

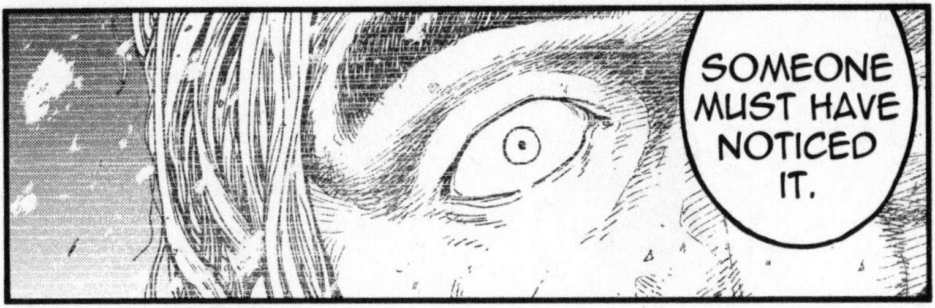
SOMEONE MUST HAVE NOTICED IT.
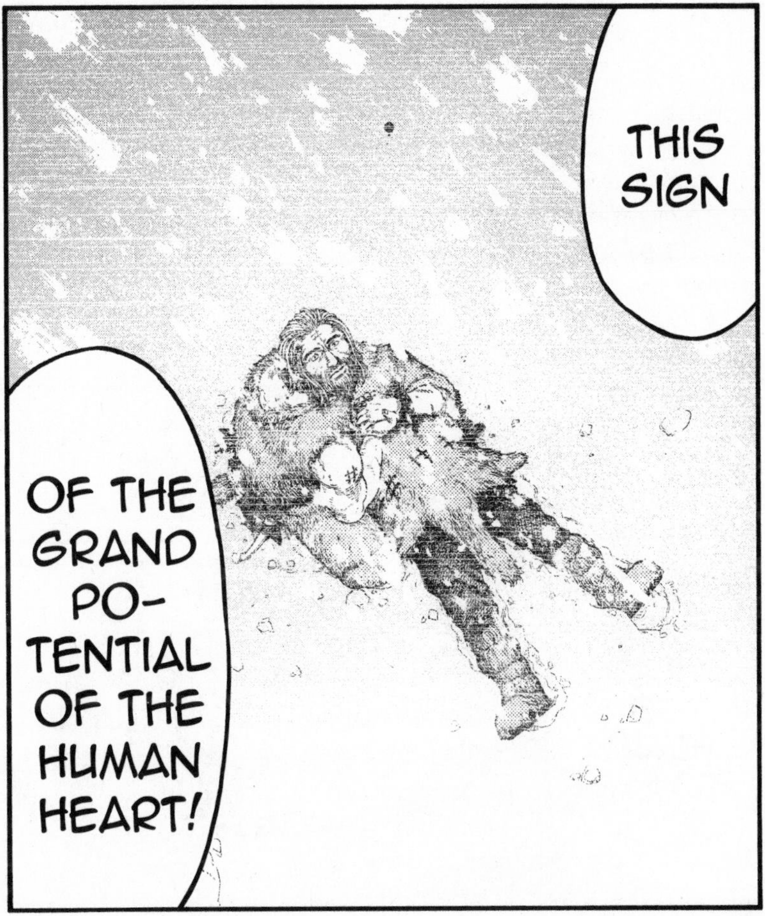
THIS SIGN
OF THE GRAND PO-TENTIAL OF THE HUMAN HEART!

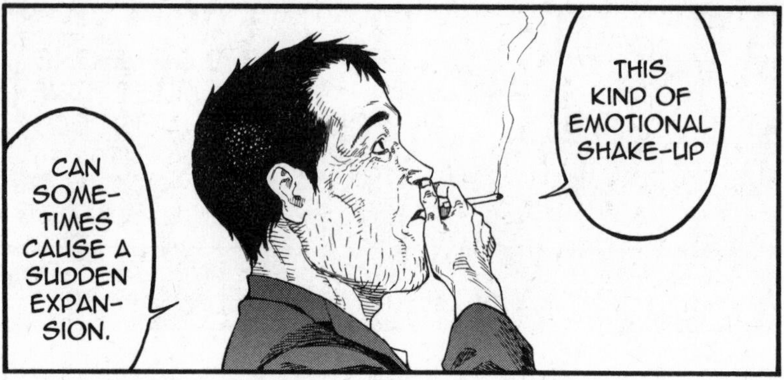
THIS KIND OF EMOTIONAL SHAKE-UP
CAN SOMETIMES CAUSE A SUDDEN EXPANSION.
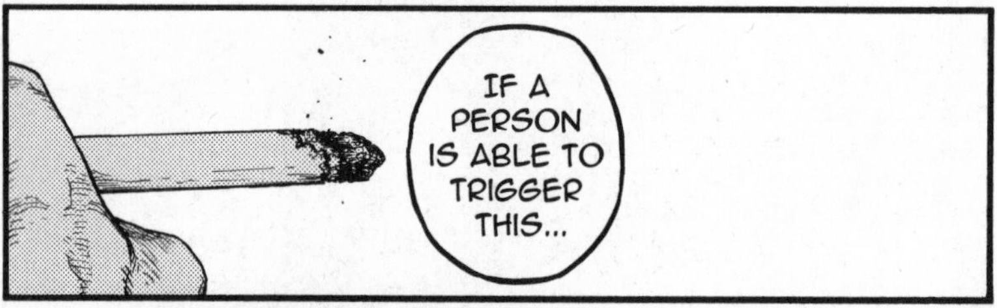
IF A PERSON IS ABLE TO TRIGGER THIS...
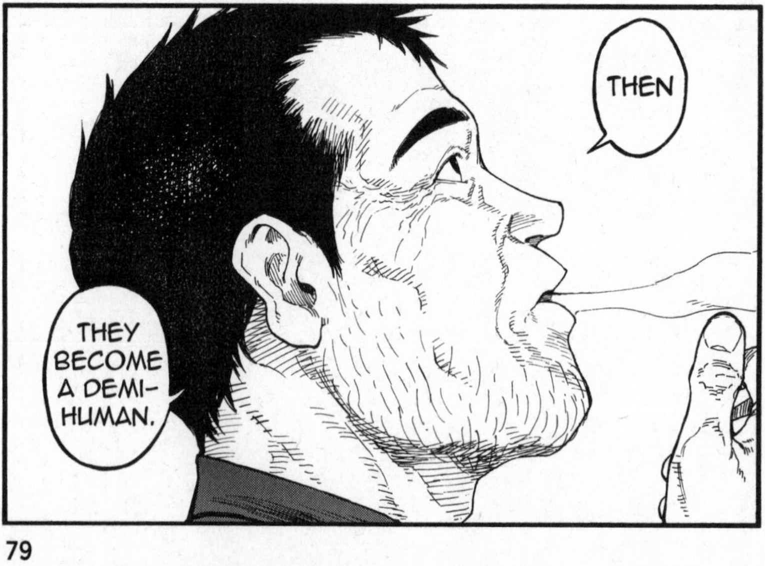
THEN
THEY BECOME A DEMI-HUMAN.

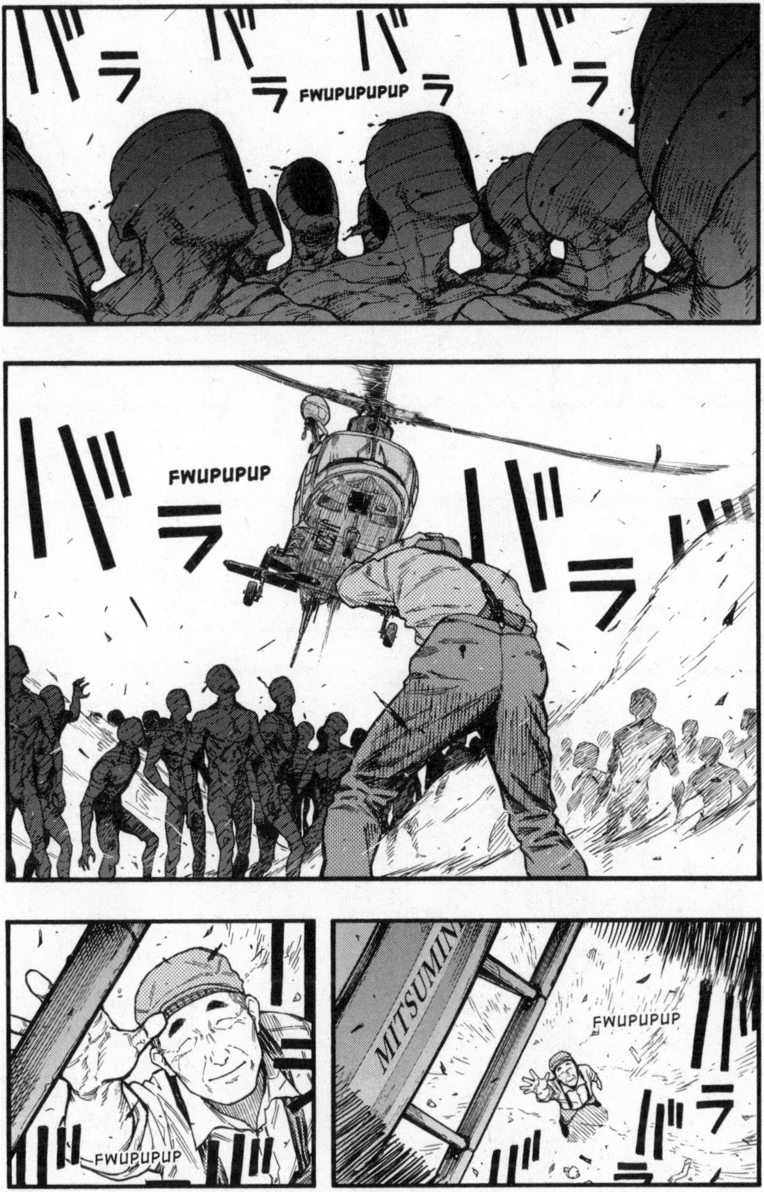
バラバラバラバラ
FWUPUPUPUP
バラ
FWUPUPUP
バラッ
FWUPUPUP
バラバラ
FWUPUPUP

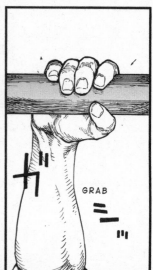

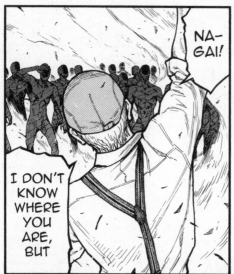

NA-GAI!

I DON'T KNOW WHERE YOU ARE, BUT

GRAB

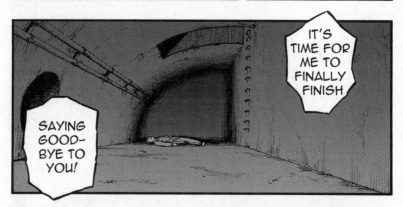

IT'S TIME FOR ME TO FINALLY FINISH

SAYING GOODBYE TO YOU!

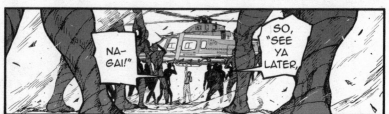

NA-GAI!"

SO, "SEE YA LATER,

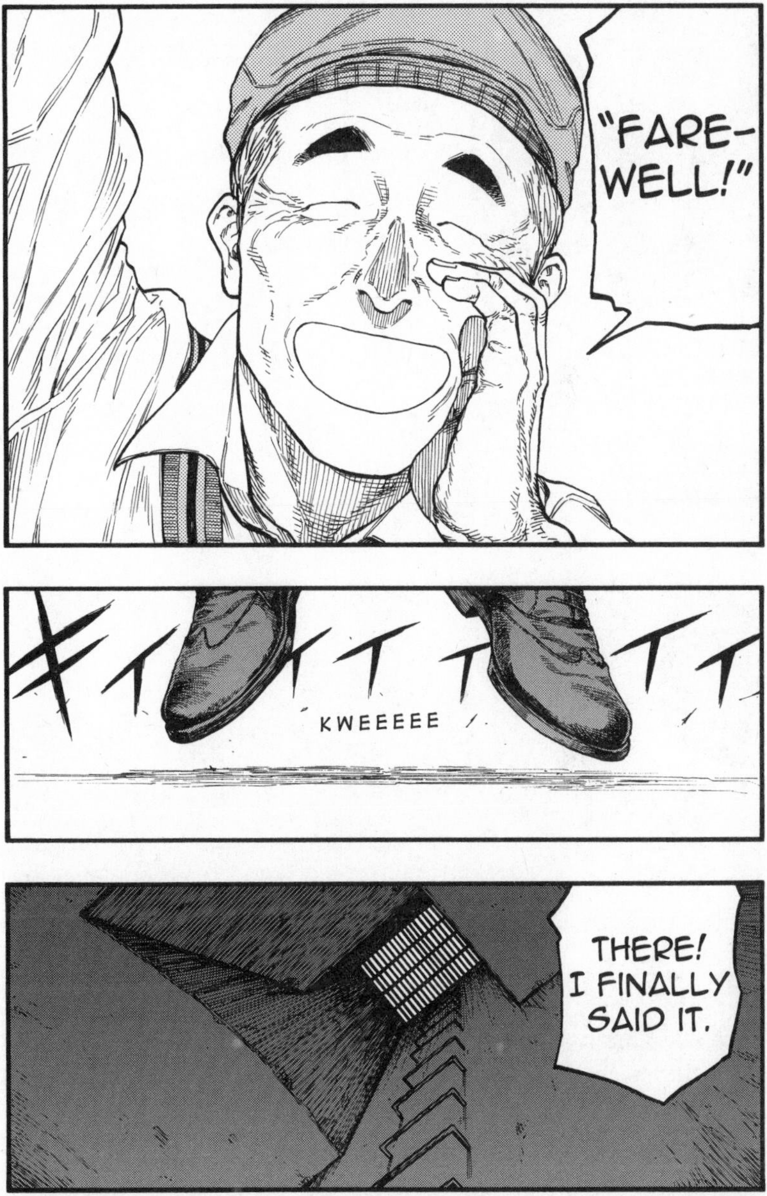
"FARE-WELL!"
KWEEEEE
THERE! I FINALLY SAID IT.

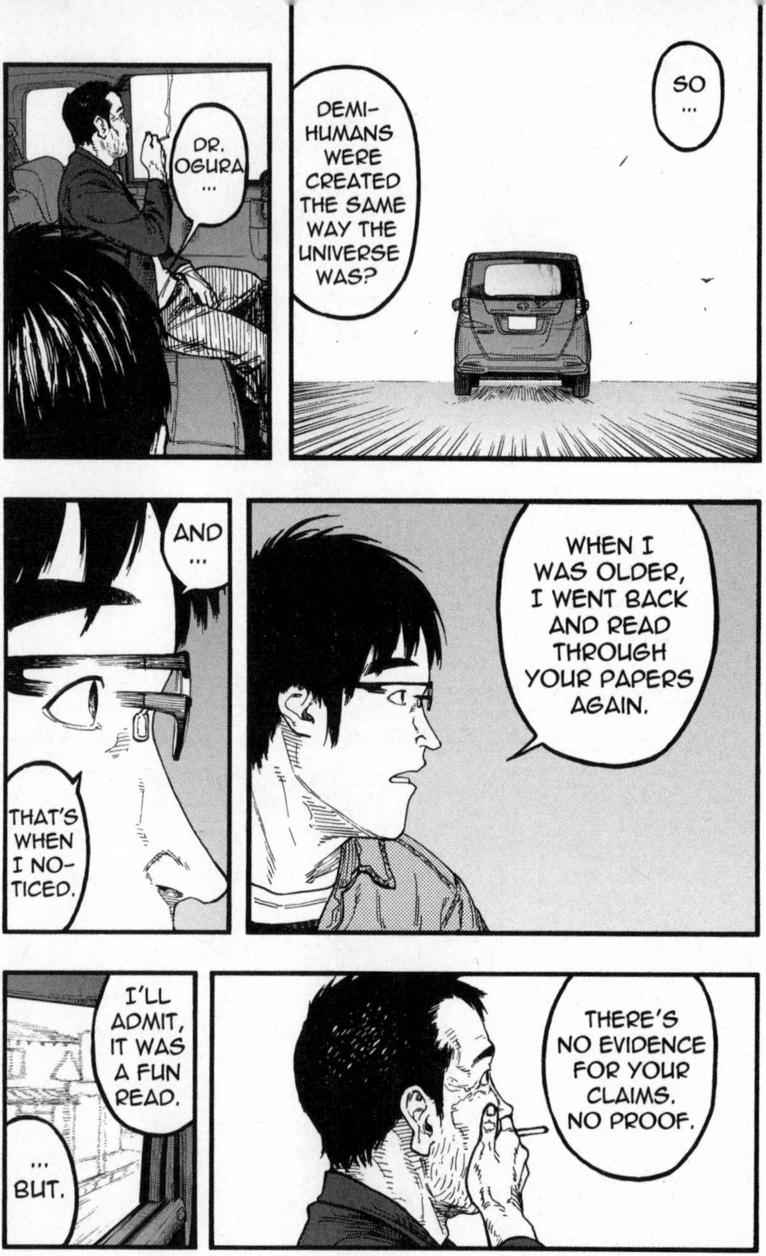
SO ...
DEMI-HUMANS WERE CREATED THE SAME WAY THE UNIVERSE WAS?
DR. OGURA ...
WHEN I WAS OLDER, I WENT BACK AND READ THROUGH YOUR PAPERS AGAIN.
AND ...
THAT'S WHEN I NOTICED.
THERE'S NO EVIDENCE FOR YOUR CLAIMS. NO PROOF.
I'LL ADMIT, IT WAS A FUN READ.
... BUT.

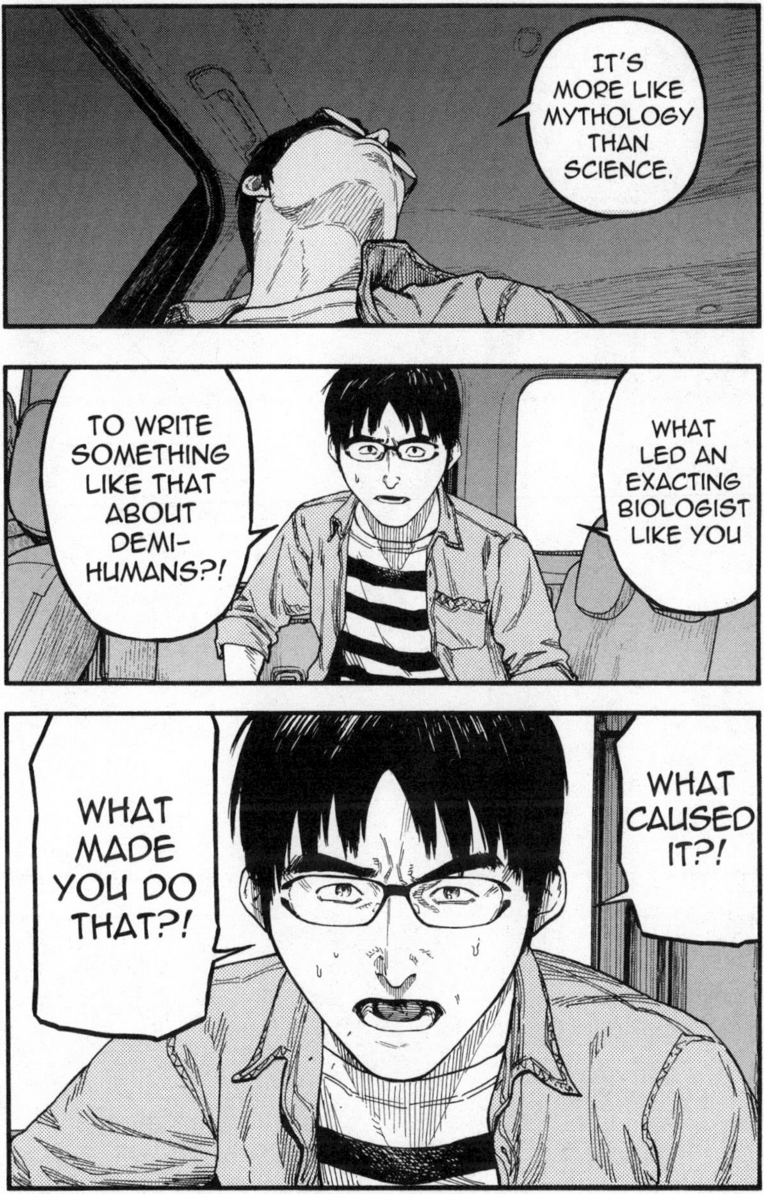
IT'S MORE LIKE MYTHOLOGY THAN SCIENCE.
WHAT LED AN EXACTING BIOLOGIST LIKE YOU
TO WRITE SOMETHING LIKE THAT ABOUT DEMI-HUMANS?!
WHAT CAUSED IT?!
WHAT MADE YOU DO THAT?!

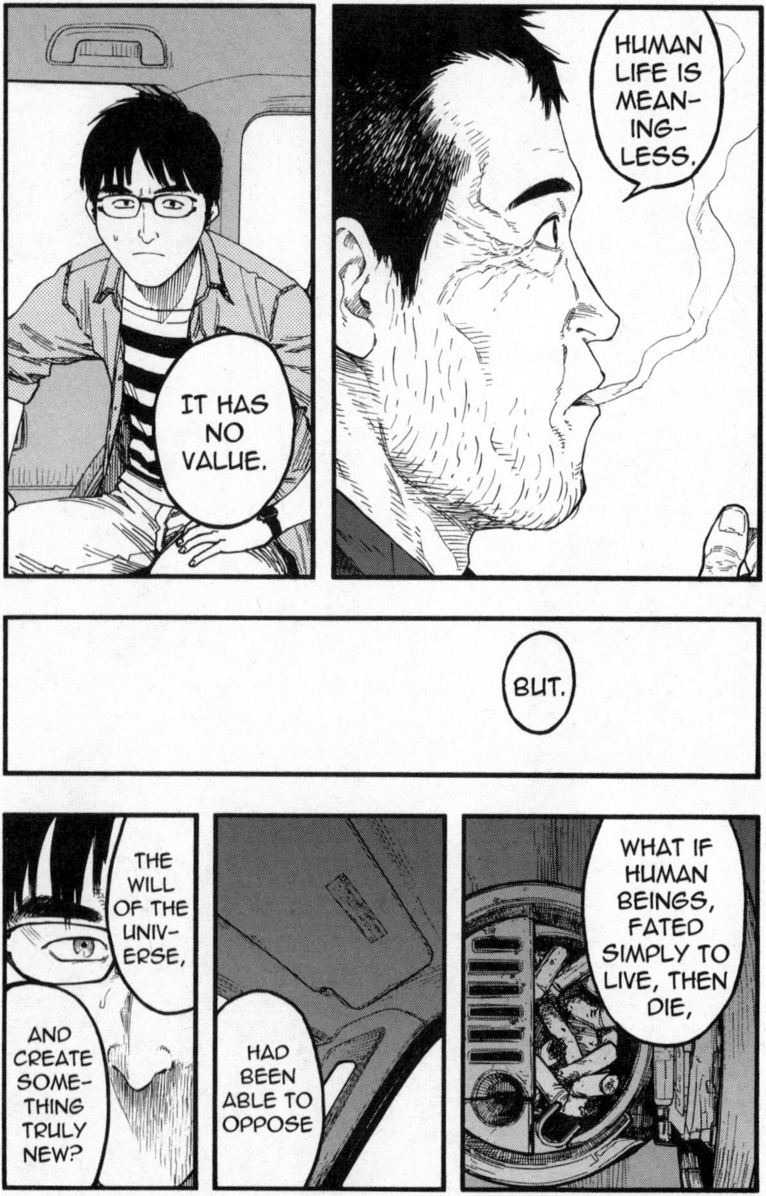
HUMAN LIFE IS MEAN-ING-LESS.
IT HAS NO VALUE.
BUT.
WHAT IF HUMAN BEINGS, FATED SIMPLY TO LIVE, THEN DIE,
HAD BEEN ABLE TO OPPOSE
THE WILL OF THE UNIV-ERSE,
AND CREATE SOME-THING TRULY NEW?

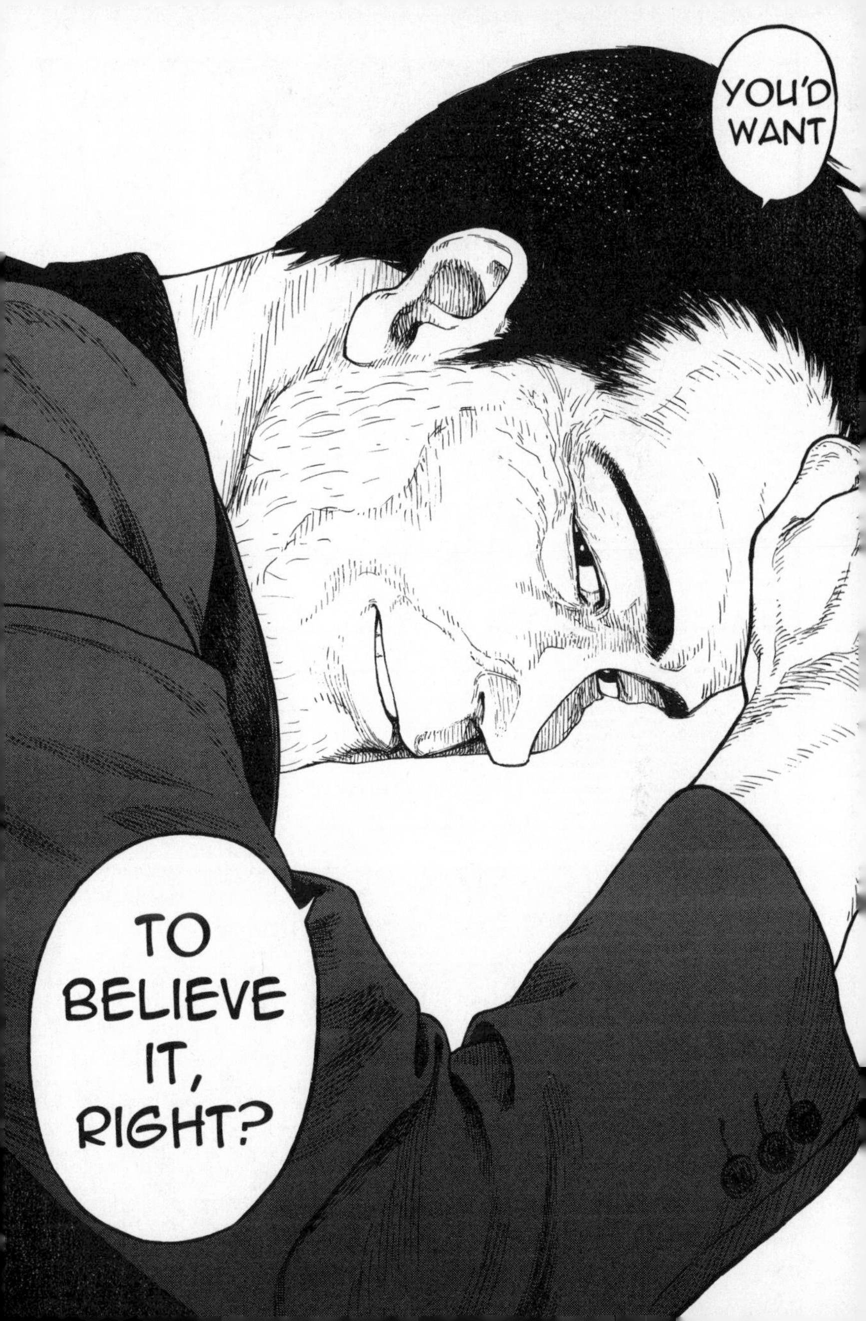
YOU'D WANT
TO BELIEVE IT, RIGHT?

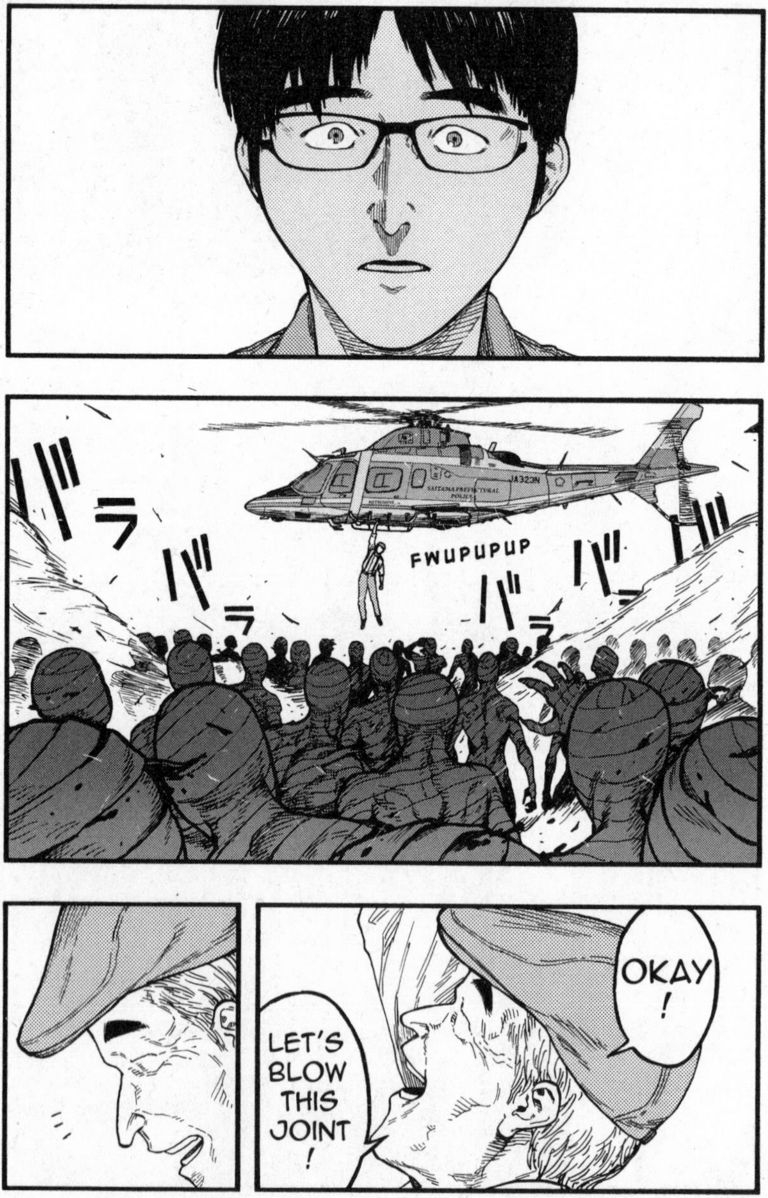
バラ
バラ
FWUPUPUP
バラ
OKAY!
LET'S BLOW THIS JOINT!

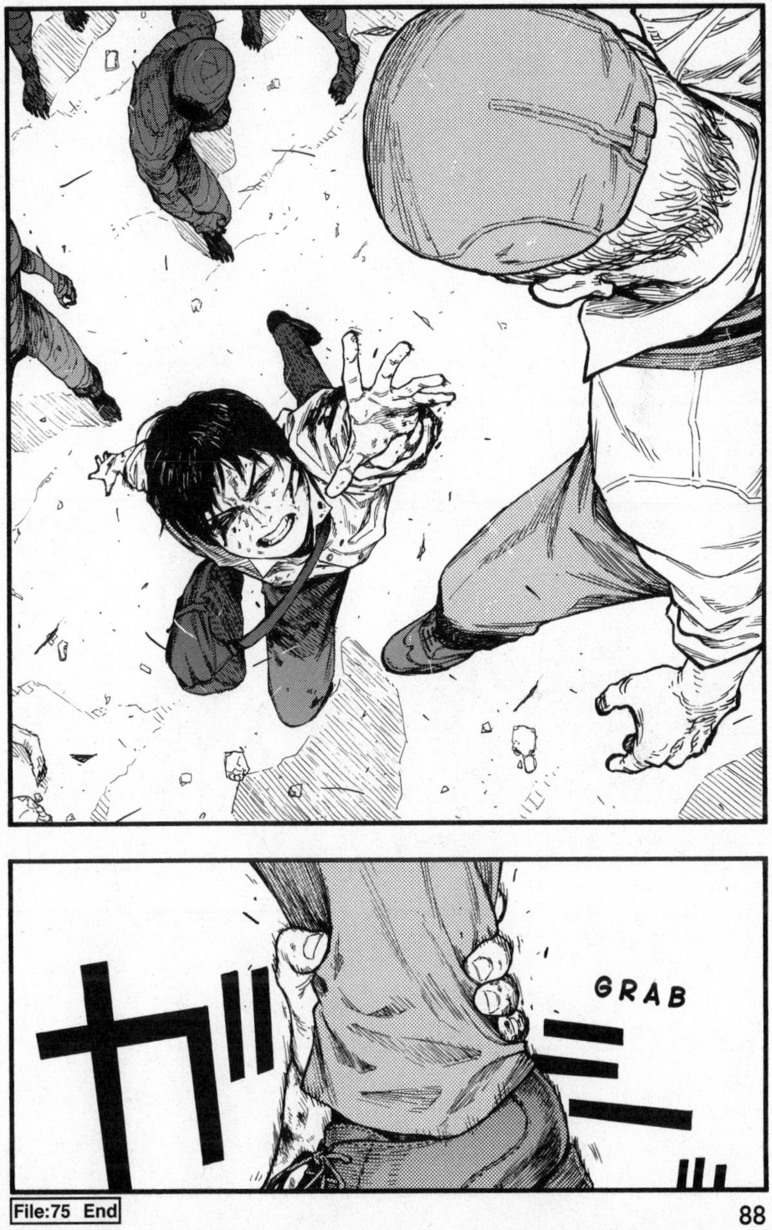
GRAB

File:75 End

File: 76

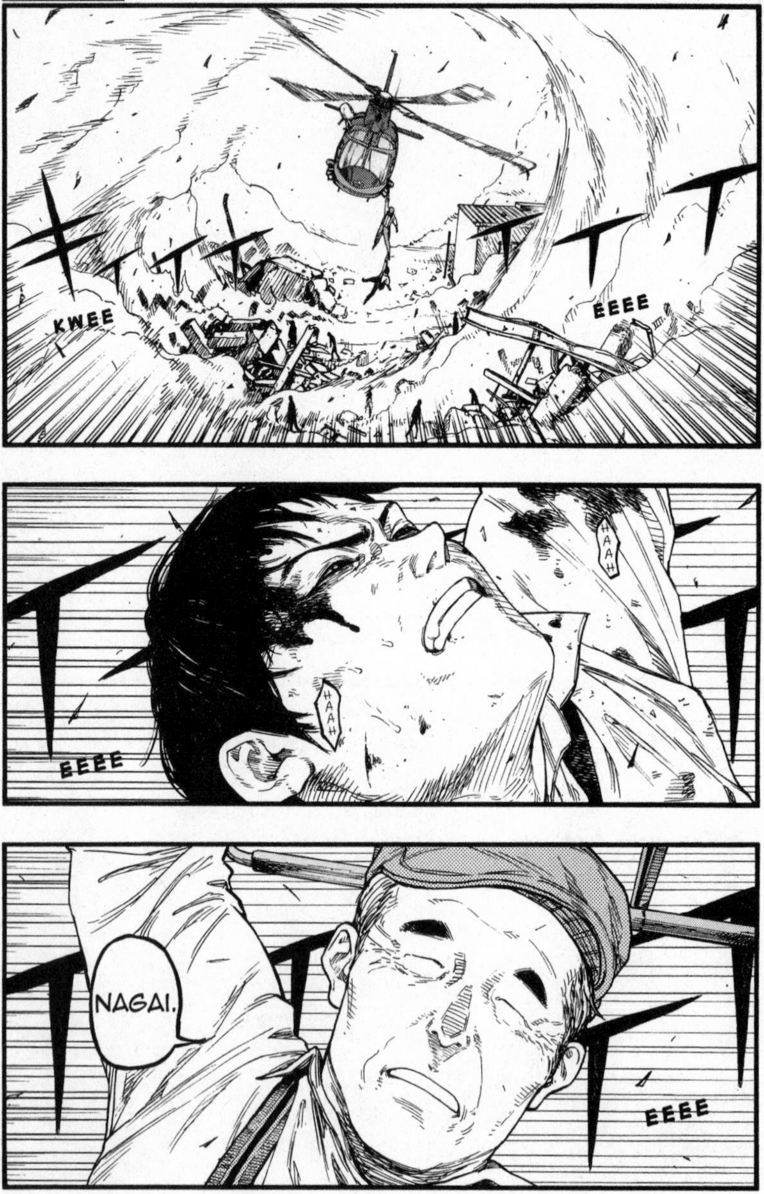
KWEE
EEEE
HAAH
HAAH
EEEE
NAGAI.
EEEE

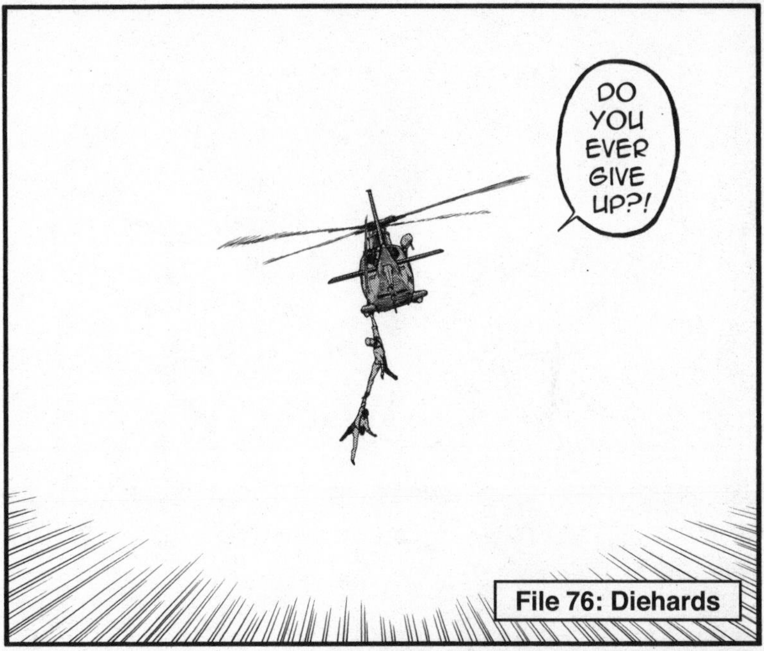
DO YOU EVER GIVE UP?!
File 76: Diehards

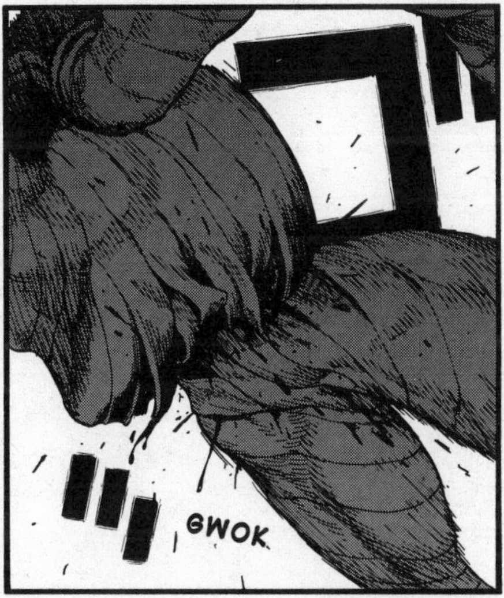
GWOK

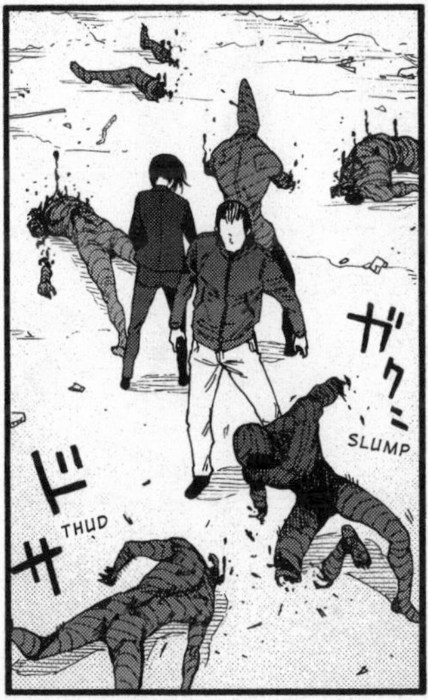
ガクッ
SLUMP
ドサ
THUD

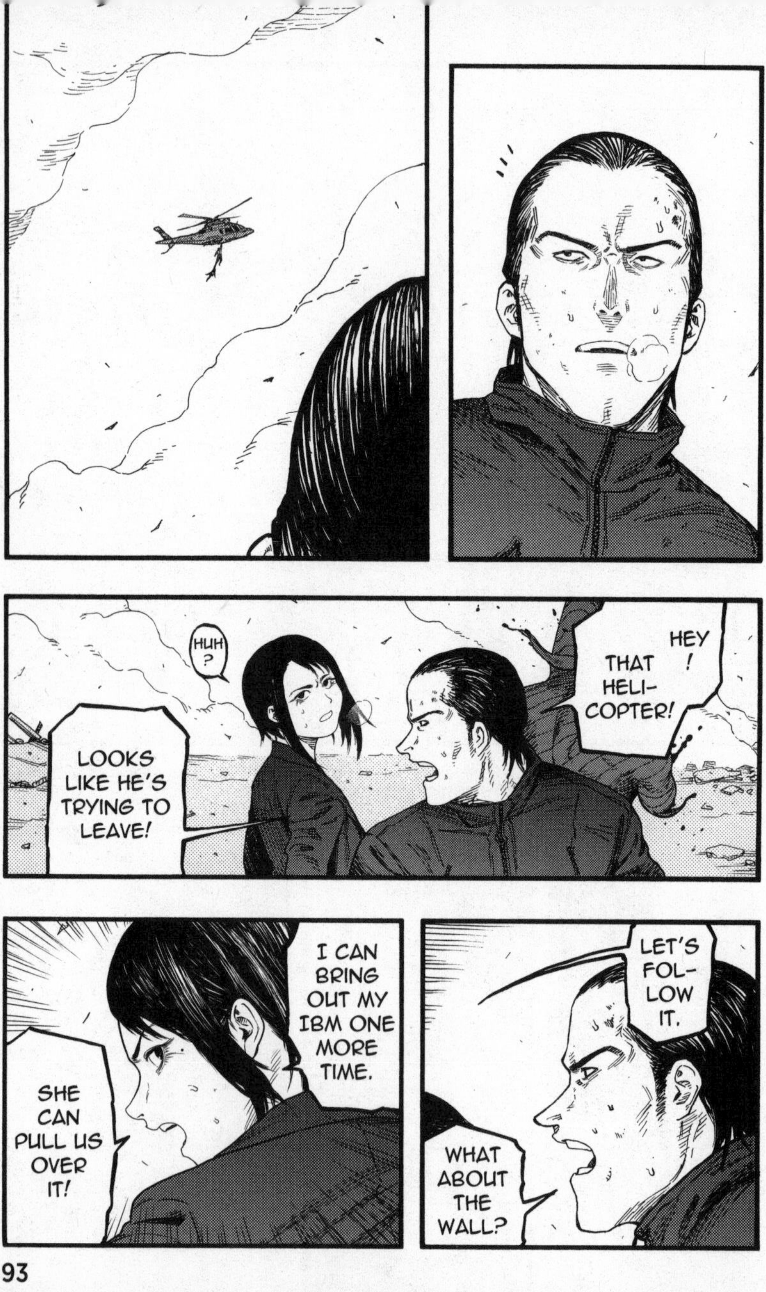
HEY! THAT HELI-COPTER!
HUH?
LOOKS LIKE HE'S TRYING TO LEAVE!
LET'S FOL-LOW IT.
WHAT ABOUT THE WALL?
I CAN BRING OUT MY IBM ONE MORE TIME.
SHE CAN PULL US OVER IT!

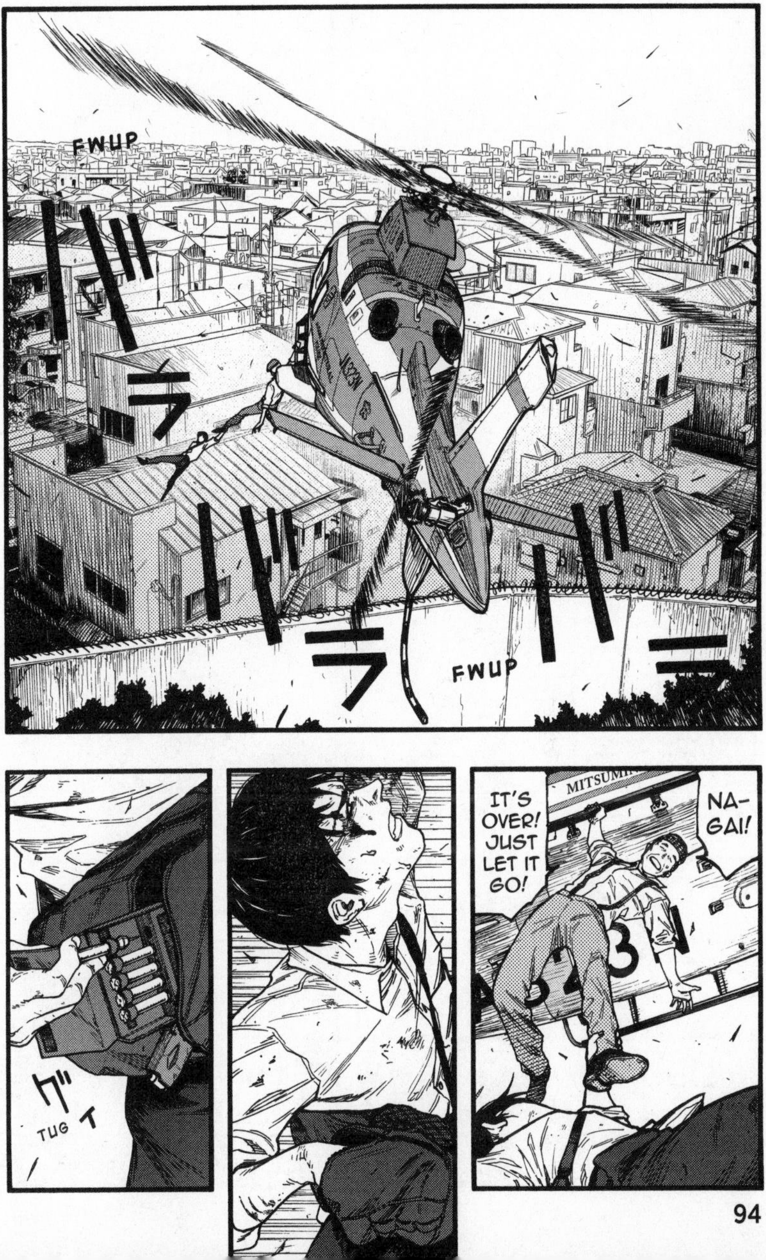
FWUP
FWUP
NA-GAI!
IT'S OVER! JUST LET IT GO!
TUG

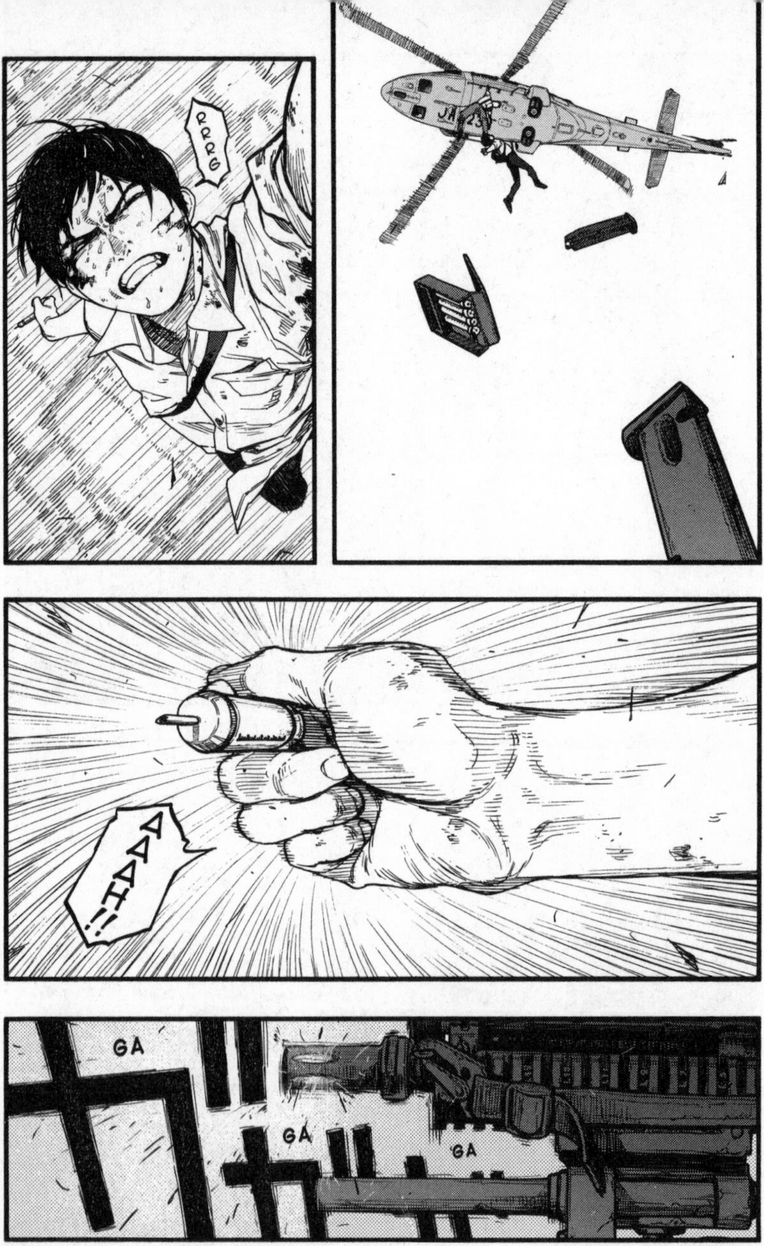
RRRG
AAAH!!
GA
GA
GA

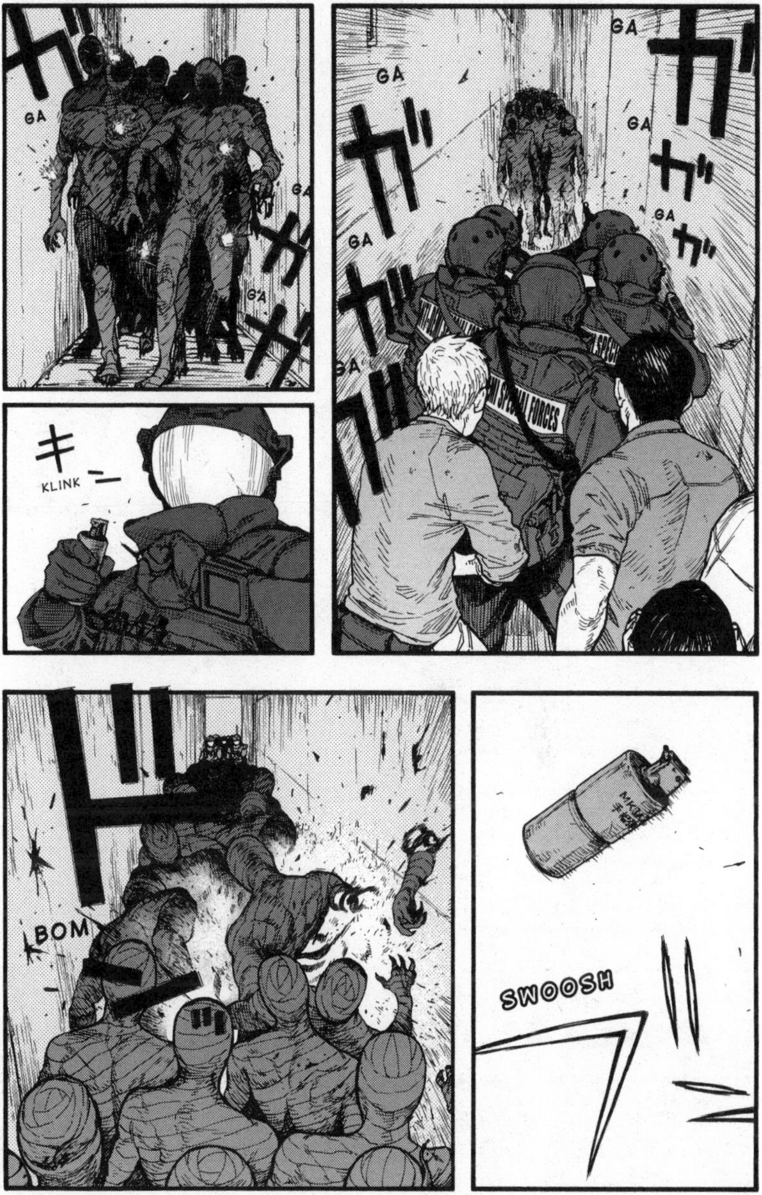
GA
GA
GA
GA
GA
GA
SPECIAL FORCES
GA
GA
GA
キ
KLINK
SWOOSH
BOM

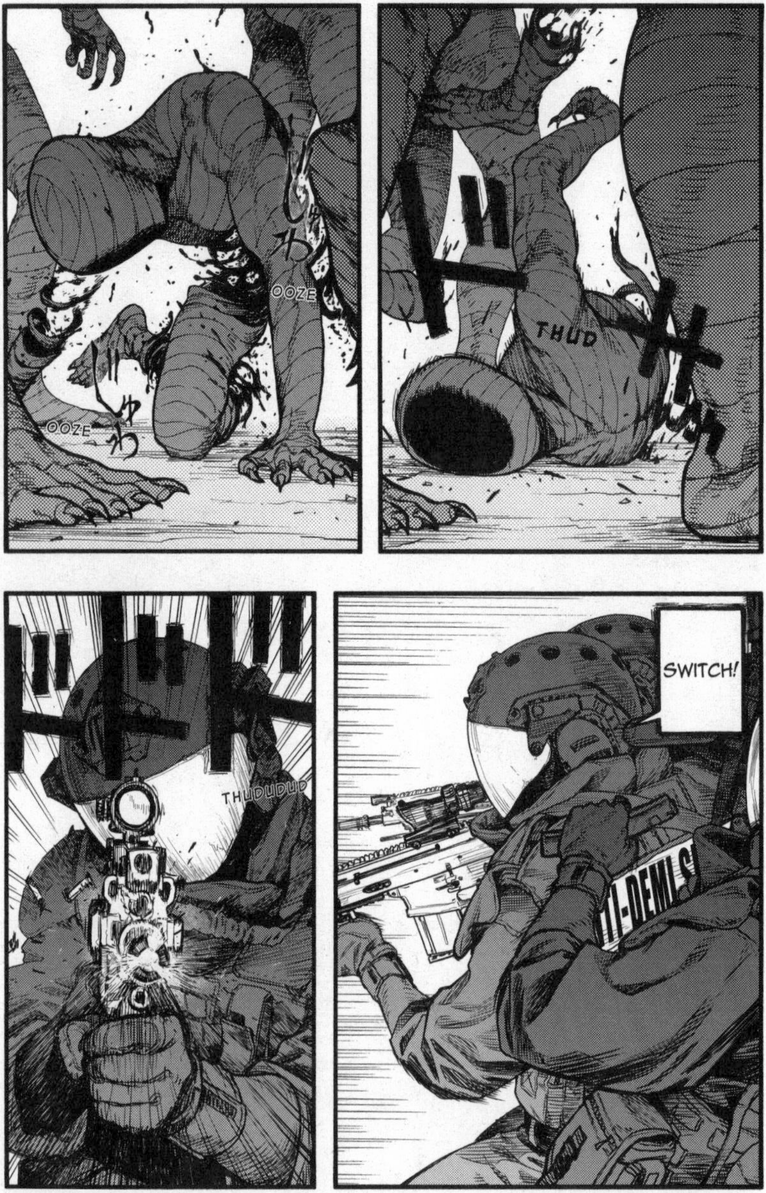
THUD
OOZE
OOZE
SWITCH!
THUDUDUD

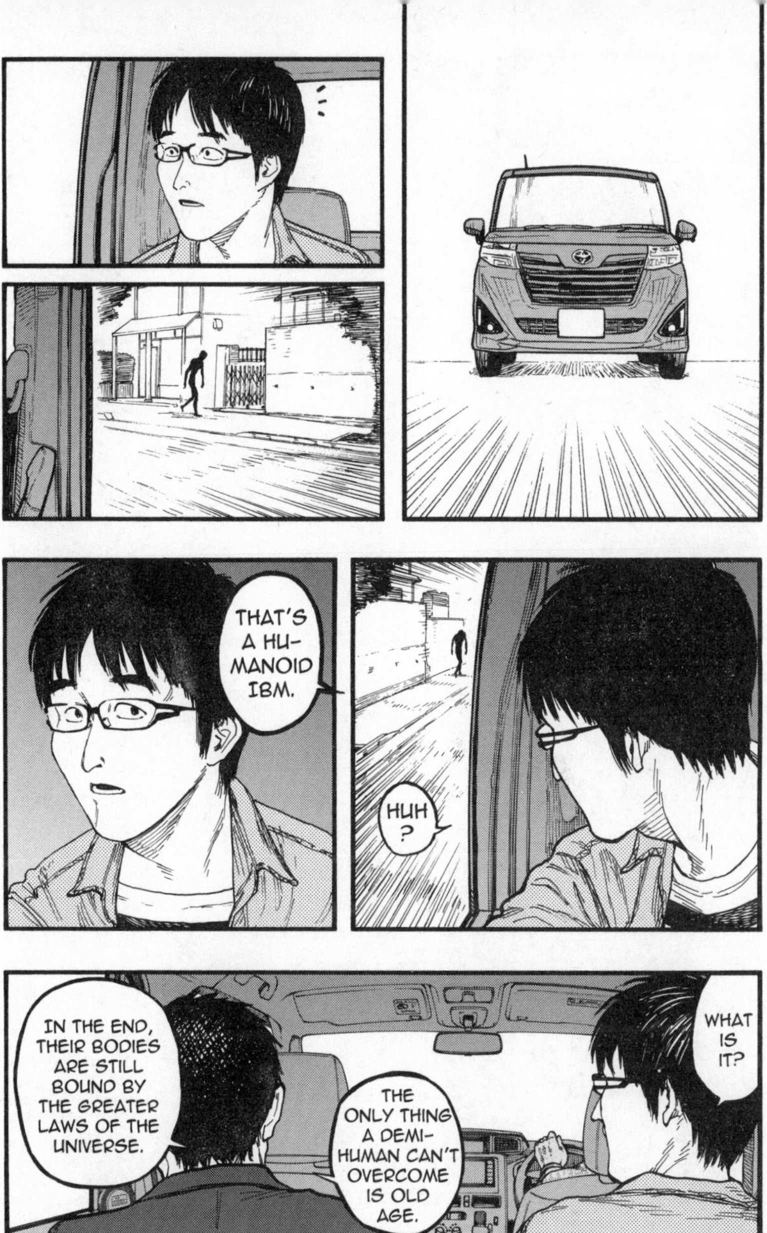
HUH?
THAT'S A HUMANOID IBM.
WHAT IS IT?
THE ONLY THING A DEMI-HUMAN CAN'T OVERCOME IS OLD AGE.
IN THE END, THEIR BODIES ARE STILL BOUND BY THE GREATER LAWS OF THE UNIVERSE.

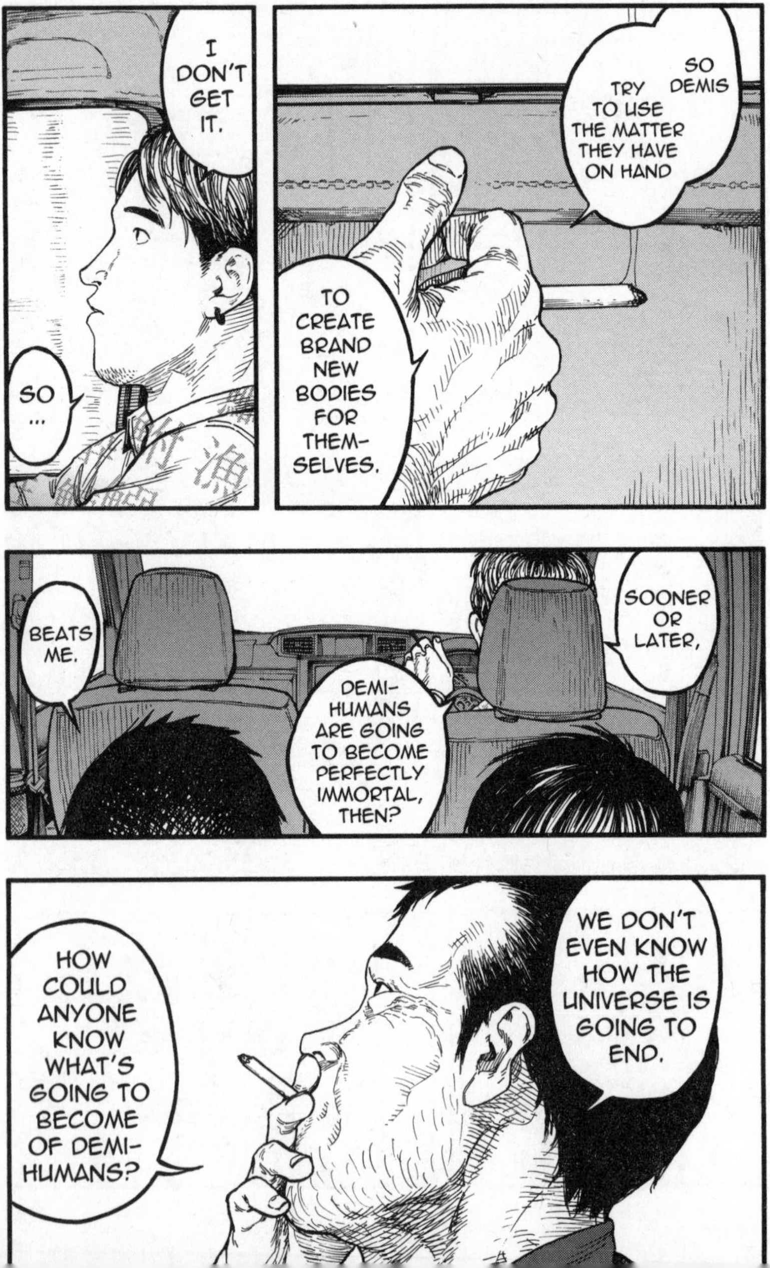
SO DEMIS TRY TO USE THE MATTER THEY HAVE ON HAND
TO CREATE BRAND NEW BODIES FOR THEM-SELVES.
I DON'T GET IT.
SO ...
SOONER OR LATER,
DEMI-HUMANS ARE GOING TO BECOME PERFECTLY IMMORTAL, THEN?
BEATS ME.
WE DON'T EVEN KNOW HOW THE UNIVERSE IS GOING TO END.
HOW COULD ANYONE KNOW WHAT'S GOING TO BECOME OF DEMI-HUMANS?

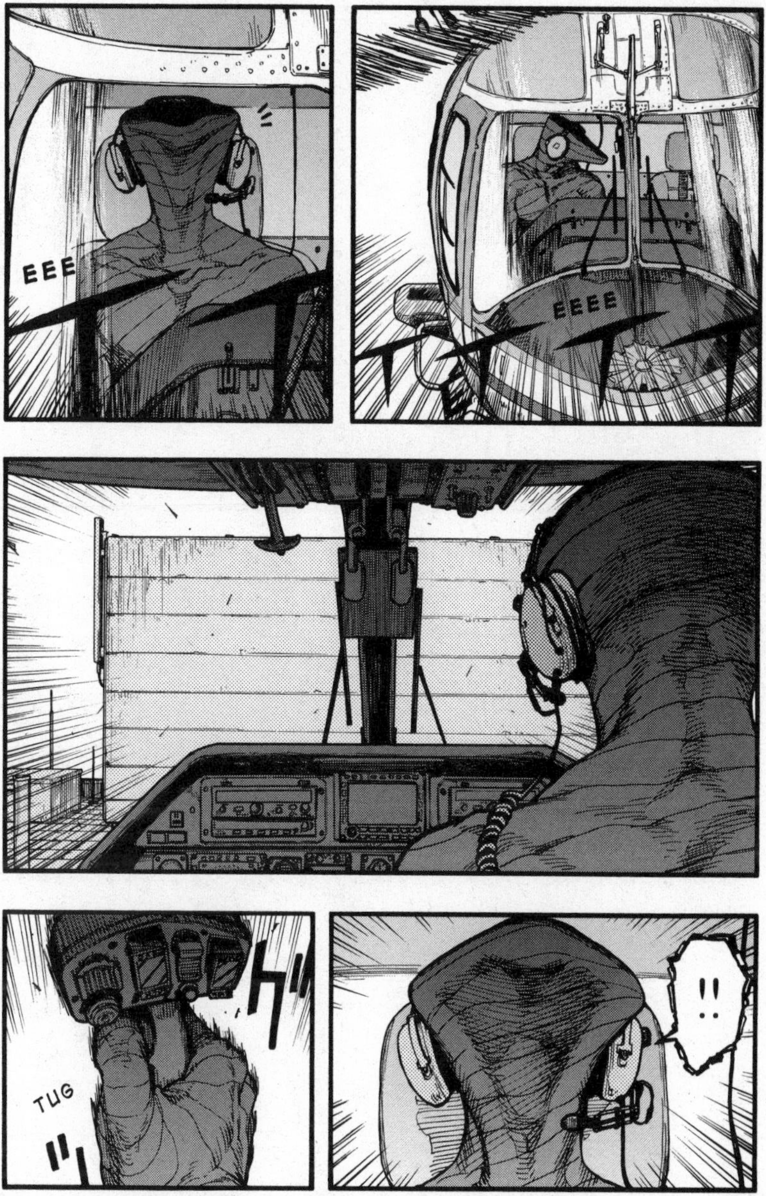
EEEE
EEE
!!
TUG

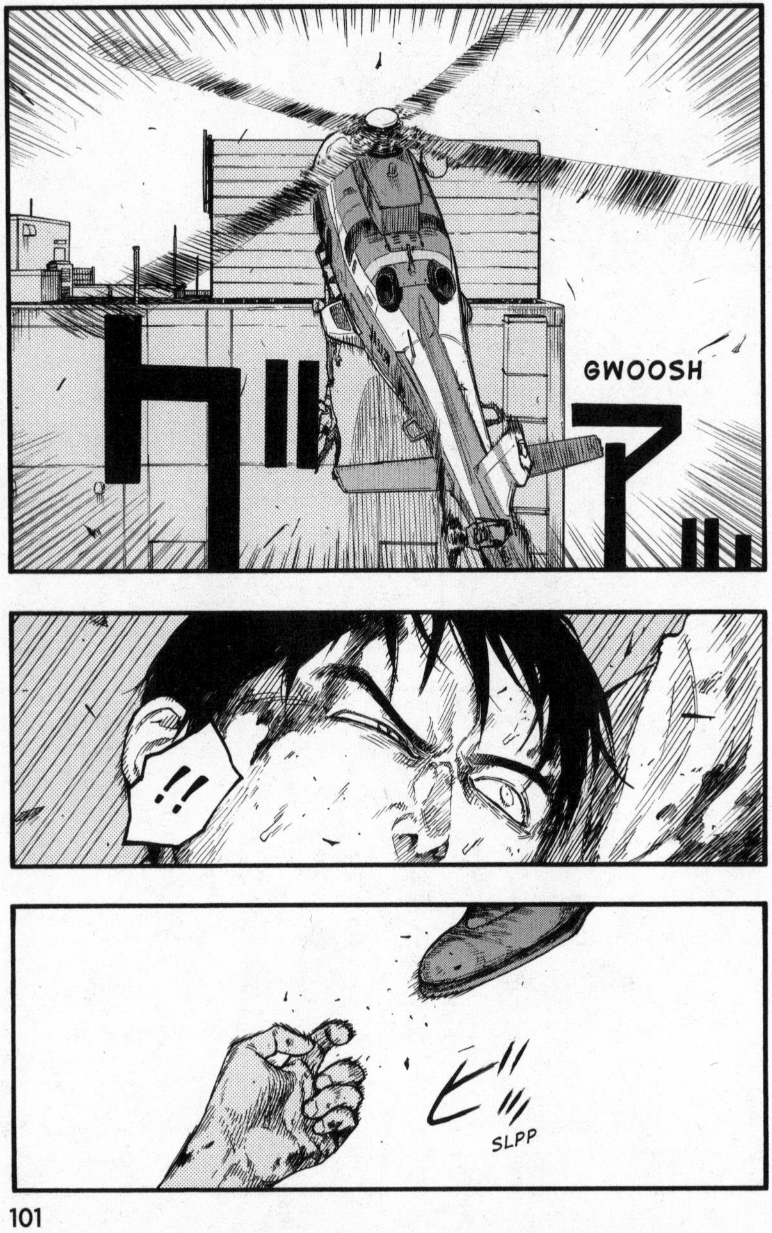
GWOOSH
!!
SLPP

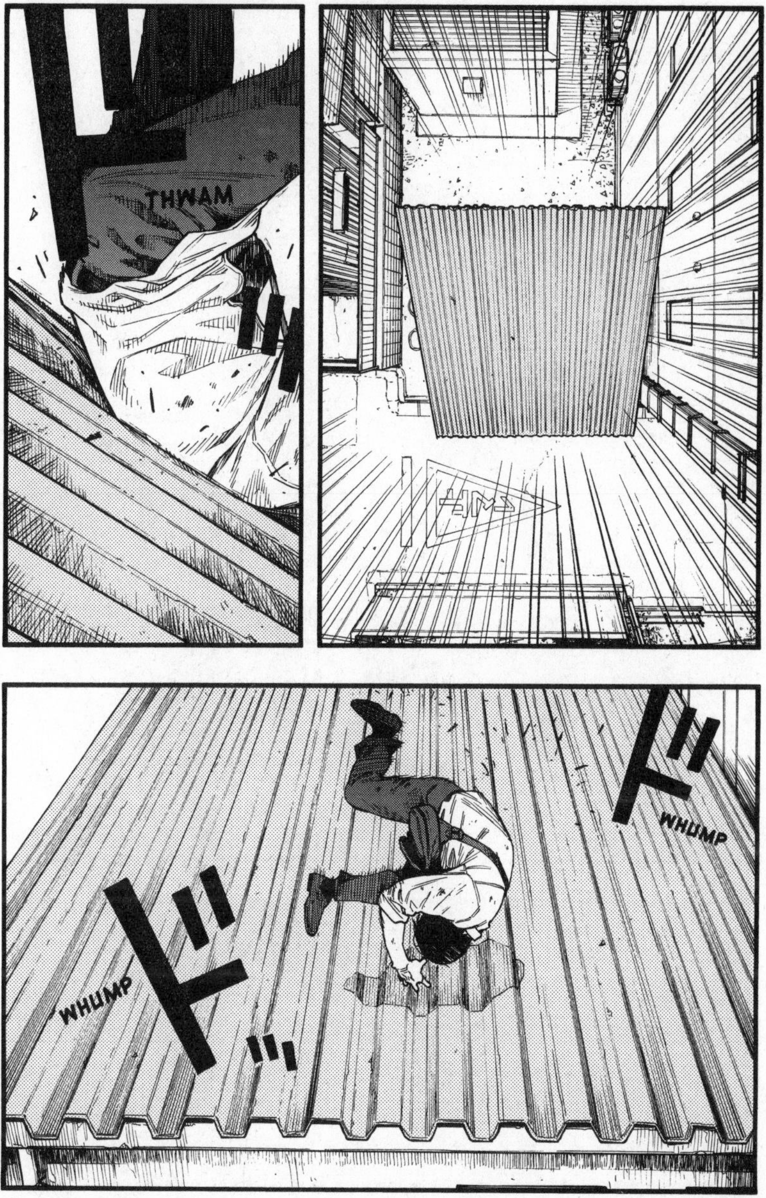
THWAM
WHUMP
WHUMP

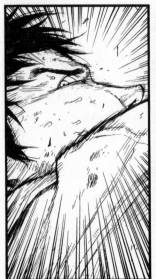

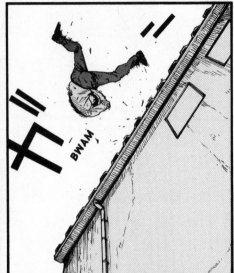

BWAM

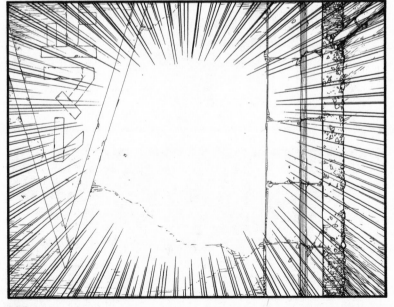

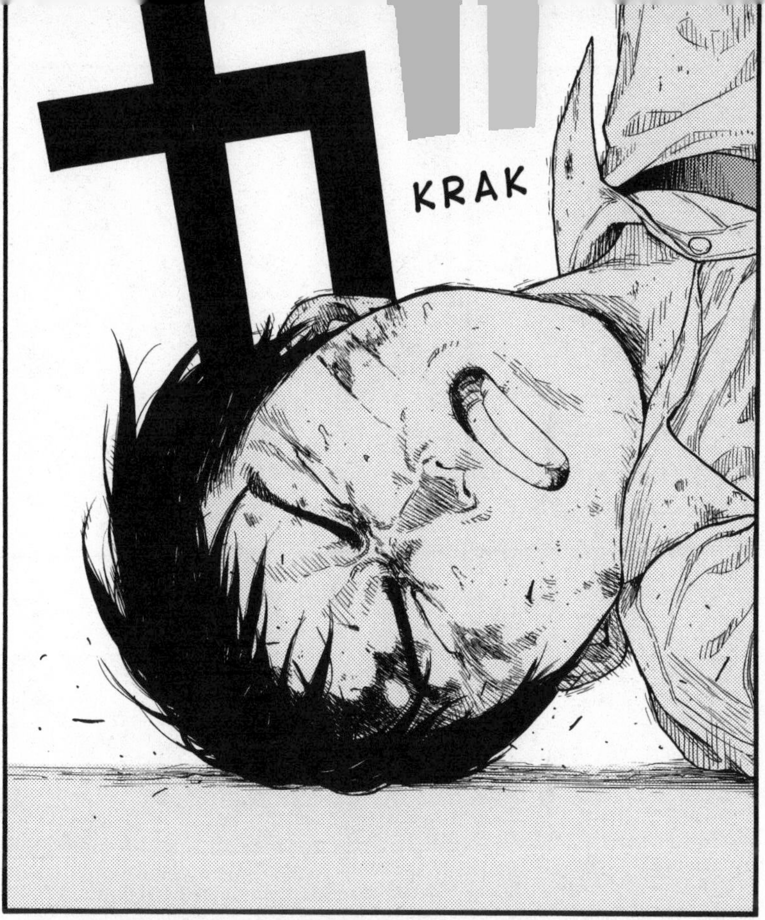
KRAK
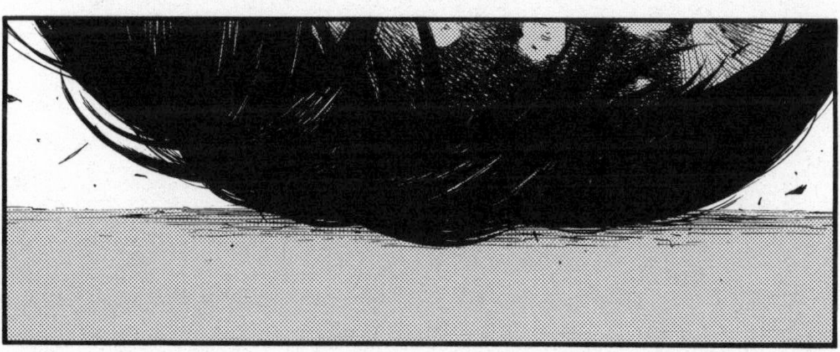

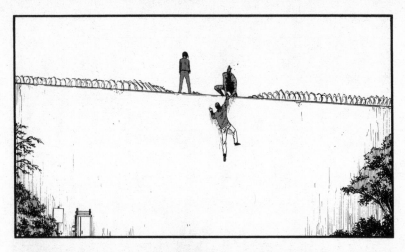

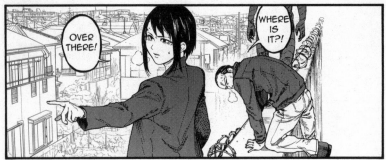

OVER THERE!

WHERE IS IT?!

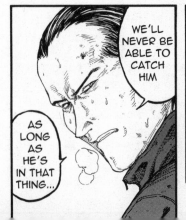

WE'LL NEVER BE ABLE TO CATCH HIM

AS LONG AS HE'S IN THAT THING...

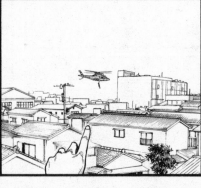

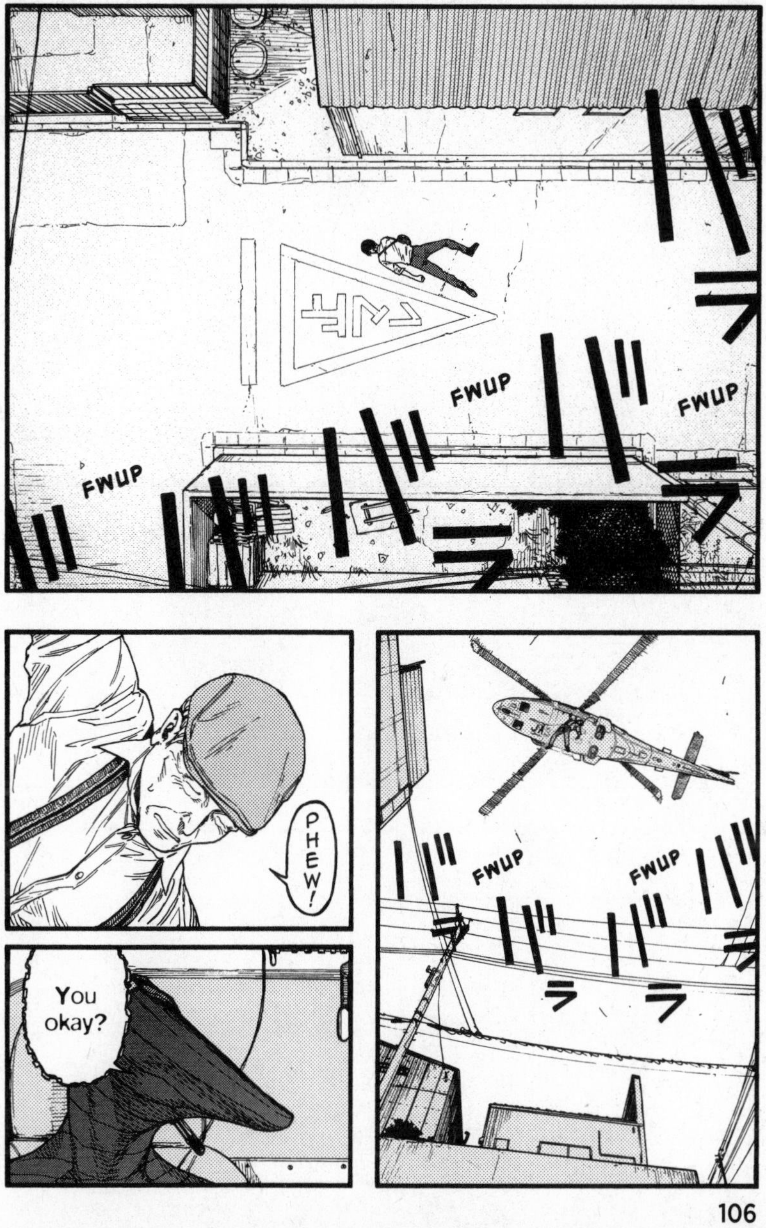
FWUP
FWUP
FWUP
FWUP
FWUP
PHEW!
You okay?

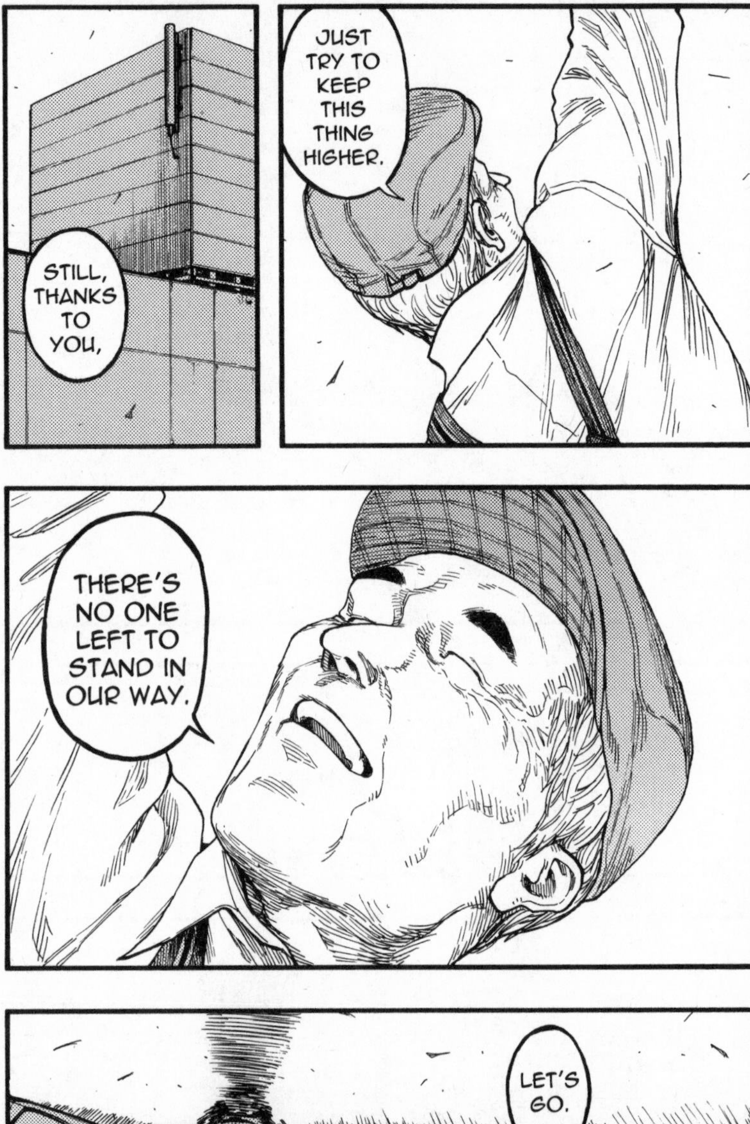
JUST TRY TO KEEP THIS THING HIGHER.
STILL, THANKS TO YOU,
THERE'S NO ONE LEFT TO STAND IN OUR WAY.
LET'S GO.

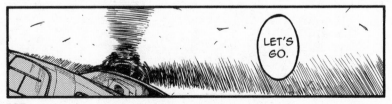

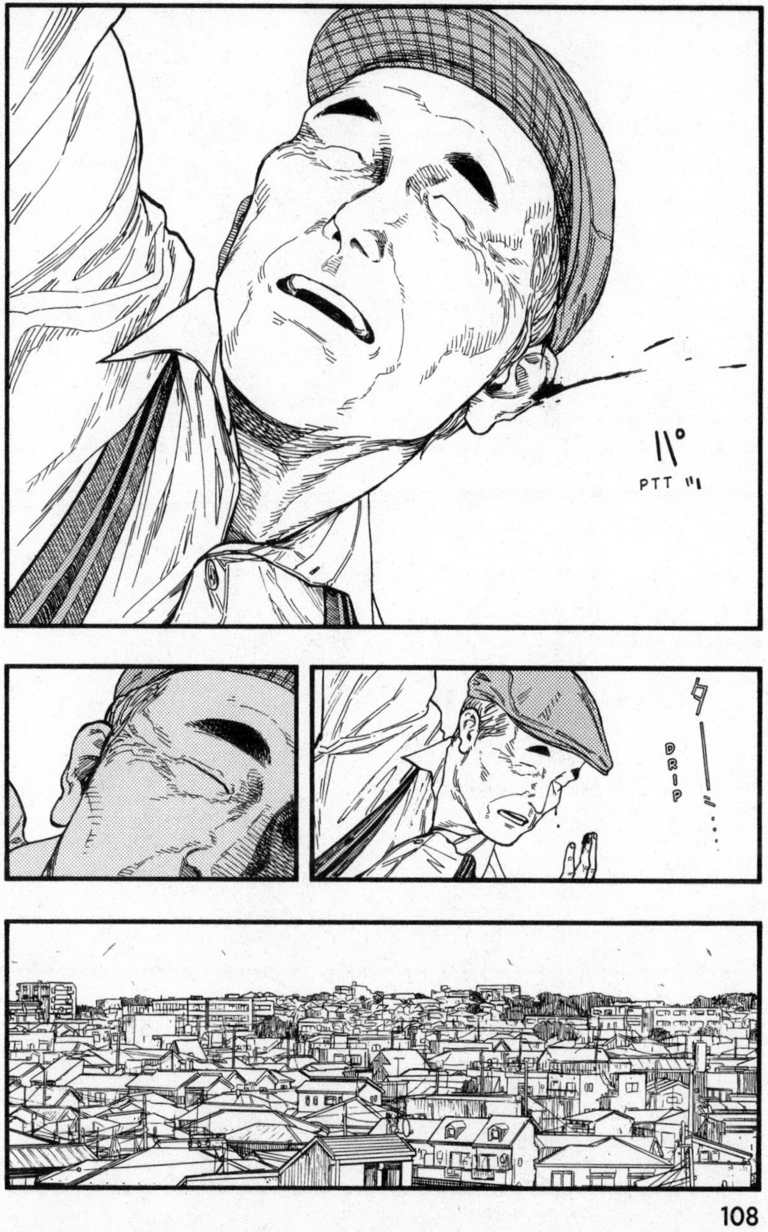
パ
PTT !!
ター…
DRIP

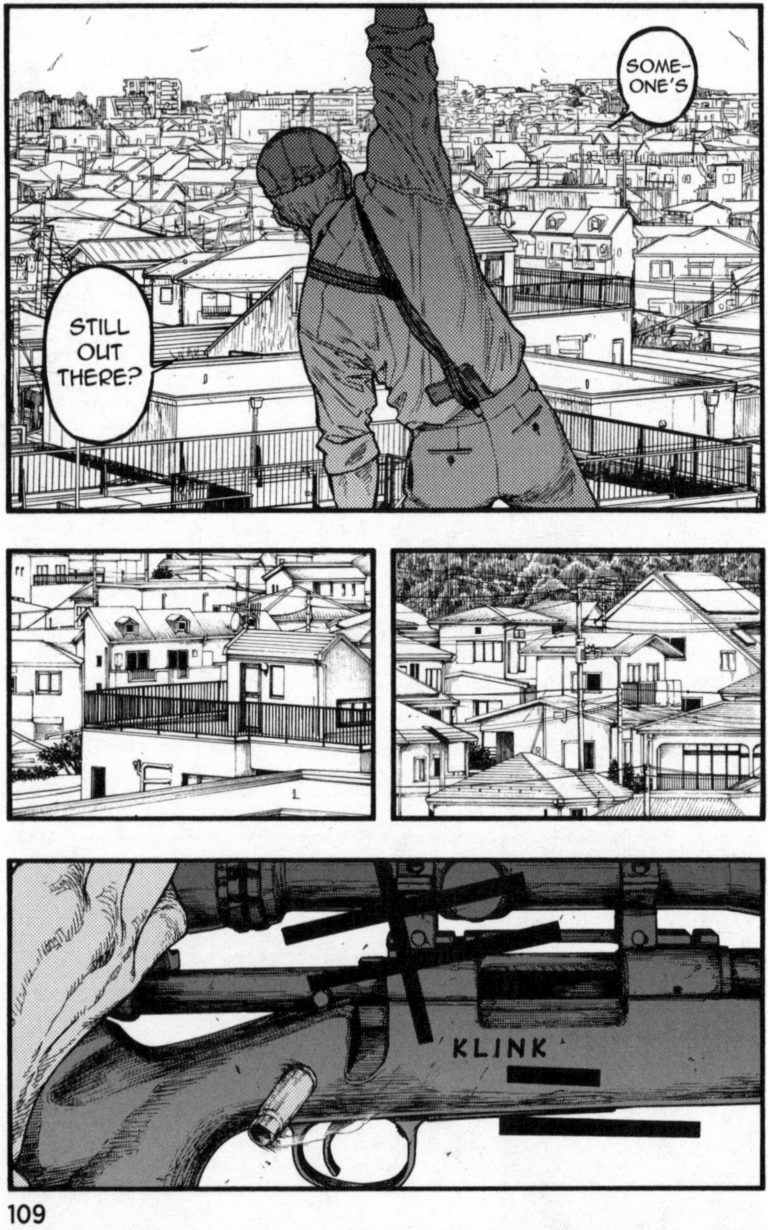
SOME-ONE'S
STILL OUT THERE?
KLINK

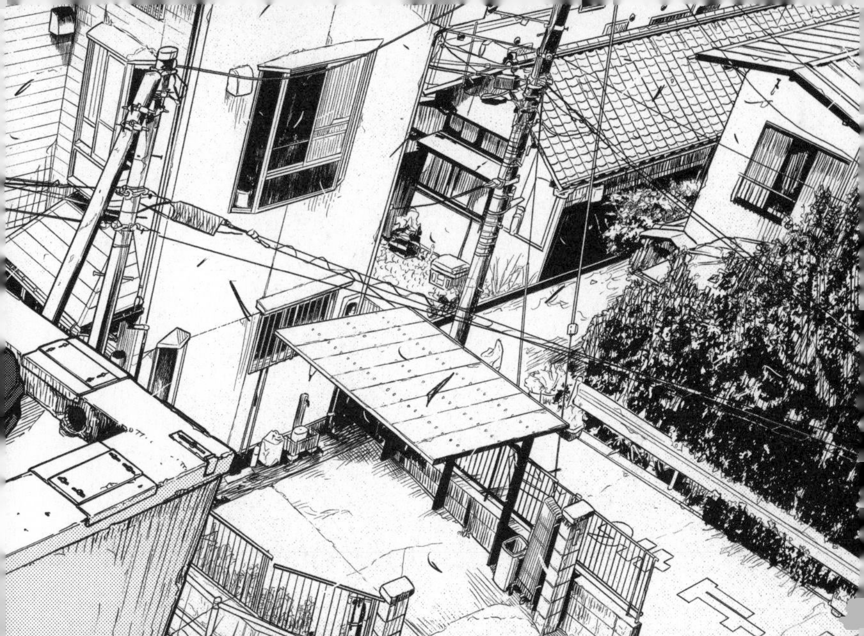

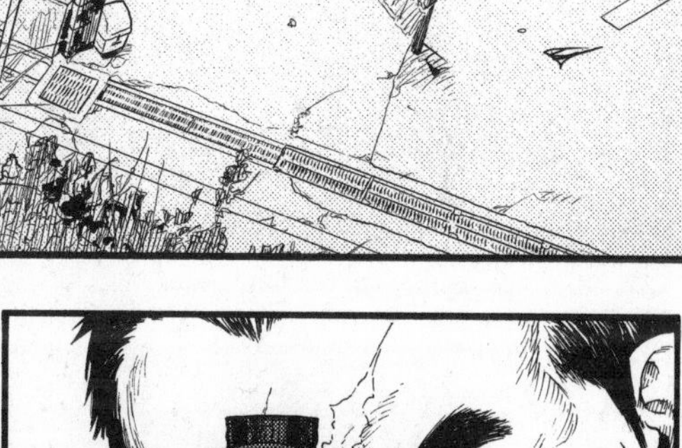

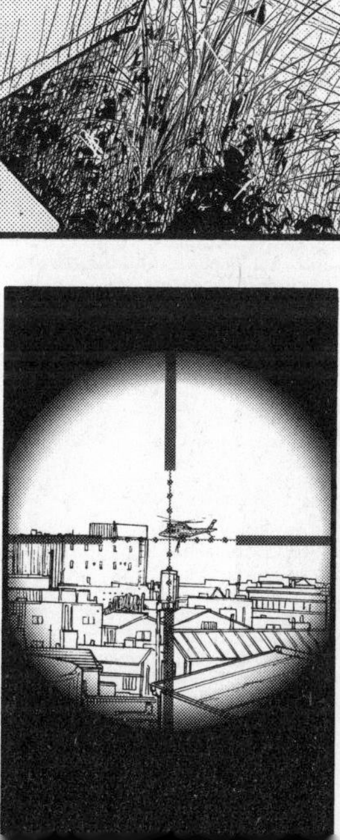

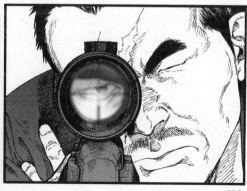

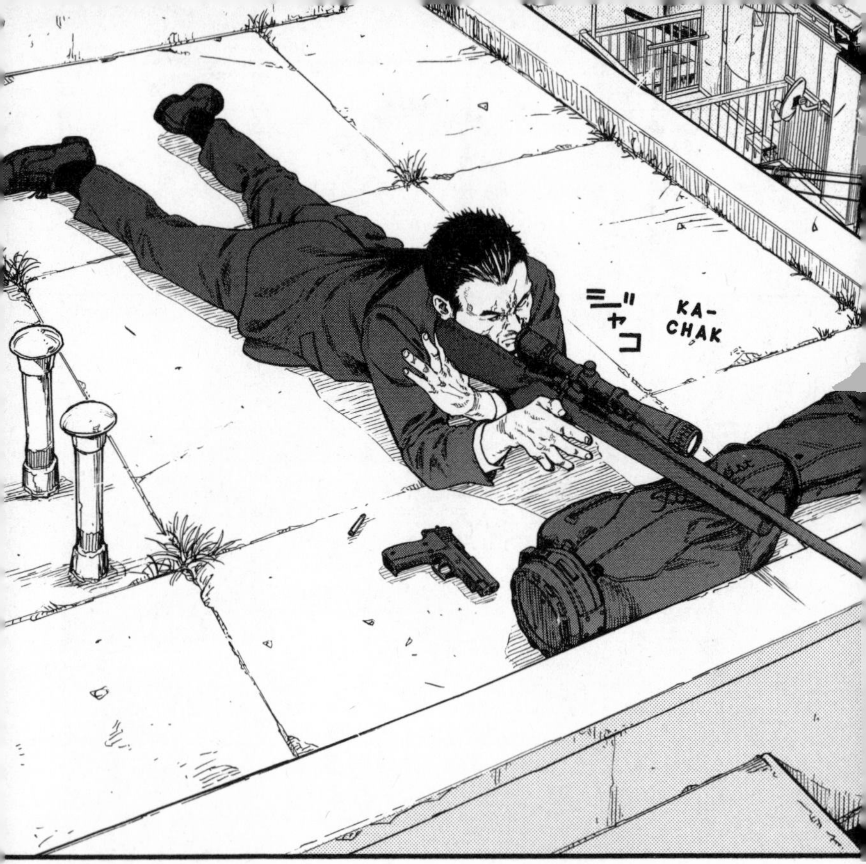
ジャコ
KA-CHAK
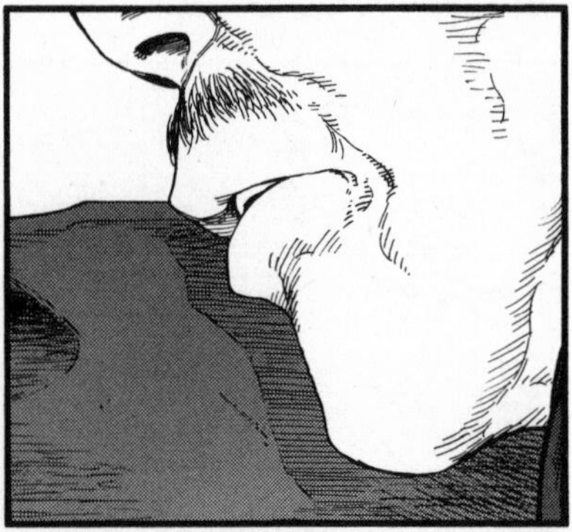
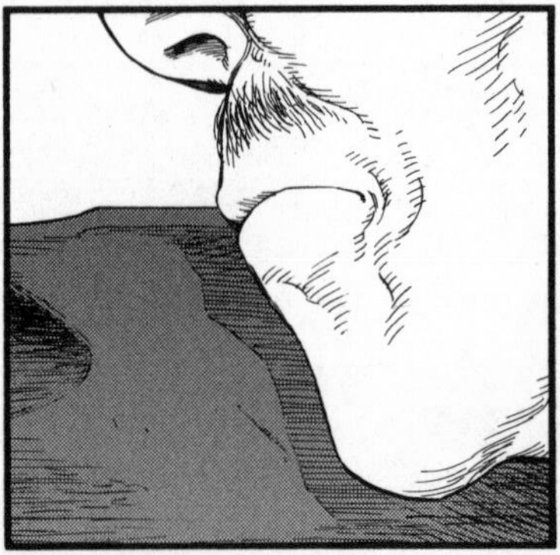

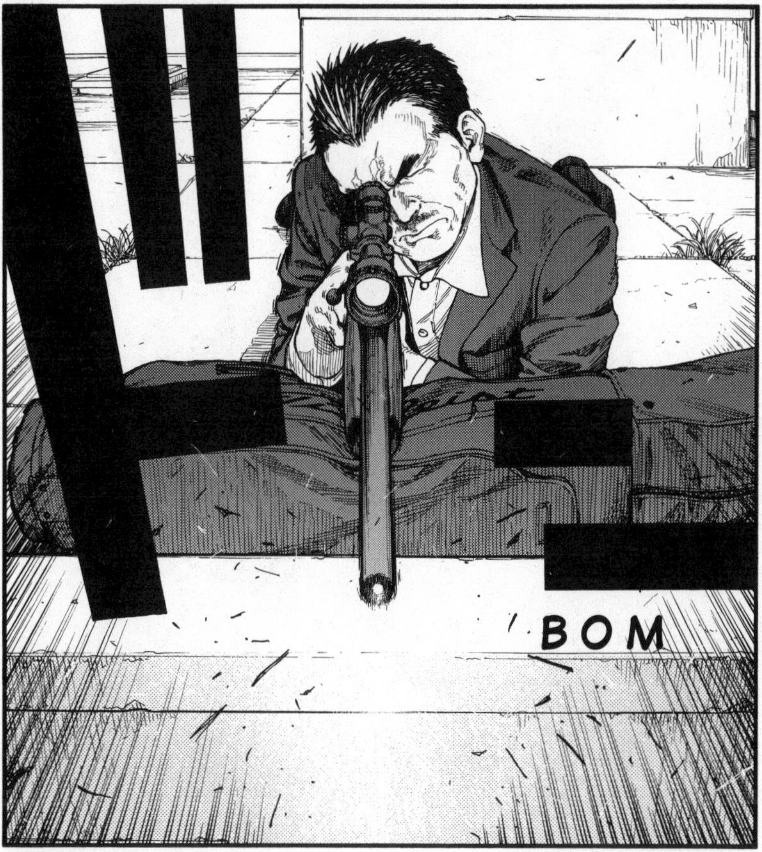
BOM

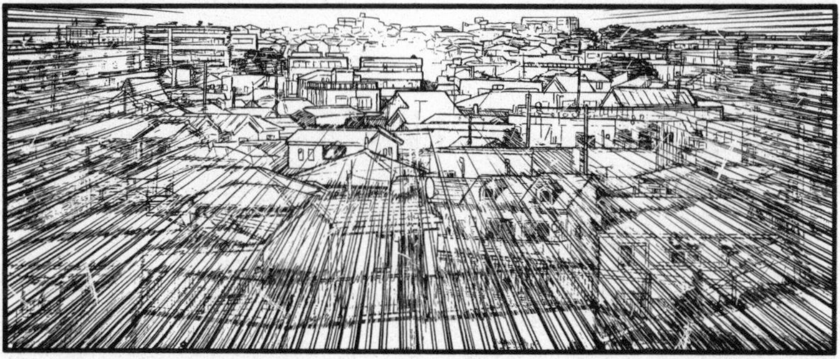

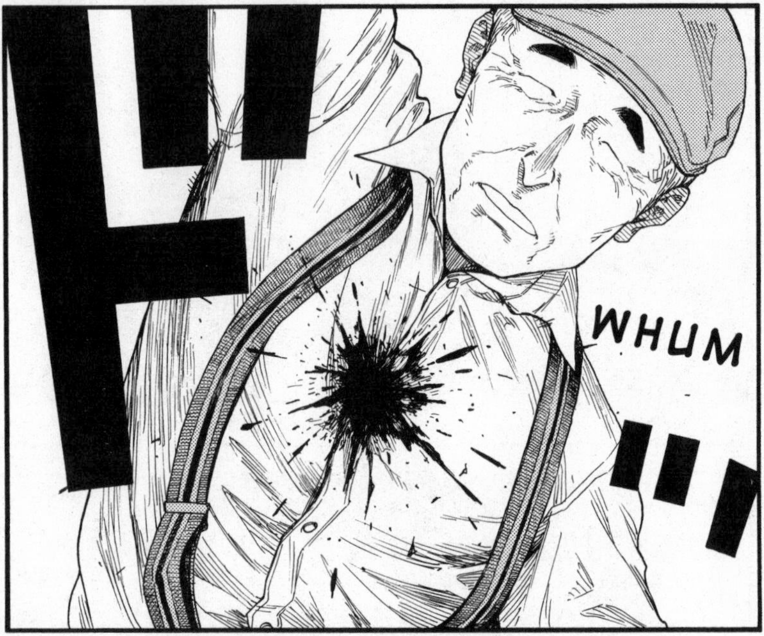
WHUM

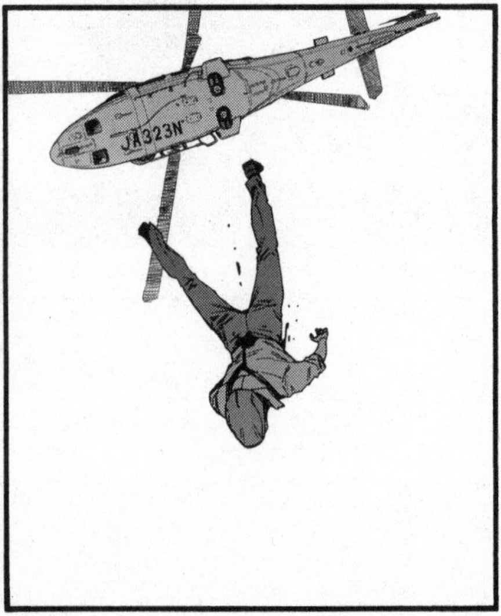
JA323N

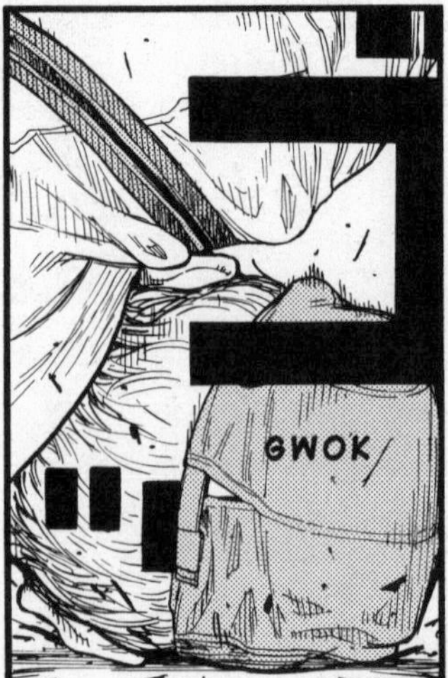
GWOK

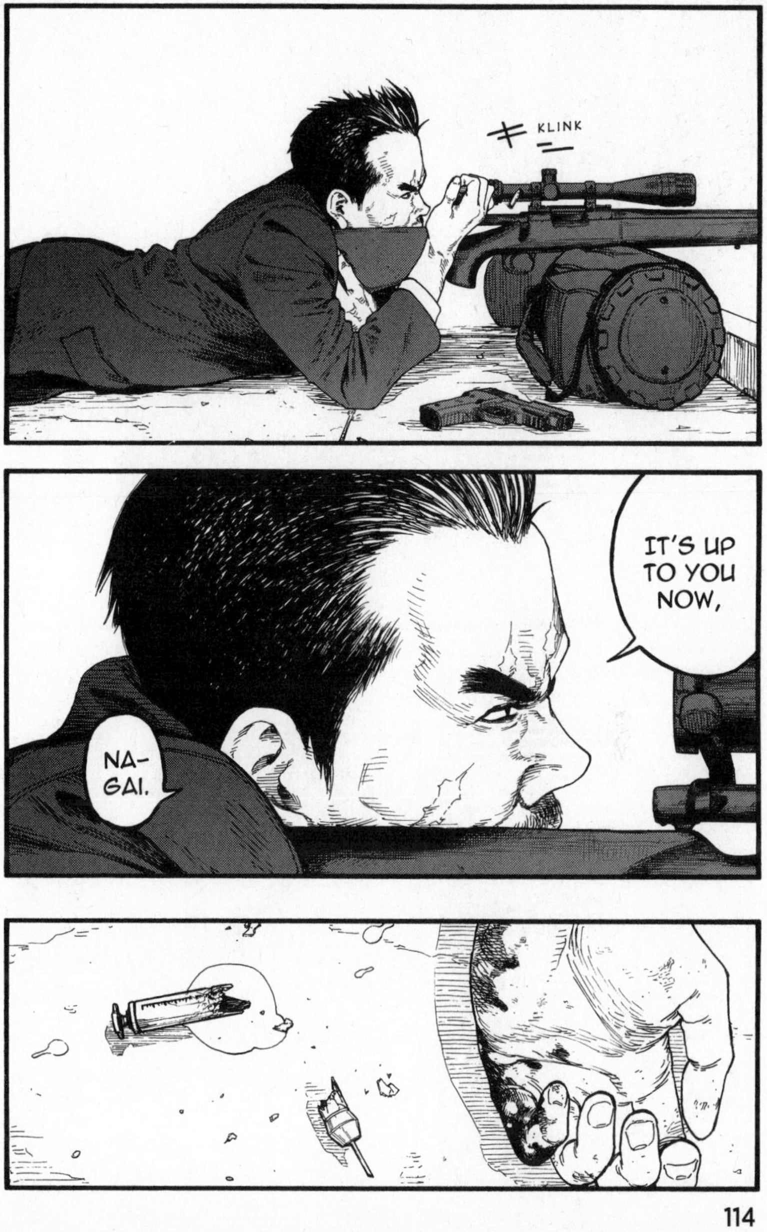
KLINK
IT'S UP TO YOU NOW,
NA-GAI.

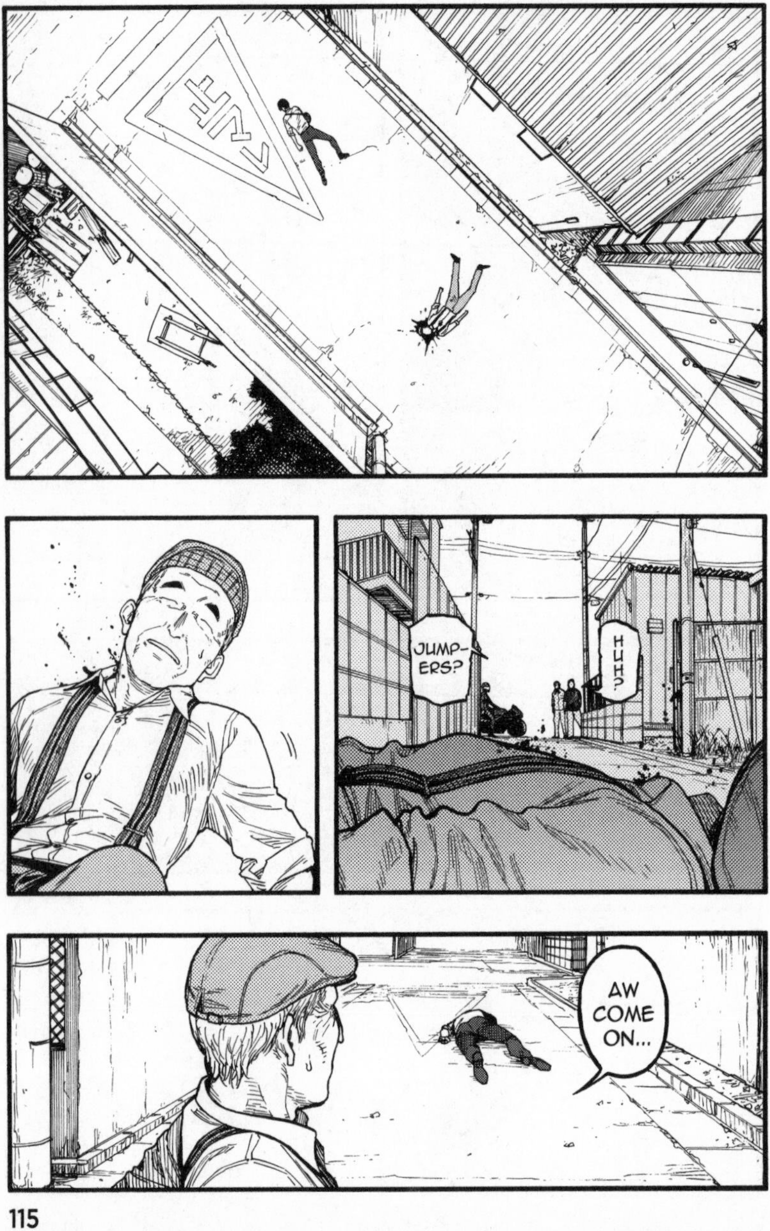
HUH?
JUMP-ERS?
AW COME ON...

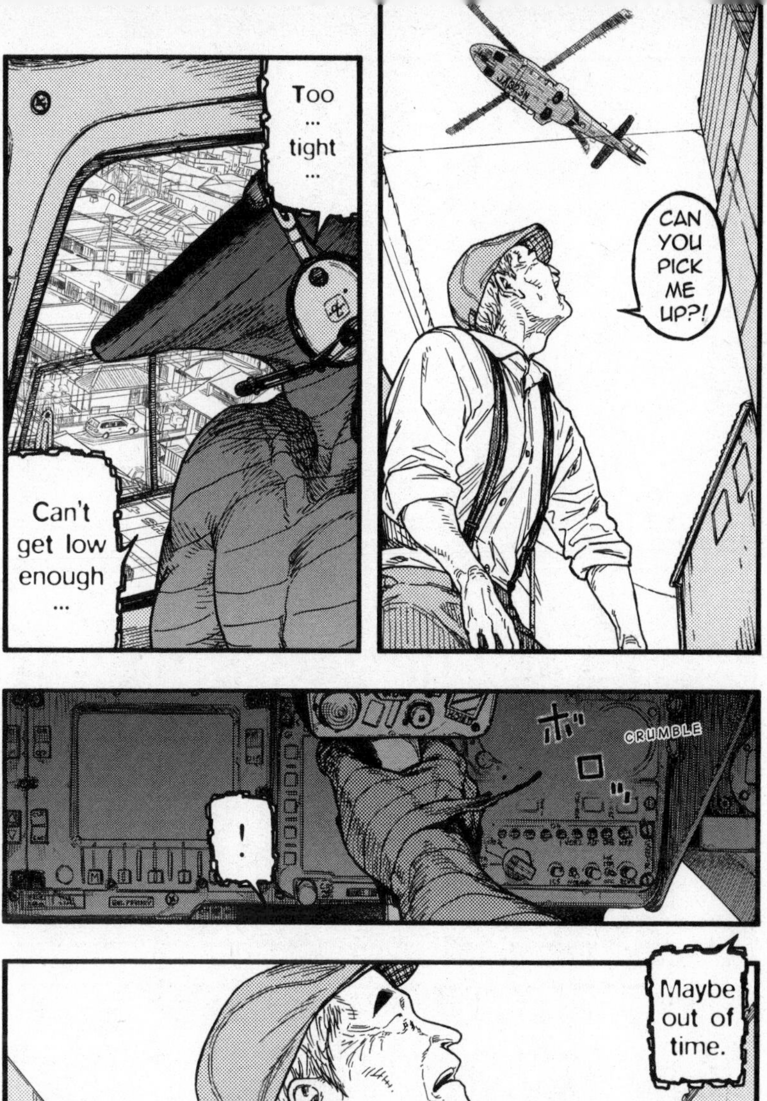
CAN YOU PICK ME UP?!
Too ... tight ...
Can't get low enough ...
ボロッ
CRUMBLE
!
Maybe out of time.
OH DEAR.

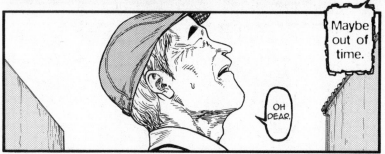

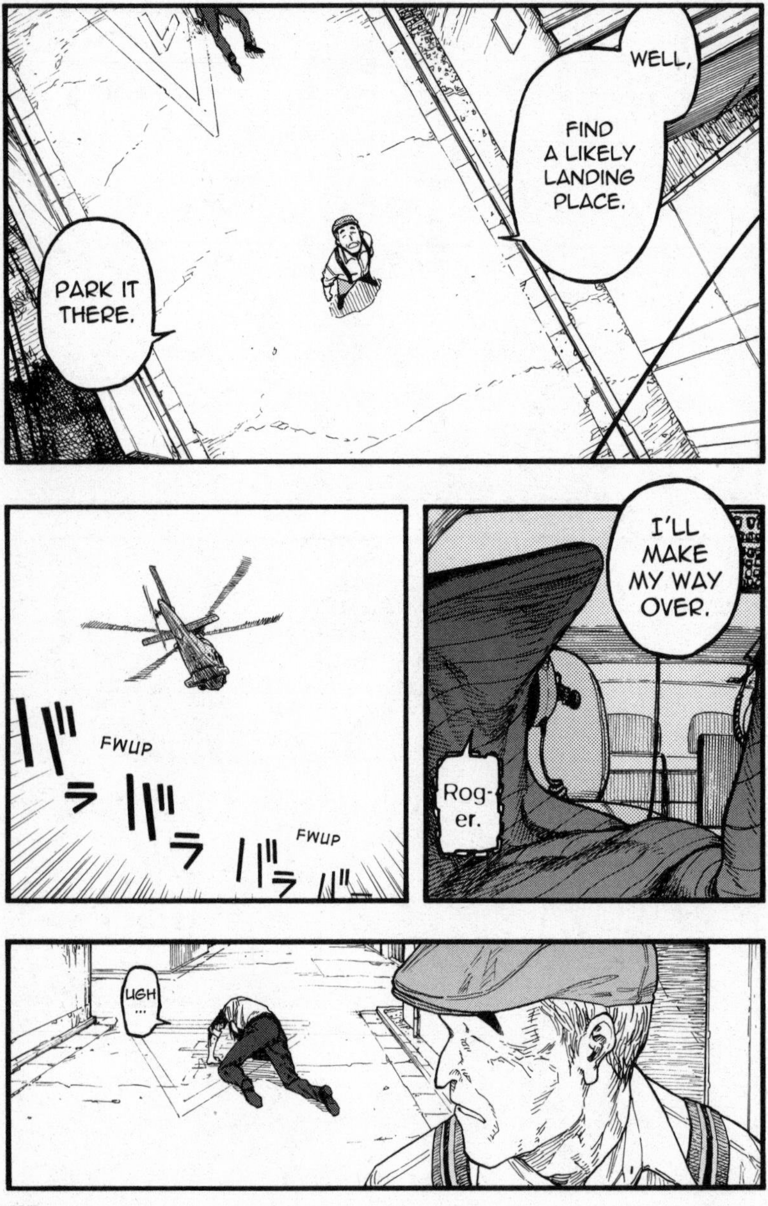
WELL,
FIND A LIKELY LANDING PLACE.
PARK IT THERE.
I'LL MAKE MY WAY OVER.
Rog-er.
バラバラバ
FWUP
FWUP
UGH...

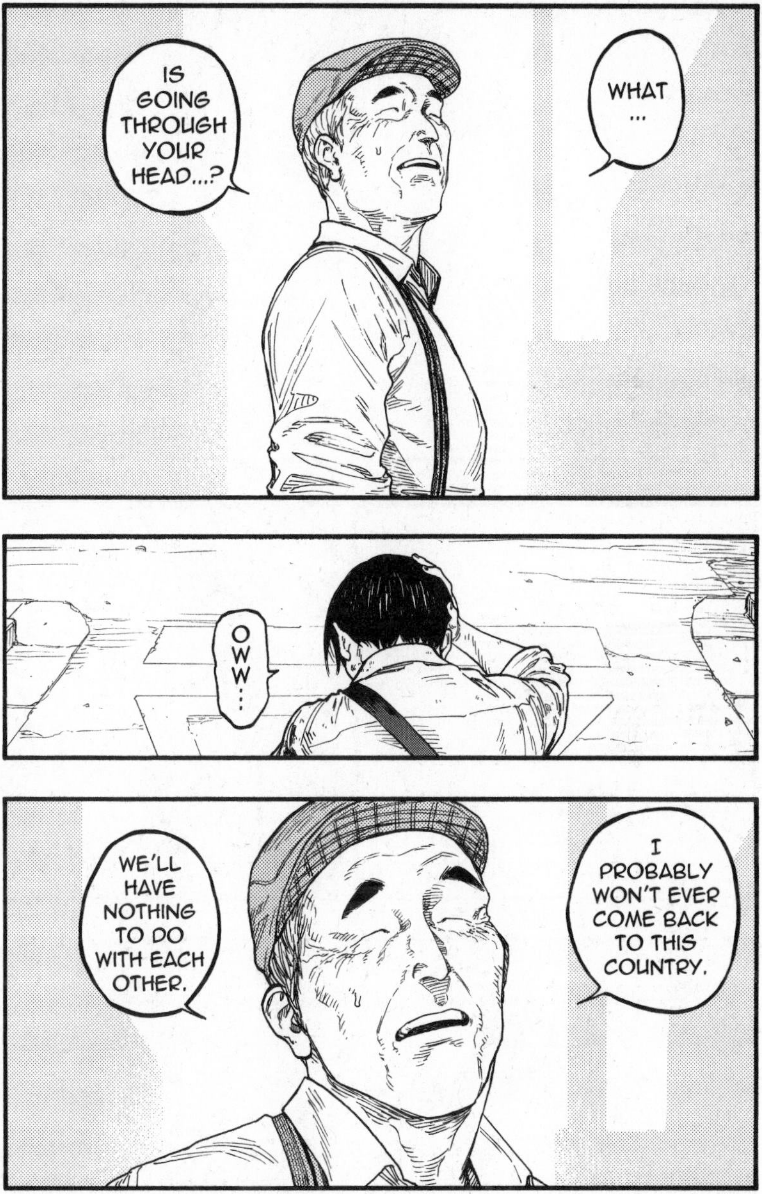
WHAT ...
IS GOING THROUGH YOUR HEAD...?
OWW...
I PROBABLY WON'T EVER COME BACK TO THIS COUNTRY.
WE'LL HAVE NOTHING TO DO WITH EACH OTHER.

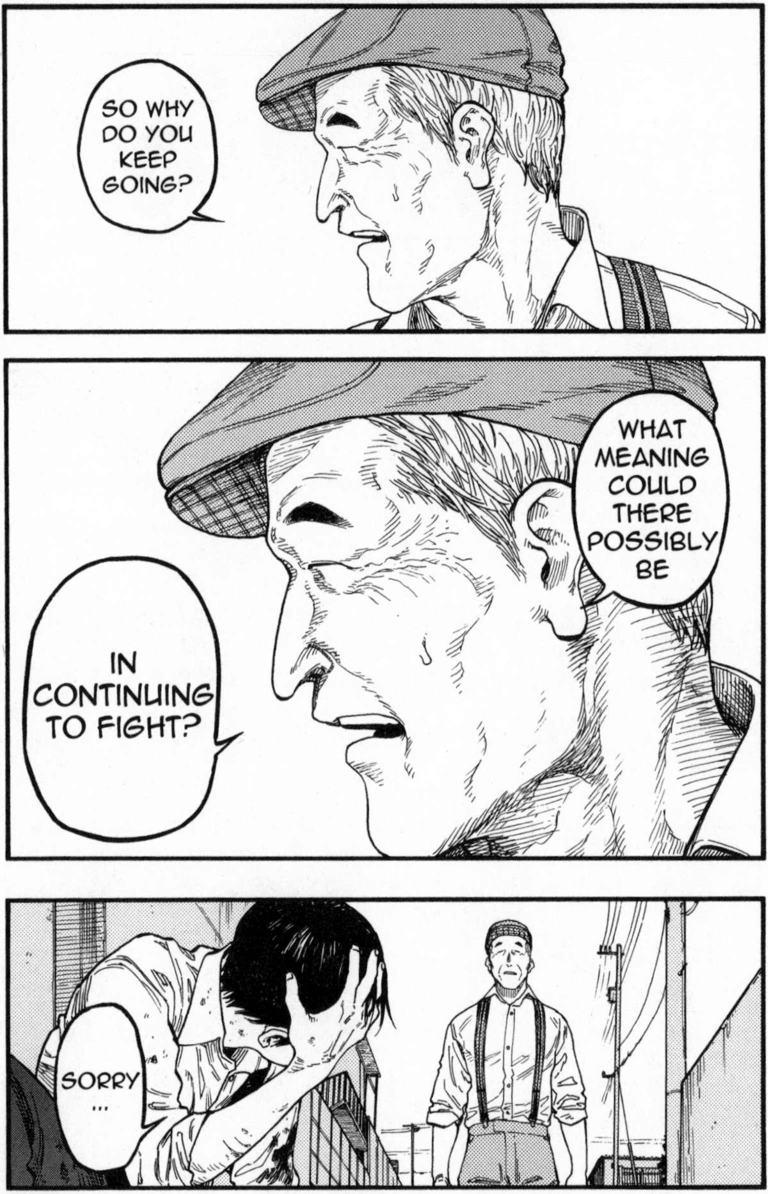
SO WHY DO YOU KEEP GOING?
WHAT MEANING COULD THERE POSSIBLY BE
IN CONTINUING TO FIGHT?
SORRY ...

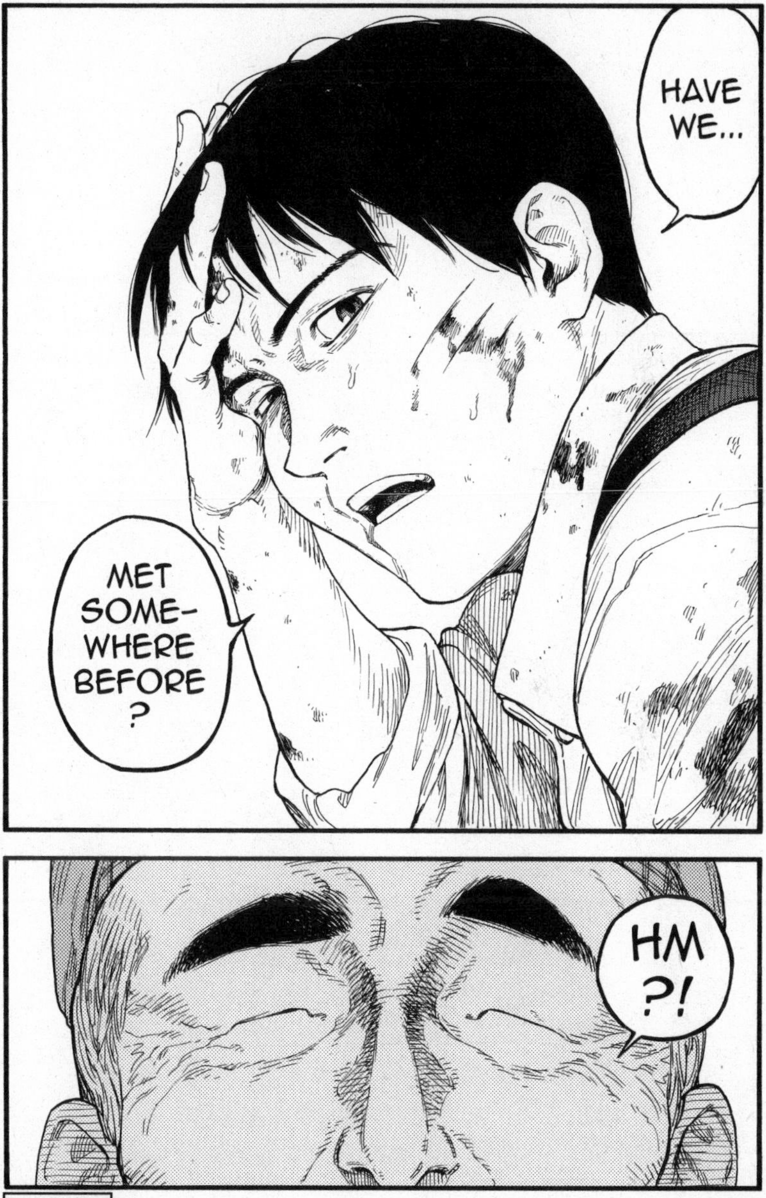
HAVE WE...
MET SOME-WHERE BEFORE ?
HM ?!

File:76 End

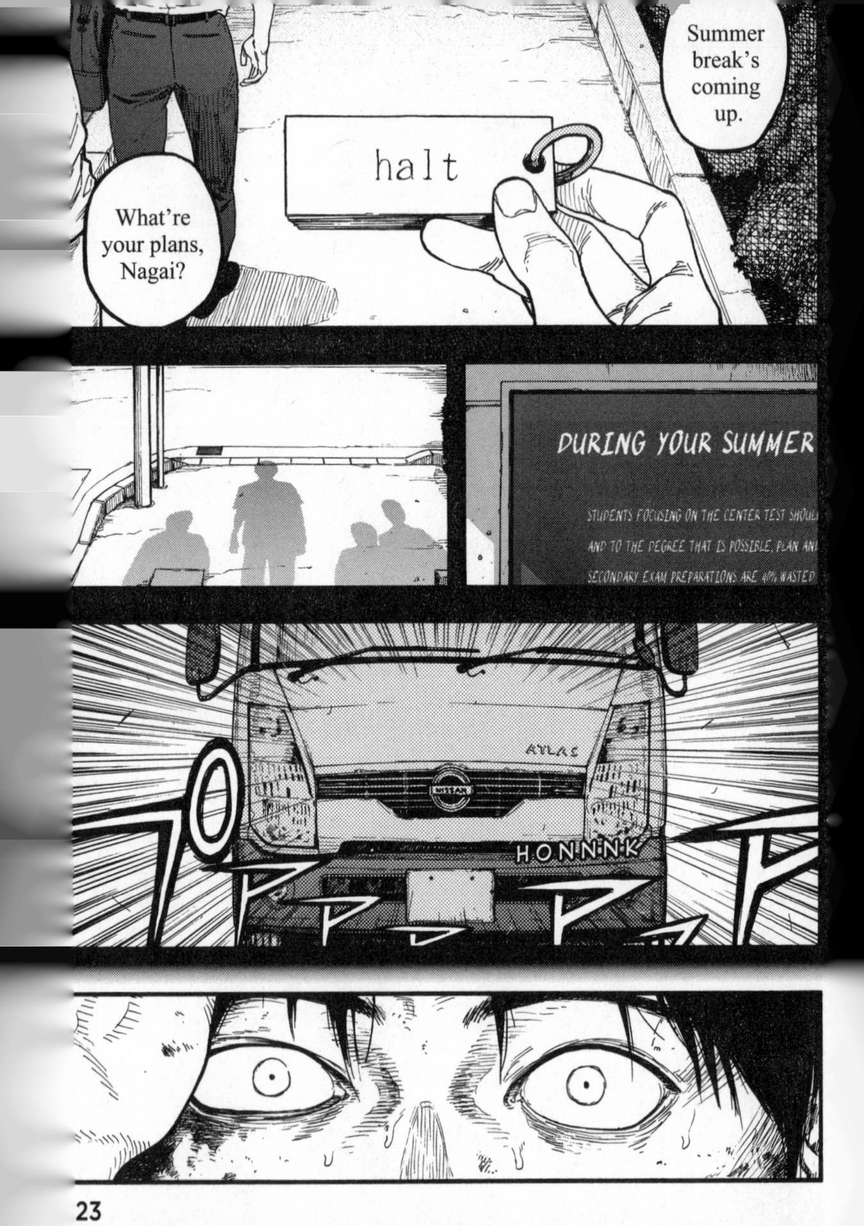
Summer break's coming up.
halt
What're your plans, Nagai?
DURING YOUR SUMMER
STUDENTS FOCUSING ON THE CENTER TEST SHOUL
AND TO THE DEGREE THAT IS POSSIBLE, PLAN AN
SECONDARY EXAM PREPARATIONS ARE 40% WASTED
ATLAS
NISSAN
HONNNK

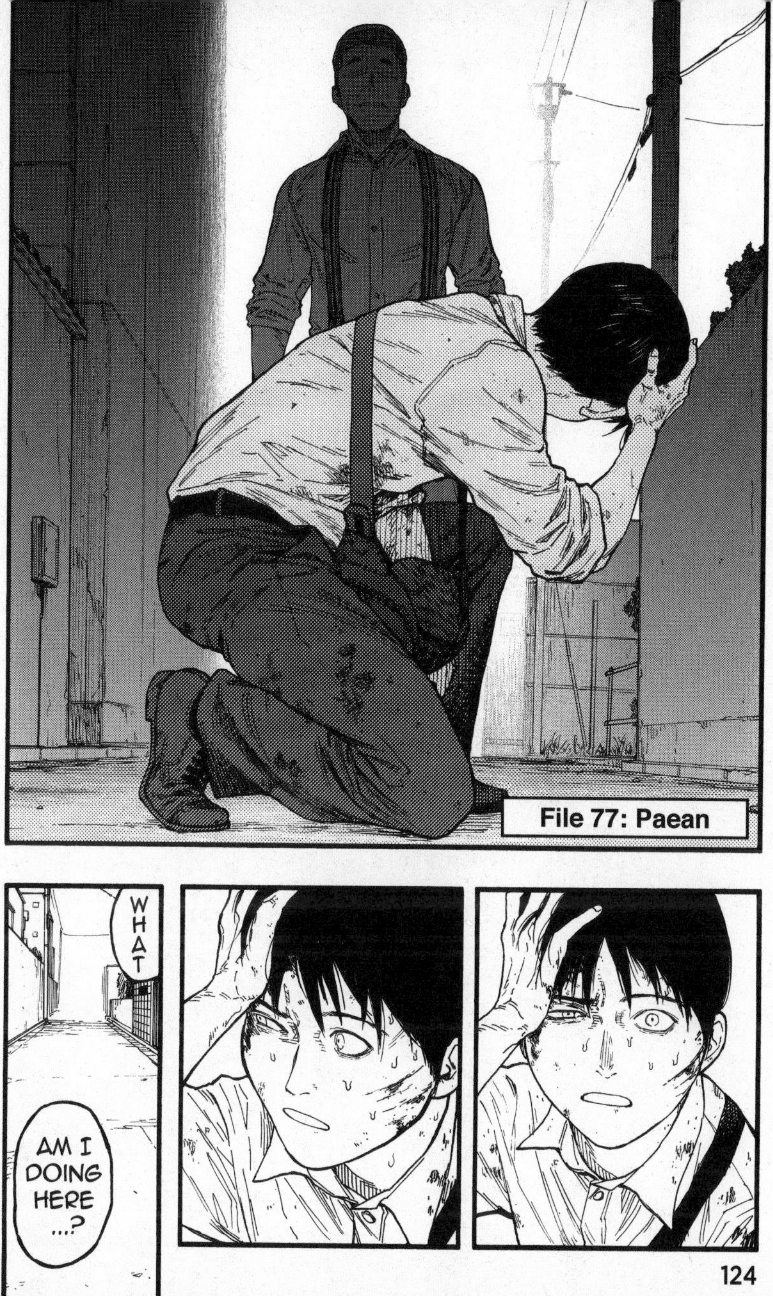
File 77: Paean
WHAT
AM I DOING HERE ...?

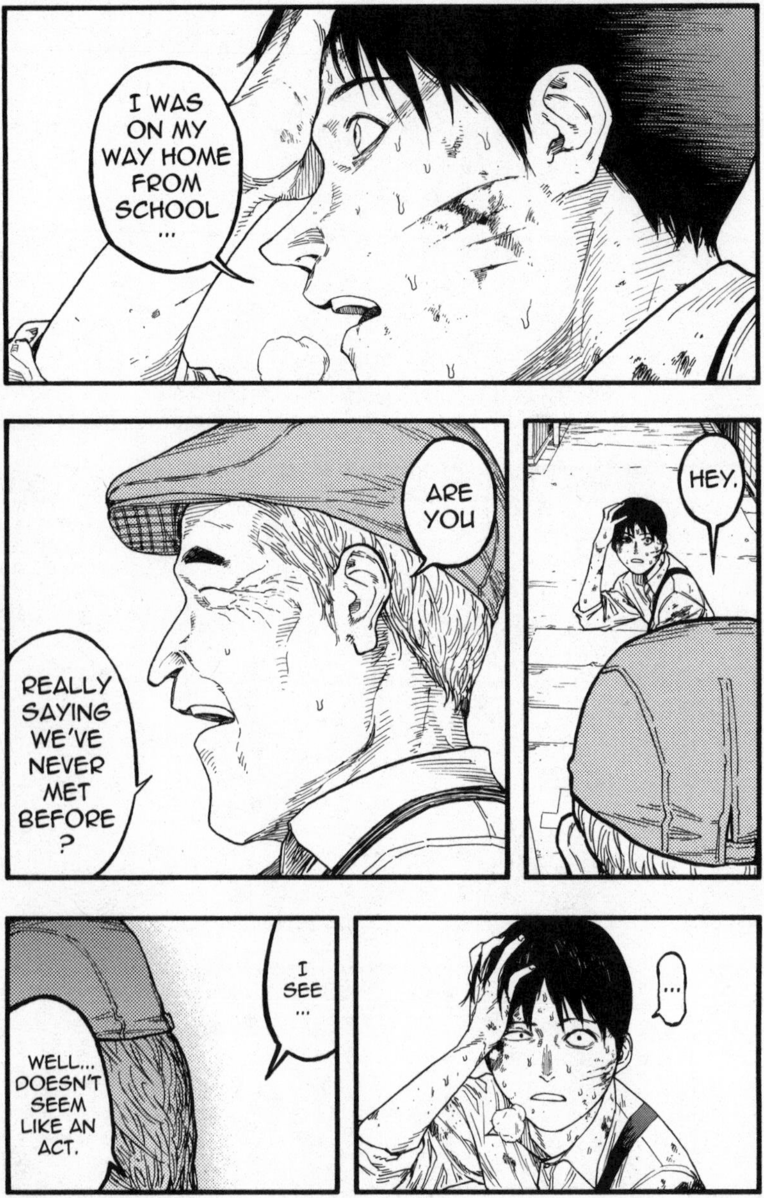
I WAS ON MY WAY HOME FROM SCHOOL ...
HEY.
ARE YOU
REALLY SAYING WE'VE NEVER MET BEFORE ?
...
I SEE ...
WELL... DOESN'T SEEM LIKE AN ACT.

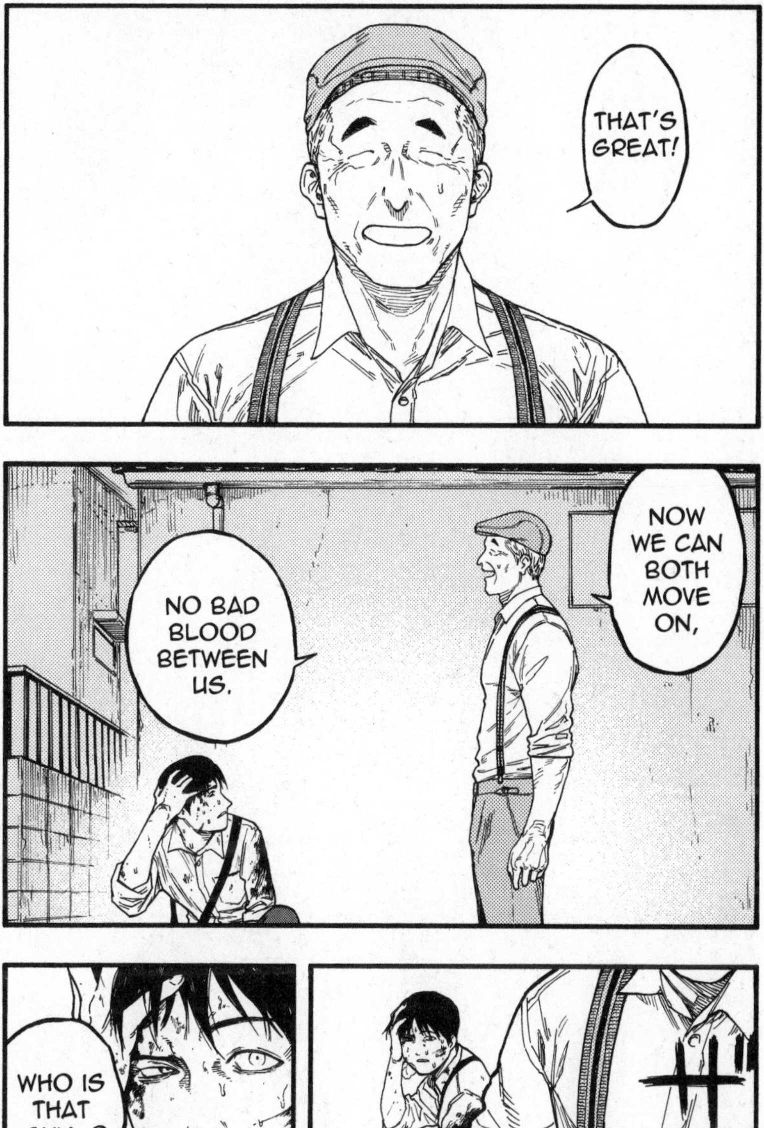
THAT'S GREAT!
NOW WE CAN BOTH MOVE ON,
NO BAD BLOOD BETWEEN US.
ZAKK
WHO IS THAT GUY...?

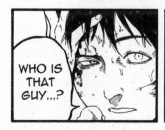

ZAKK
WHAT-EVER. STILL.
SOME-THING'S WEIRD HERE...
ZAKK
ZAKK
NEED AN AMBU-LANCE ...
ZAKK
WHERE'S ...
MY PHONE ...?
HUH ?!

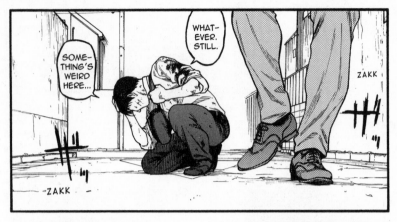

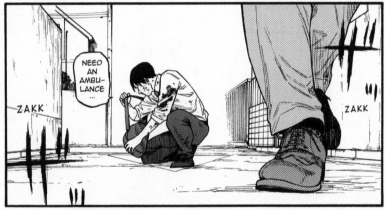

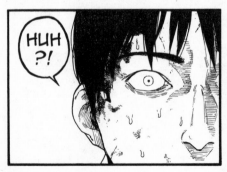

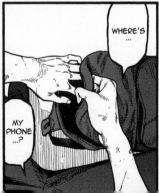

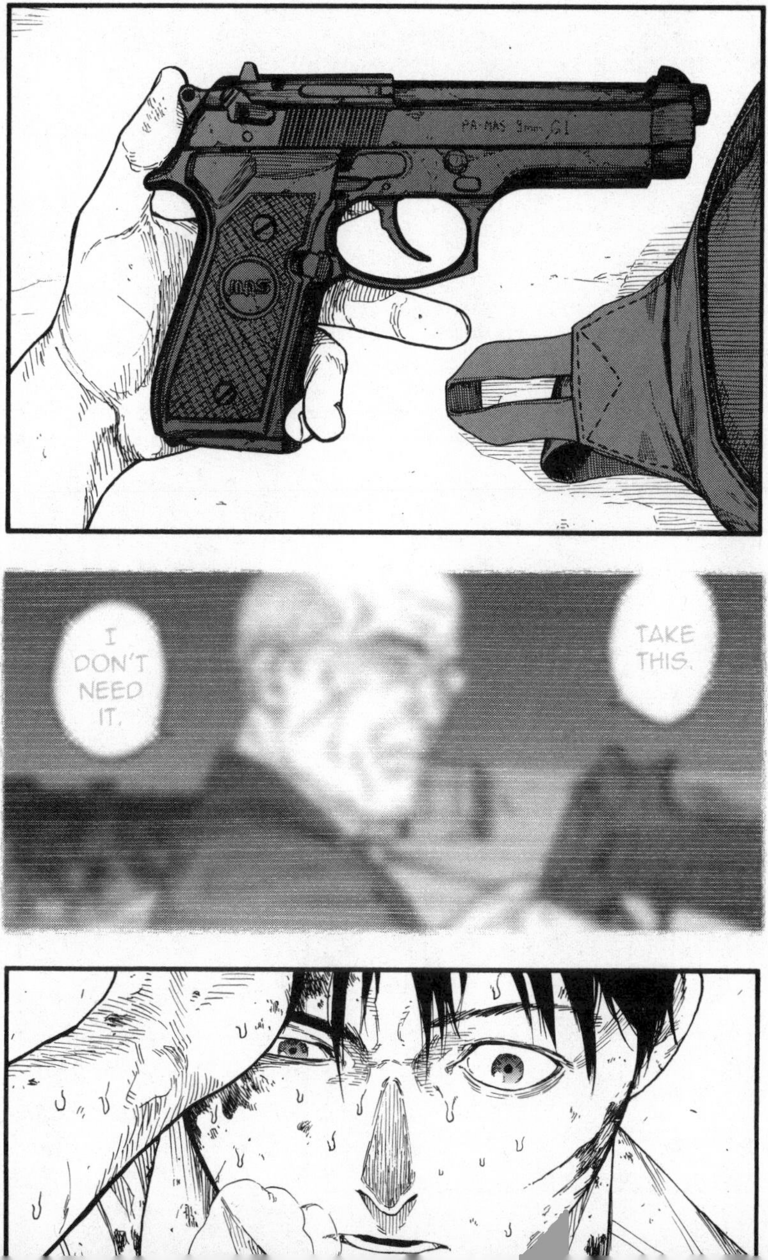
PA-MAS 9mm G1
MAS
TAKE THIS.
I DON'T NEED IT.

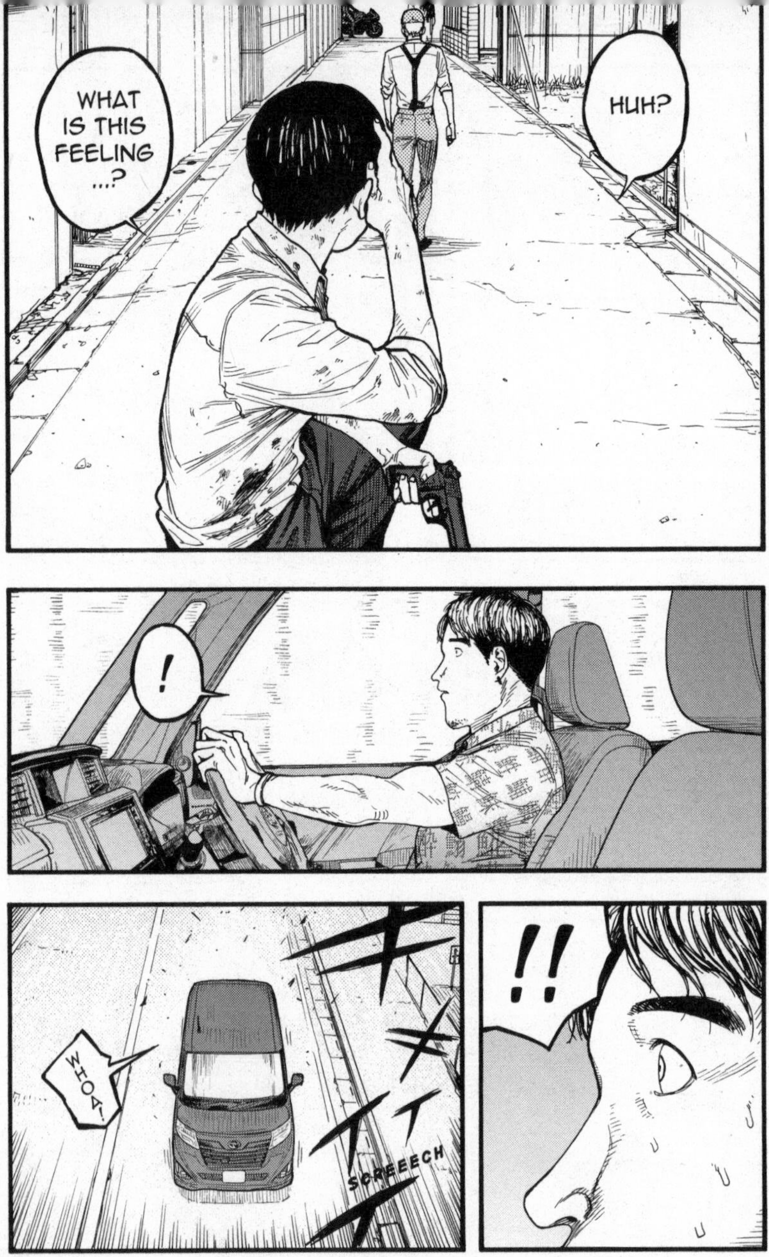
HUH?
WHAT IS THIS FEELING ...?
!
!!
WHOA!
SCREEECH

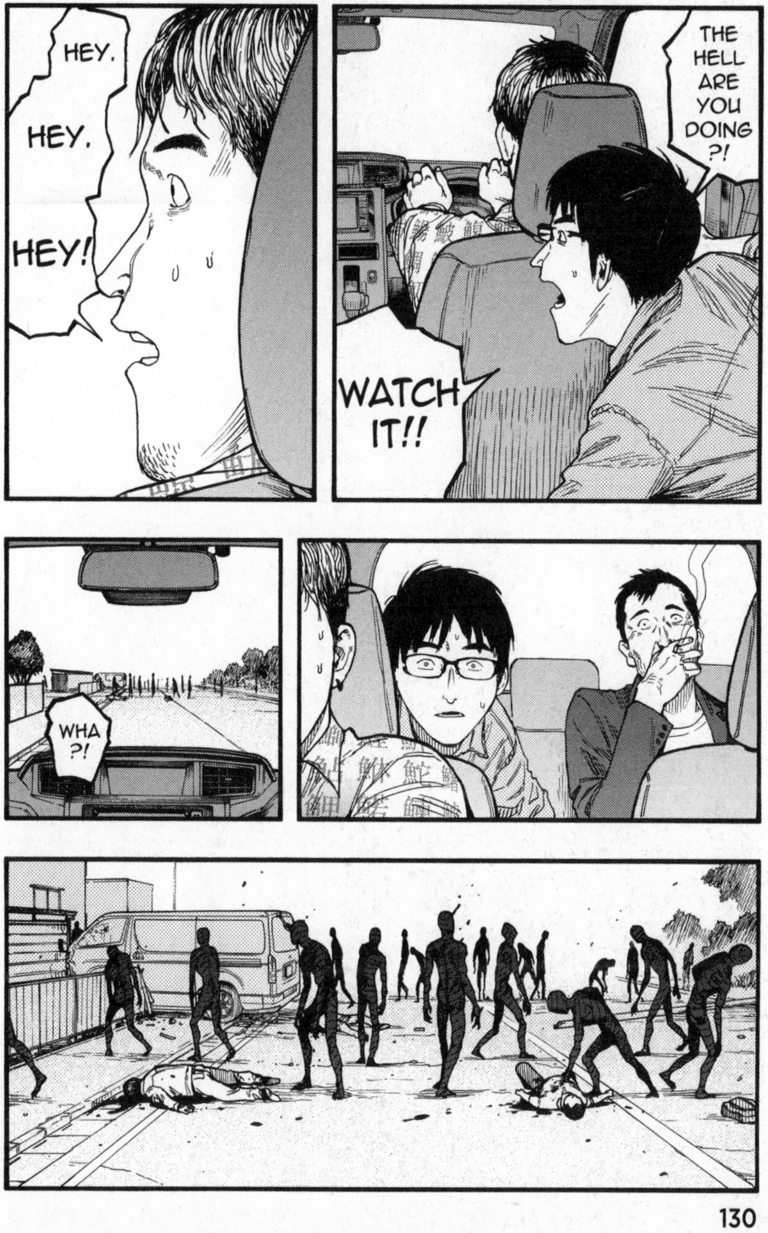
THE HELL ARE YOU DOING ?!
WATCH IT!!
HEY. HEY. HEY!
WHA ?!

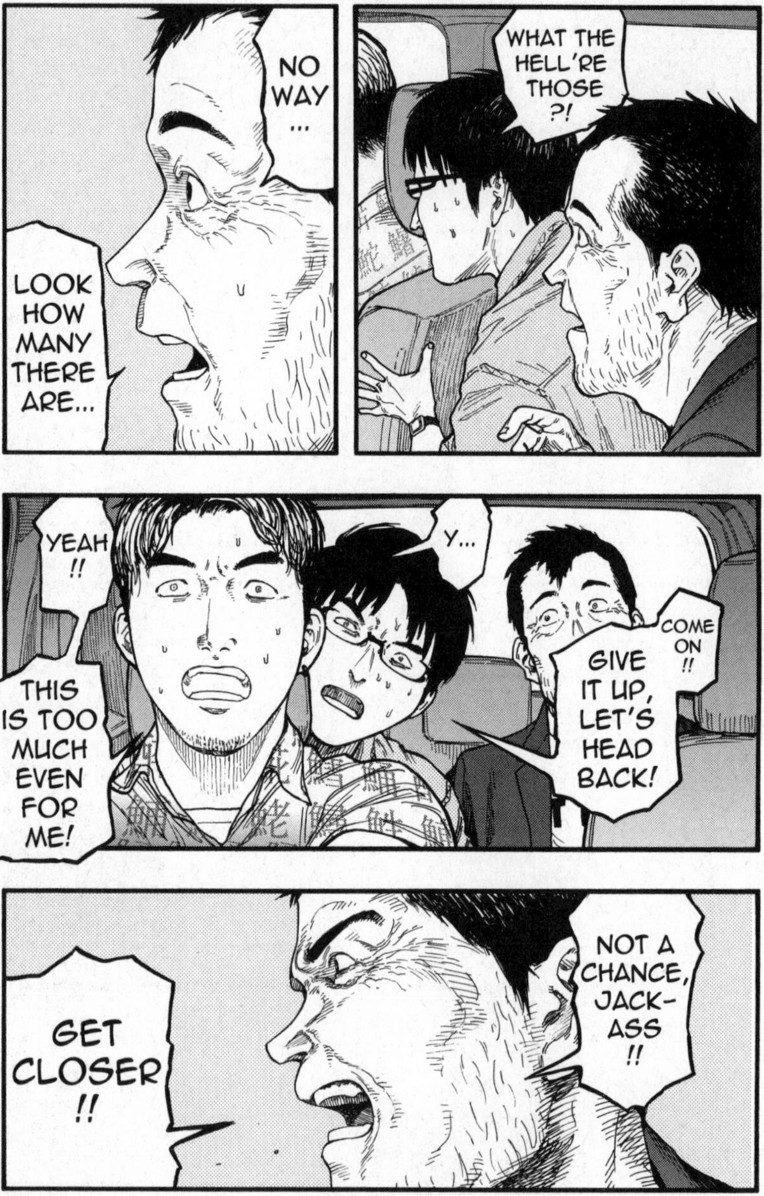
WHAT THE HELL'RE THOSE ?!
NO WAY ...
LOOK HOW MANY THERE ARE...
Y...
COME ON !!
GIVE IT UP, LET'S HEAD BACK!
YEAH !!
THIS IS TOO MUCH EVEN FOR ME!
NOT A CHANCE, JACK-ASS !!
GET CLOSER !!

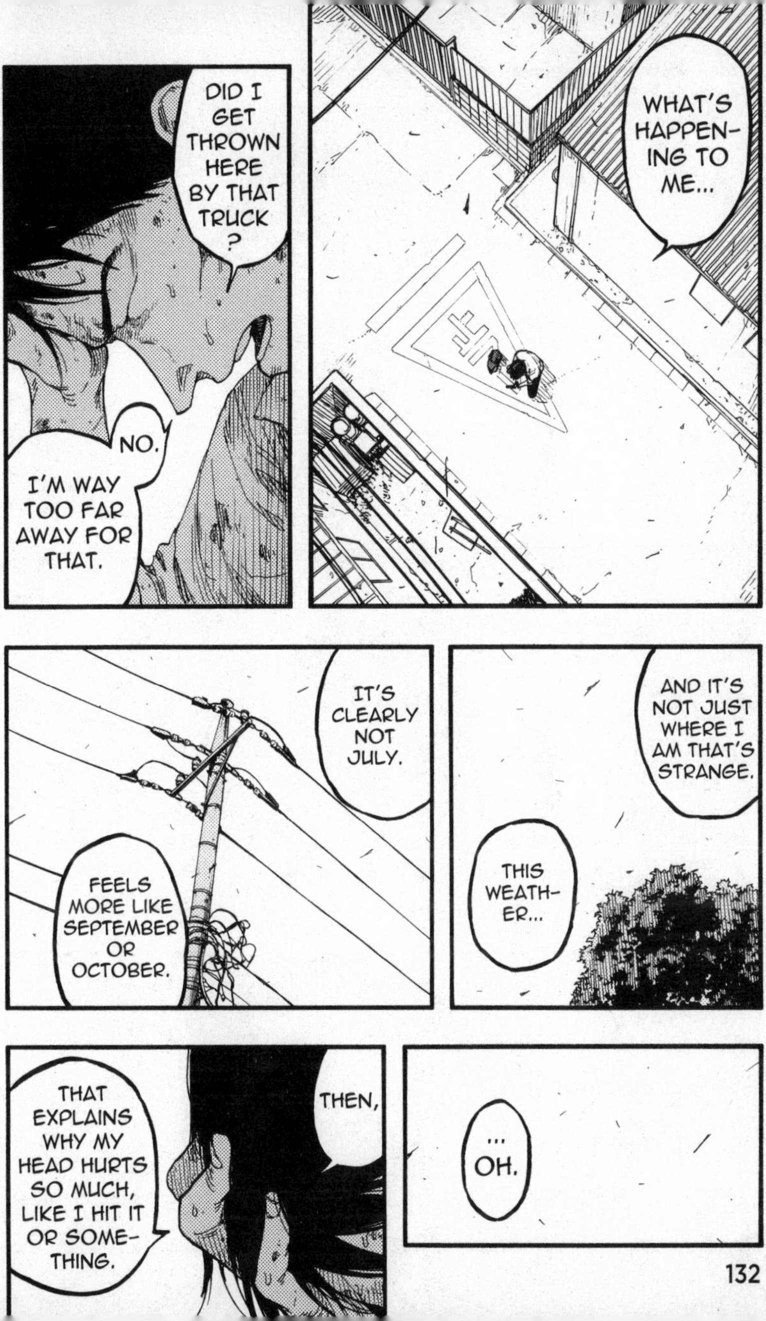
WHAT'S HAPPENING TO ME...
DID I GET THROWN HERE BY THAT TRUCK ?
NO.
I'M WAY TOO FAR AWAY FOR THAT.
AND IT'S NOT JUST WHERE I AM THAT'S STRANGE.
THIS WEATHER...
IT'S CLEARLY NOT JULY.
FEELS MORE LIKE SEPTEMBER OR OCTOBER.
... OH.
THEN,
THAT EXPLAINS WHY MY HEAD HURTS SO MUCH, LIKE I HIT IT OR SOMETHING.

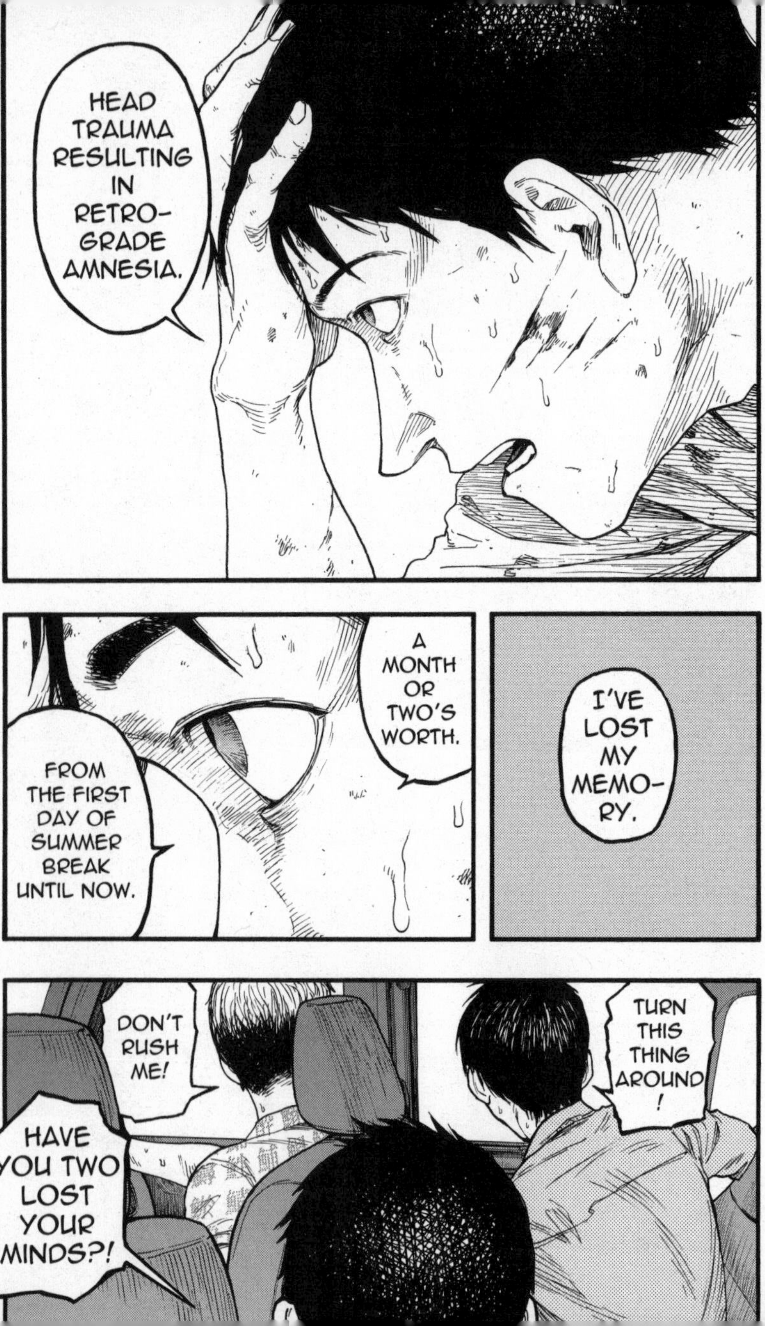
HEAD TRAUMA RESULTING IN RETRO-GRADE AMNESIA.
I'VE LOST MY MEMO-RY.
A MONTH OR TWO'S WORTH.
FROM THE FIRST DAY OF SUMMER BREAK UNTIL NOW.
TURN THIS THING AROUND!
DON'T RUSH ME!
HAVE YOU TWO LOST YOUR MINDS?!

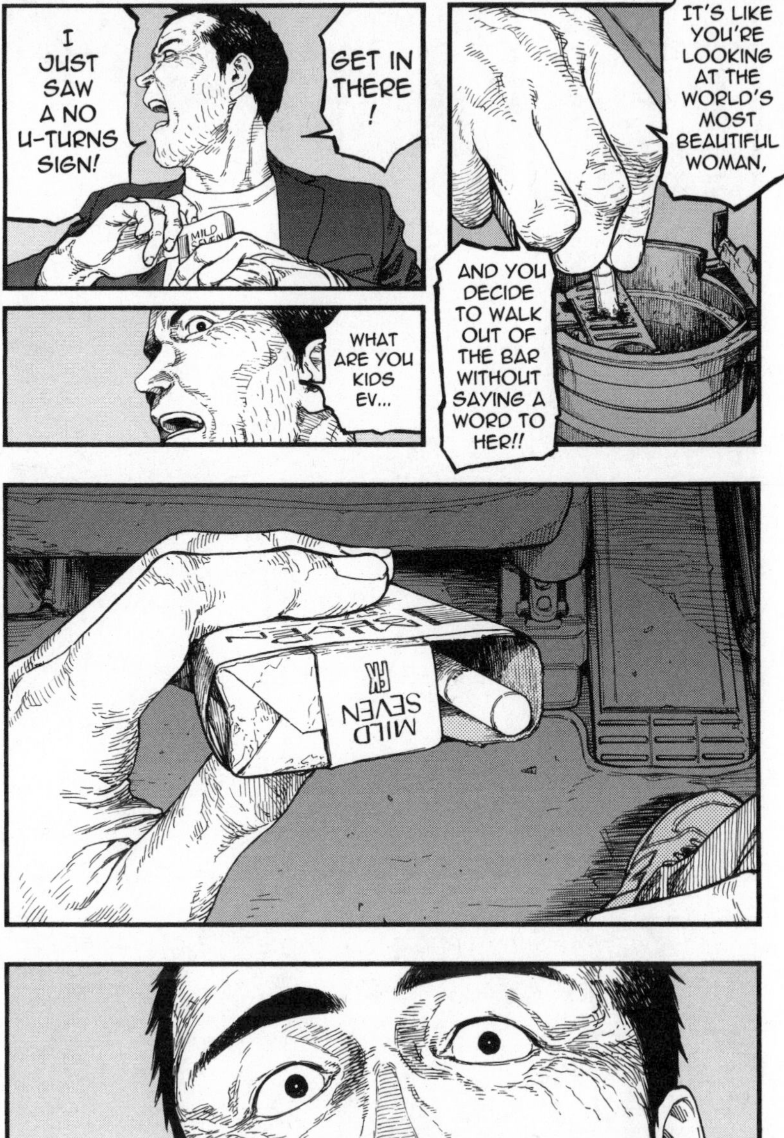
IT'S LIKE YOU'RE LOOKING AT THE WORLD'S MOST BEAUTIFUL WOMAN,
AND YOU DECIDE TO WALK OUT OF THE BAR WITHOUT SAYING A WORD TO HER!!
GET IN THERE !
I JUST SAW A NO U-TURNS SIGN!
MILD SEVEN
WHAT ARE YOU KIDS EV...
MILD SEVEN

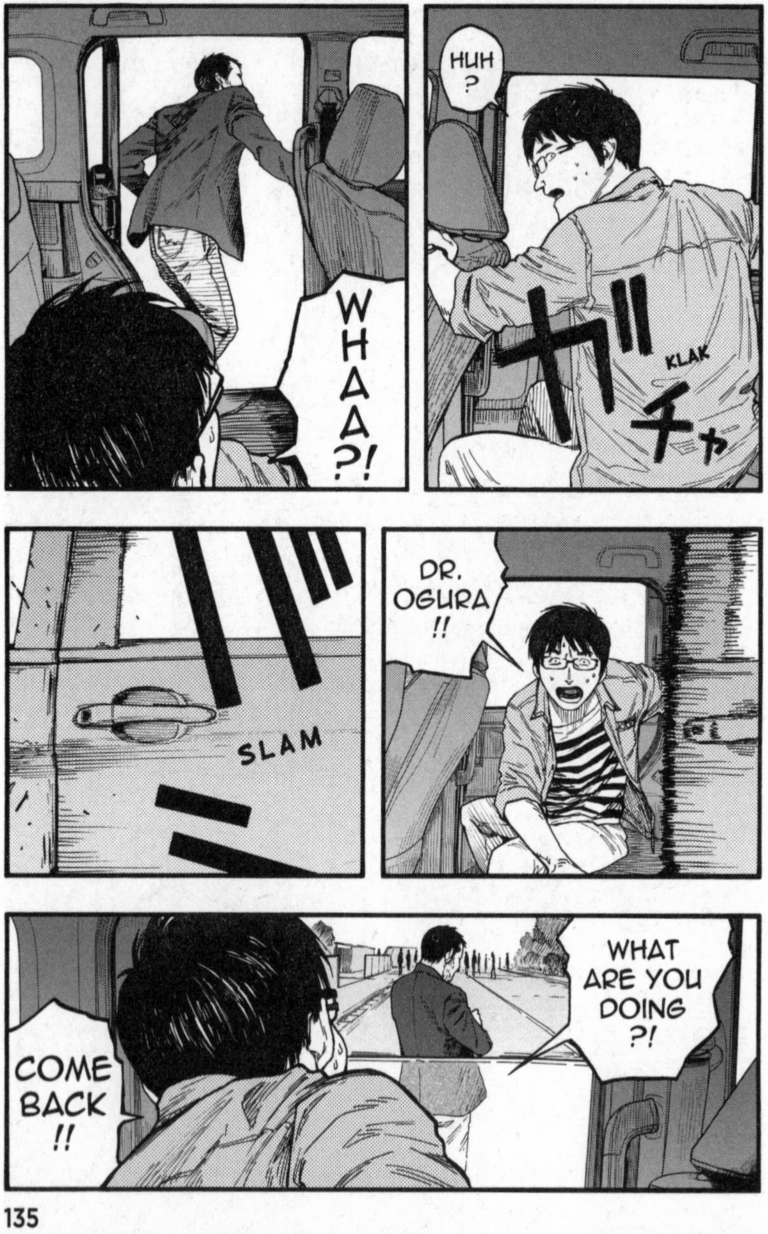
HUH?
ガチャ
KLAK
WHAA?!
DR. OGURA!!
SLAM
WHAT ARE YOU DOING?!
COME BACK!!

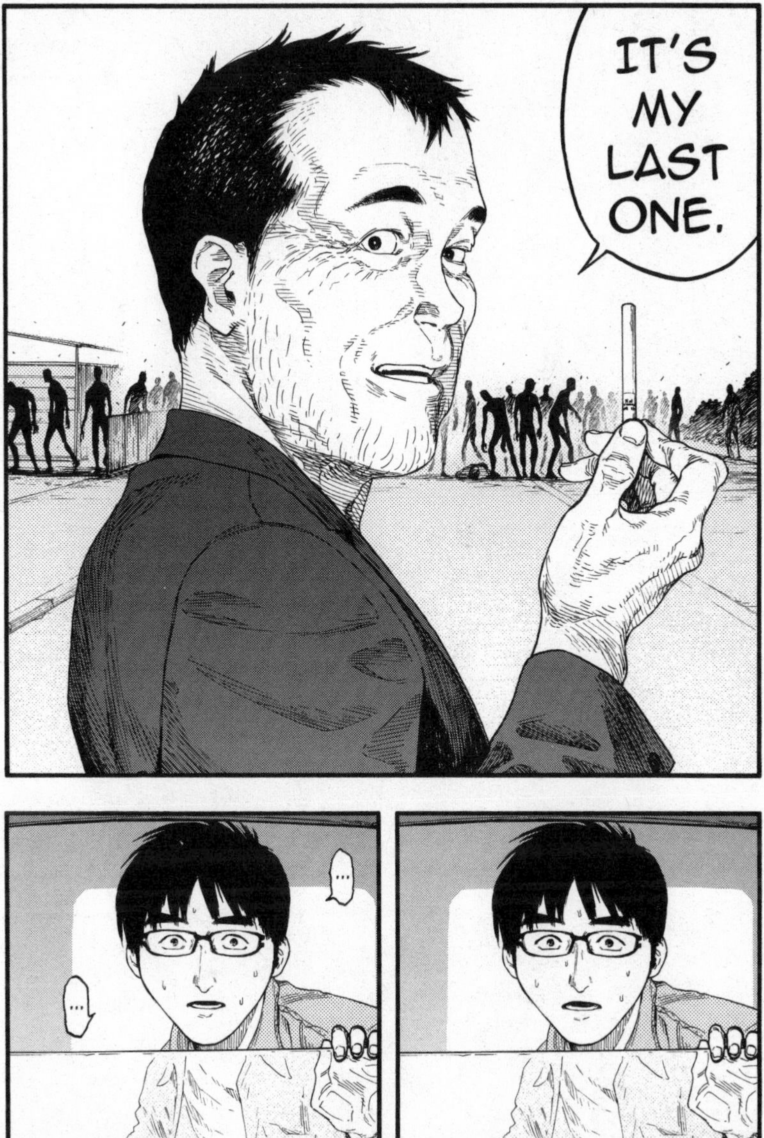
IT'S MY LAST ONE.
...
...

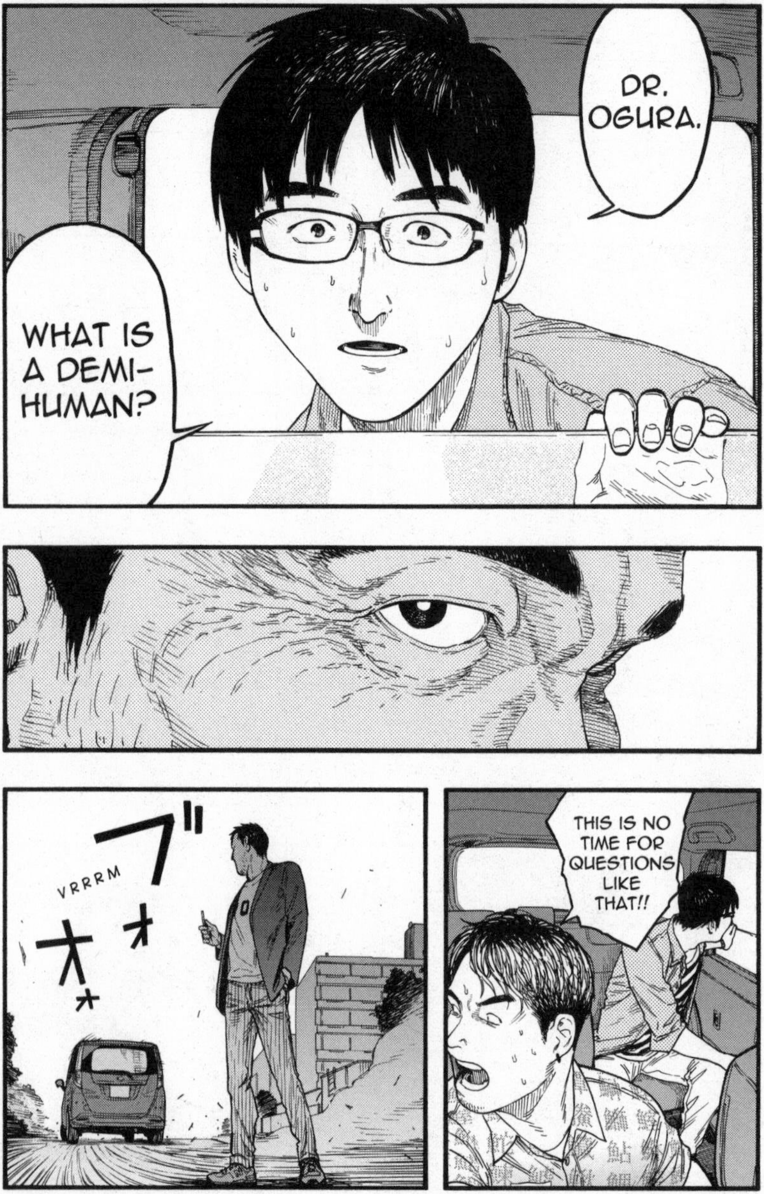
DR. OGURA.
WHAT IS A DEMI-HUMAN?
THIS IS NO TIME FOR QUESTIONS LIKE THAT!!
ブォォ
VRRRM

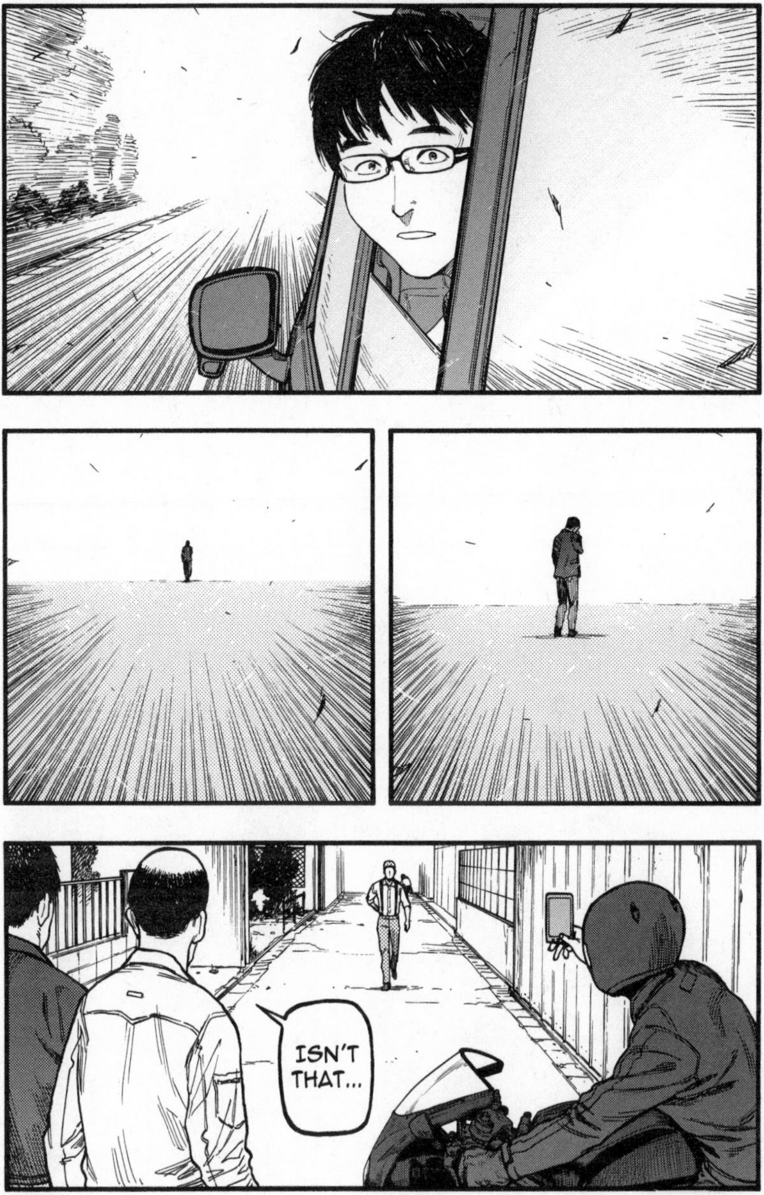
ISN'T THAT...

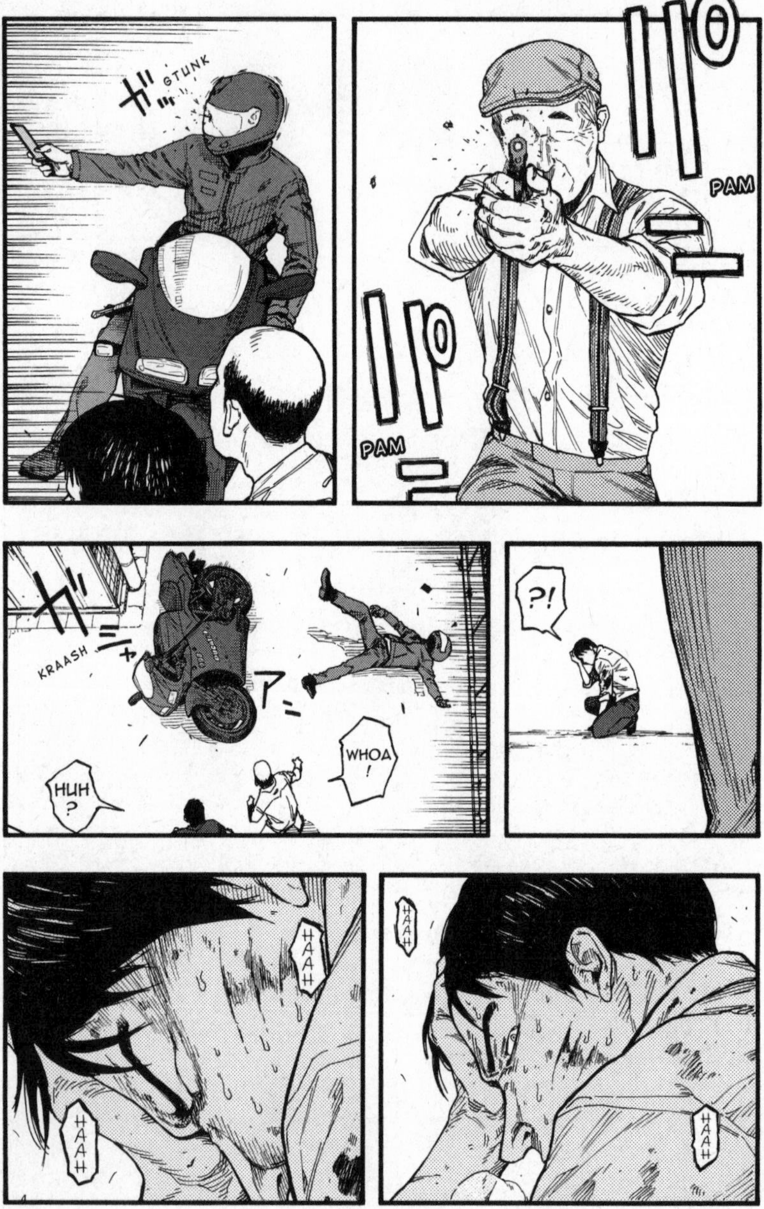
PAM
PAM
GTUNK
?!
WHOA!
KRAASH
HUH?
HAAH
HAAH
HAAH
HAAH

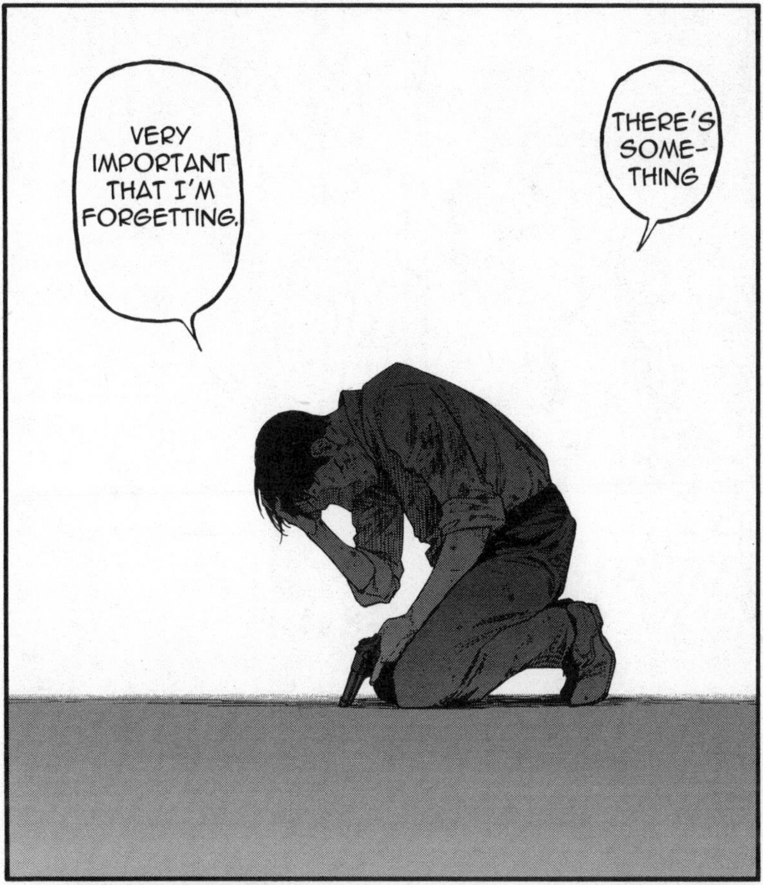
THERE'S SOME-THING
VERY IMPORTANT THAT I'M FORGETTING.
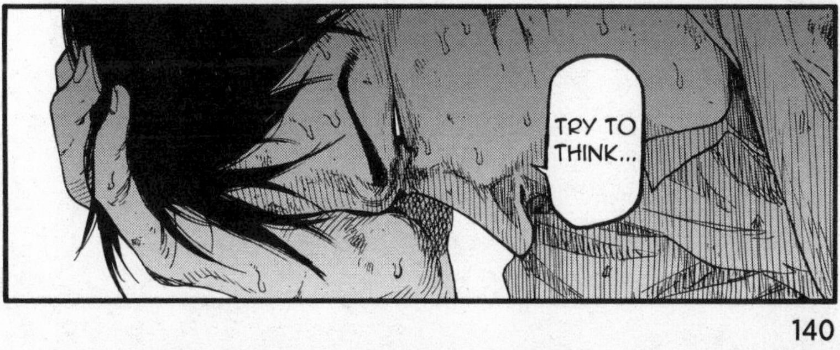
TRY TO THINK...

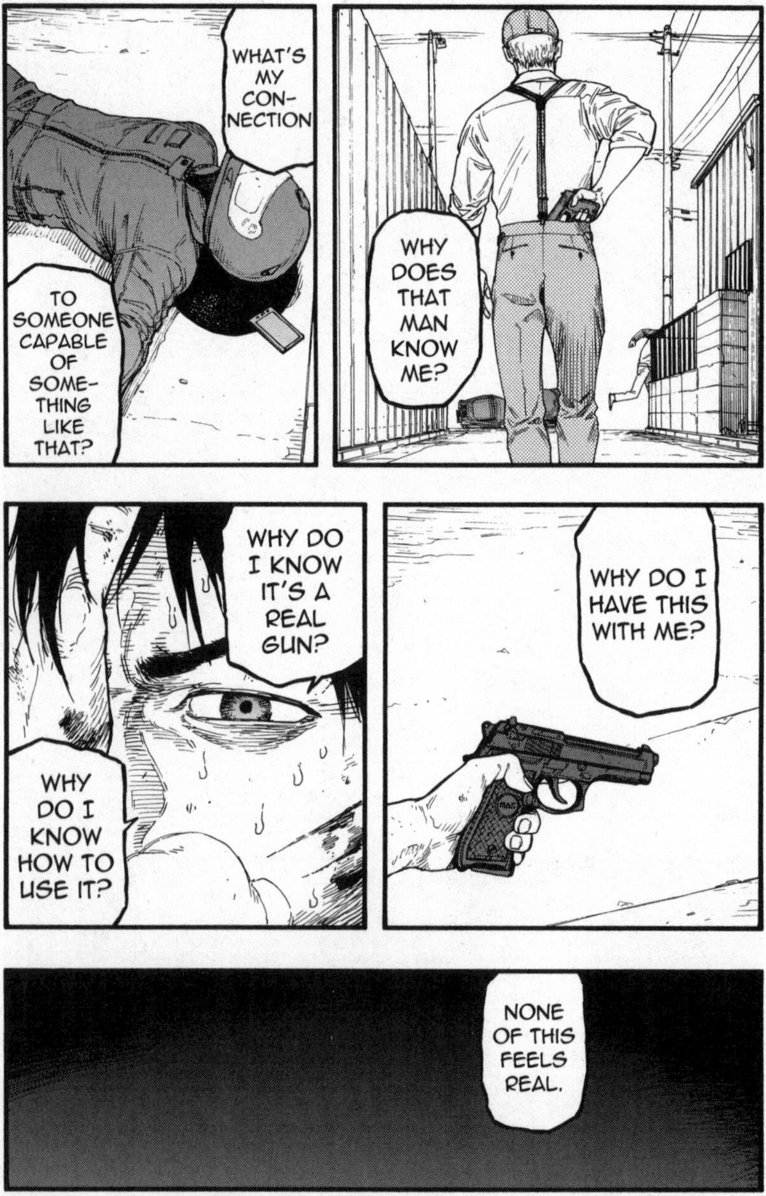

WHY DOES THAT MAN KNOW ME?
WHAT'S MY CONNECTION
TO SOMEONE CAPABLE OF SOMETHING LIKE THAT?
WHY DO I HAVE THIS WITH ME?
WHY DO I KNOW IT'S A REAL GUN?
WHY DO I KNOW HOW TO USE IT?
NONE OF THIS FEELS REAL.

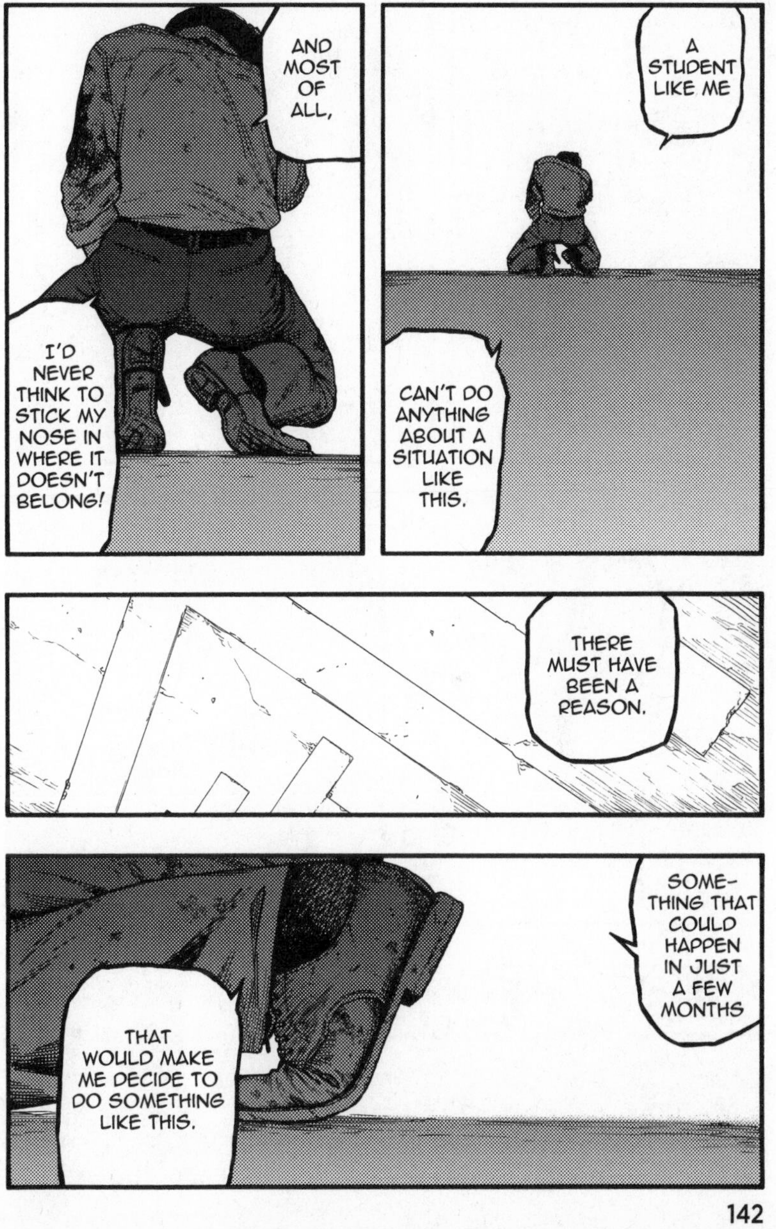
A STUDENT LIKE ME
CAN'T DO ANYTHING ABOUT A SITUATION LIKE THIS.
AND MOST OF ALL,
I'D NEVER THINK TO STICK MY NOSE IN WHERE IT DOESN'T BELONG!
THERE MUST HAVE BEEN A REASON.
SOME-THING THAT COULD HAPPEN IN JUST A FEW MONTHS
THAT WOULD MAKE ME DECIDE TO DO SOMETHING LIKE THIS.

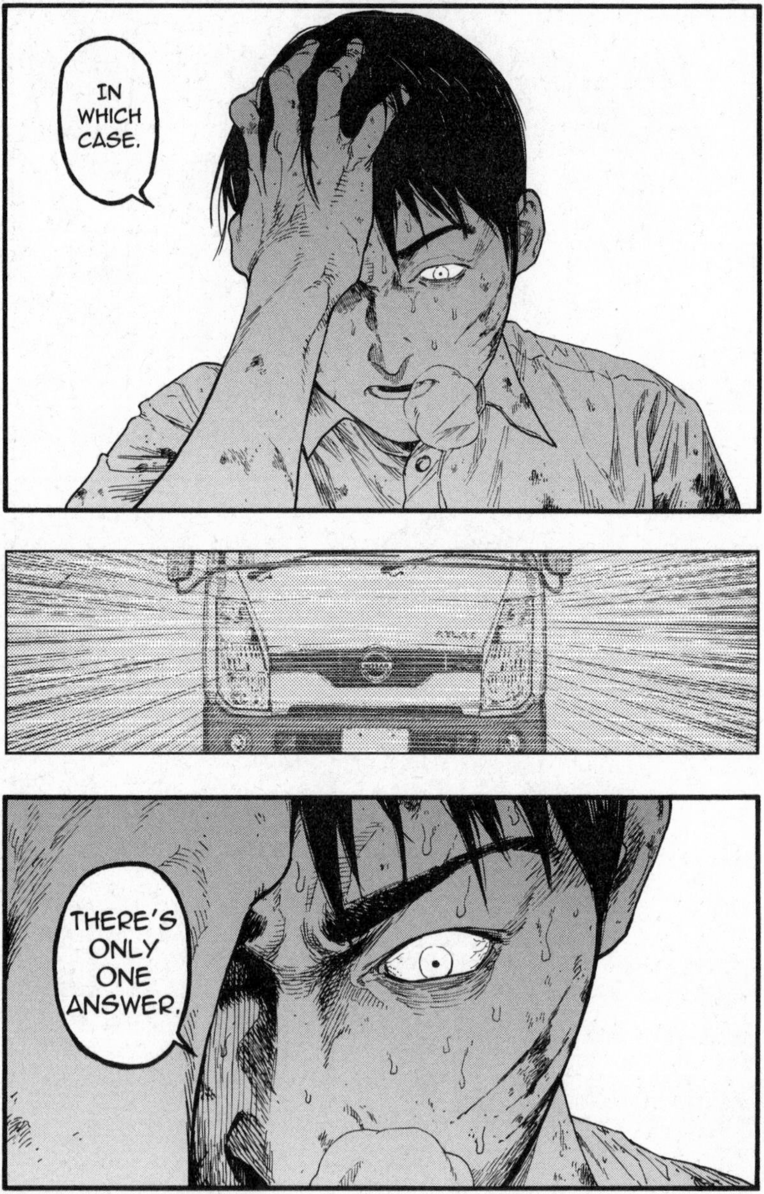
IN WHICH CASE.
THERE'S ONLY ONE ANSWER.

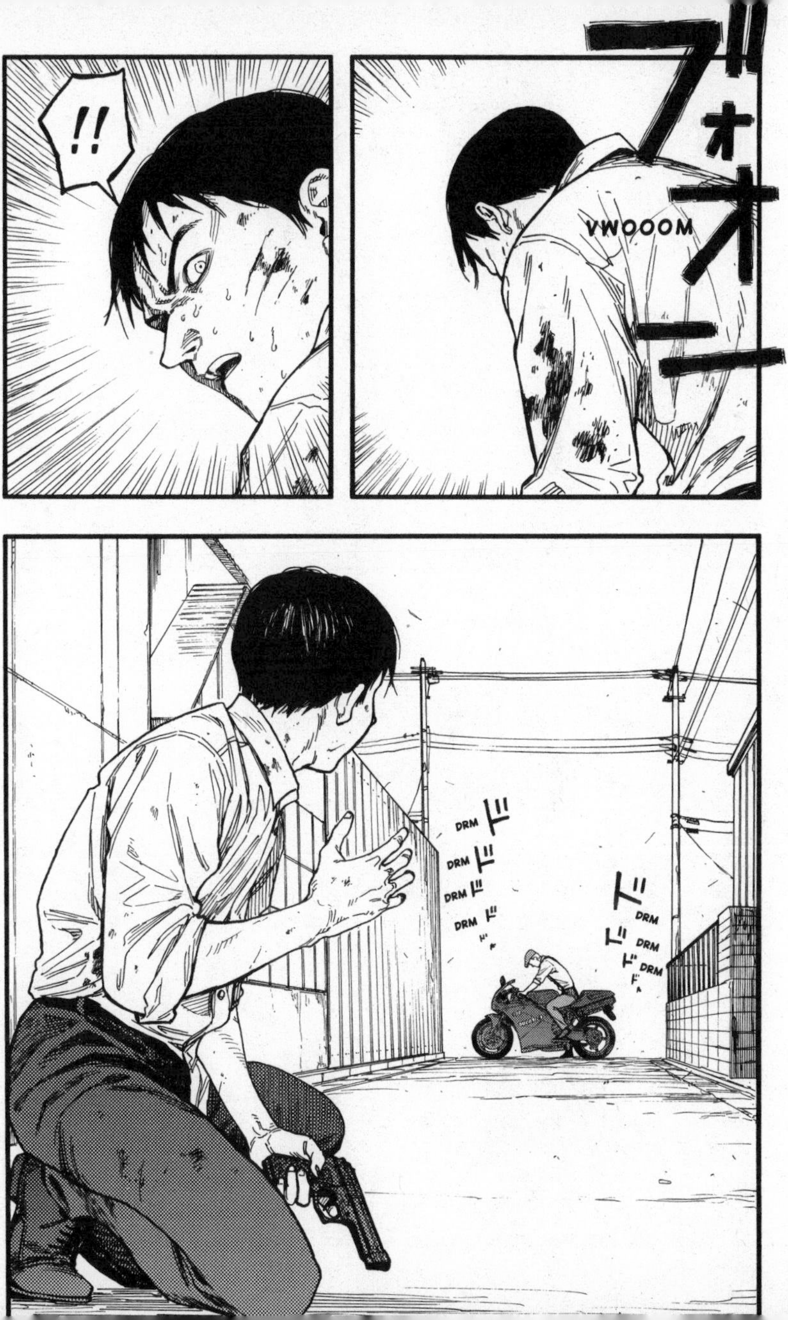
ブォオーー
VWOOOM
!!
ドドドド
DRM DRM DRM DRM
ドドドド
DRM DRM DRM

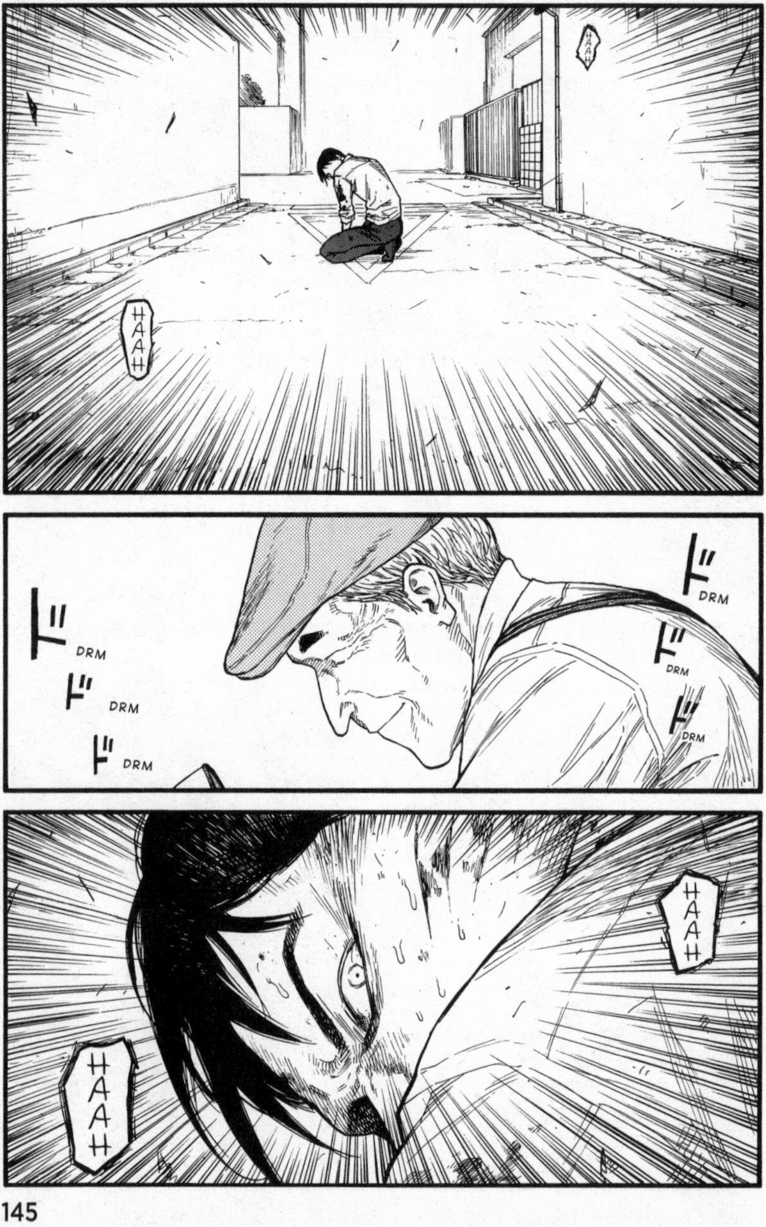
HAAAH
HAAAH
ド DRM
ド DRM
ド DRM
ド DRM
ド DRM
ド DRM
HAAAH
HAAAH

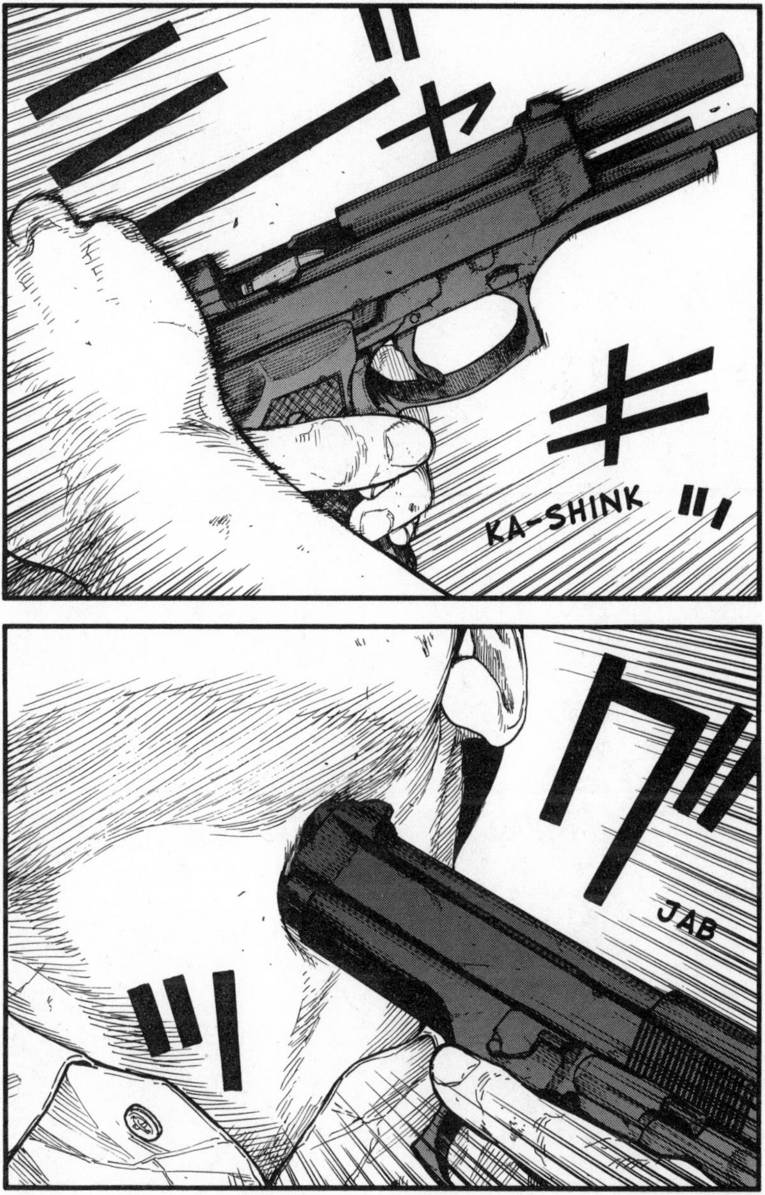
ジャキッ
KA-SHINK
グッ
JAB

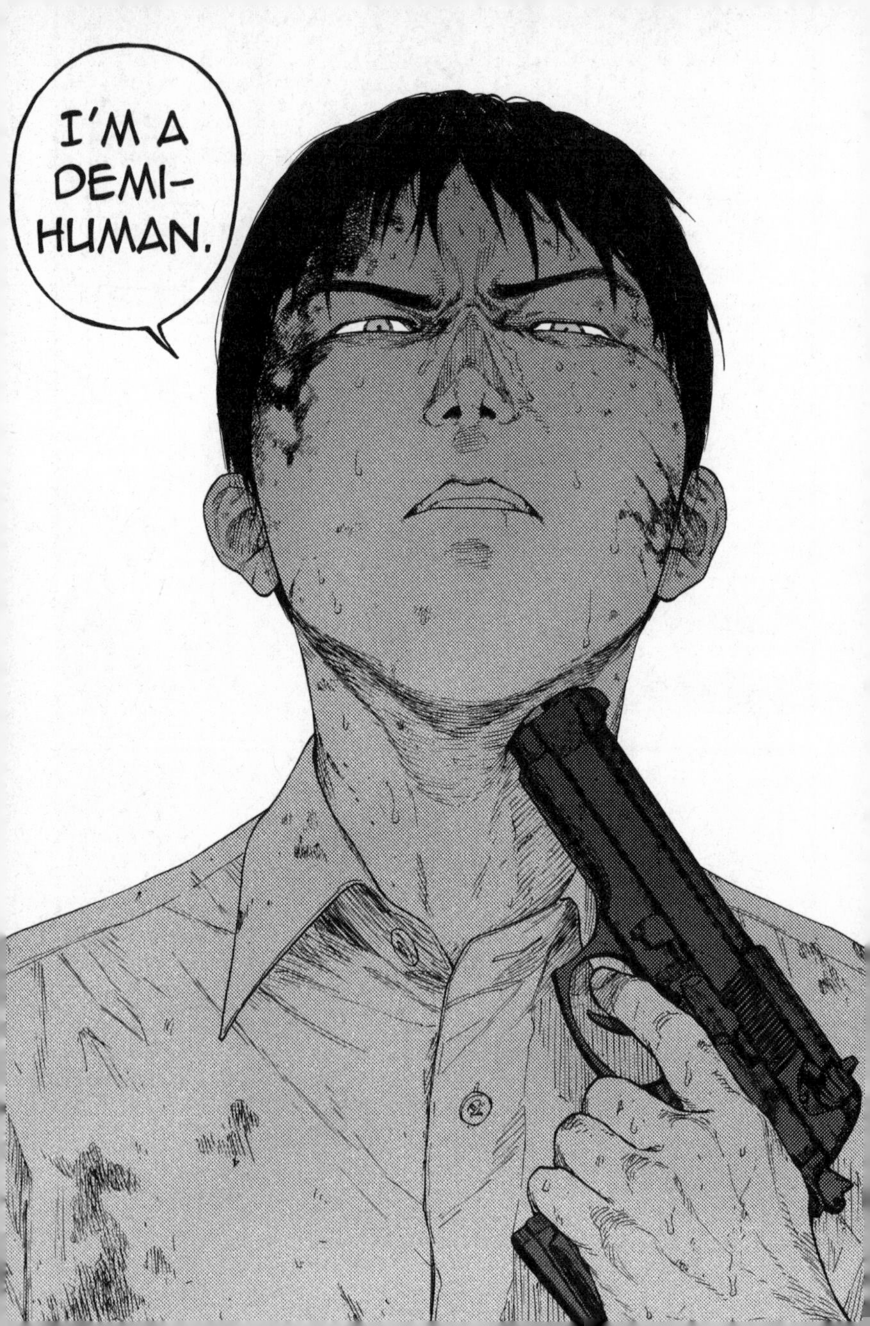
I'M A DEMI-HUMAN.

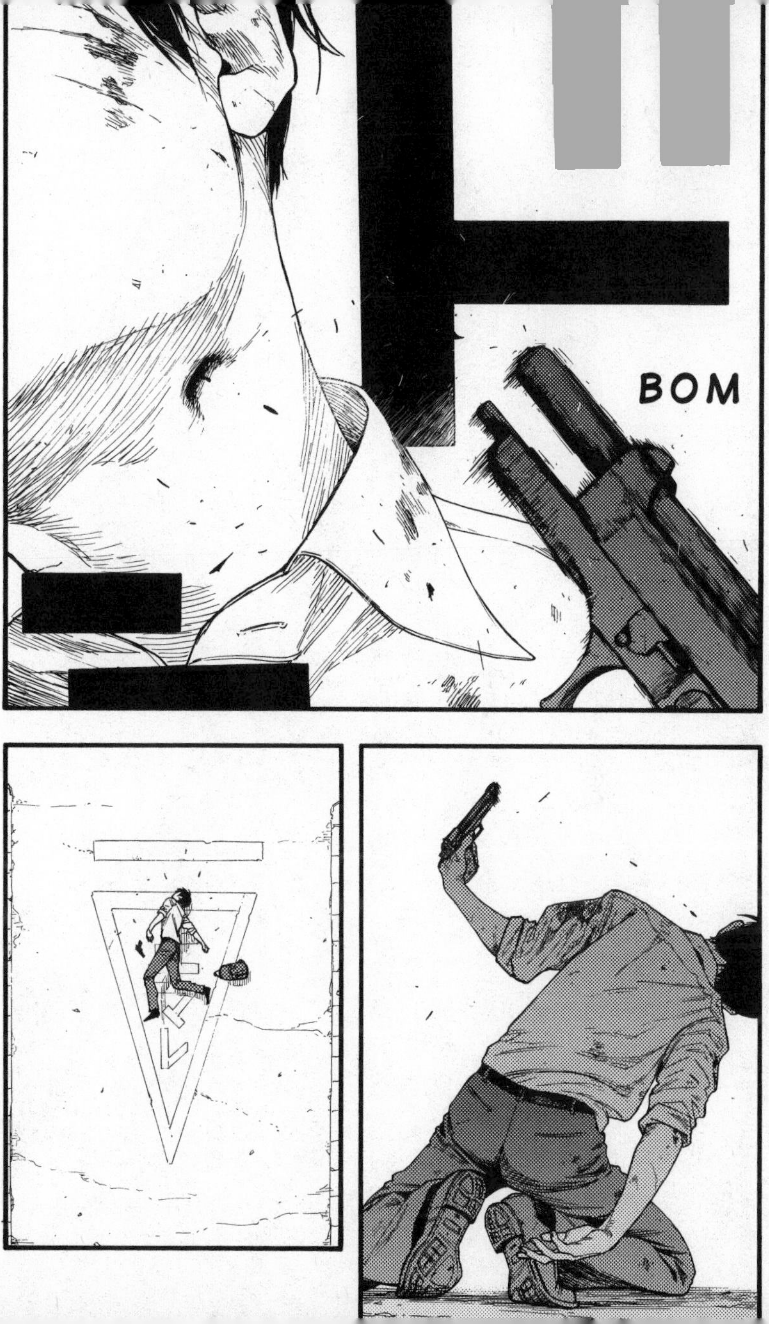
BOM

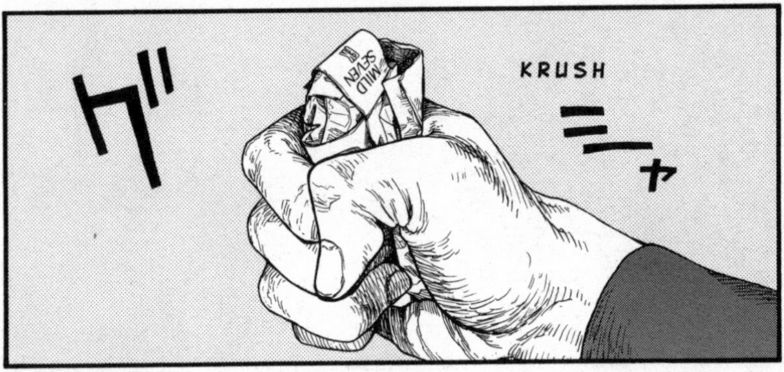
KRUSH
グシャ
MILD SEVEN

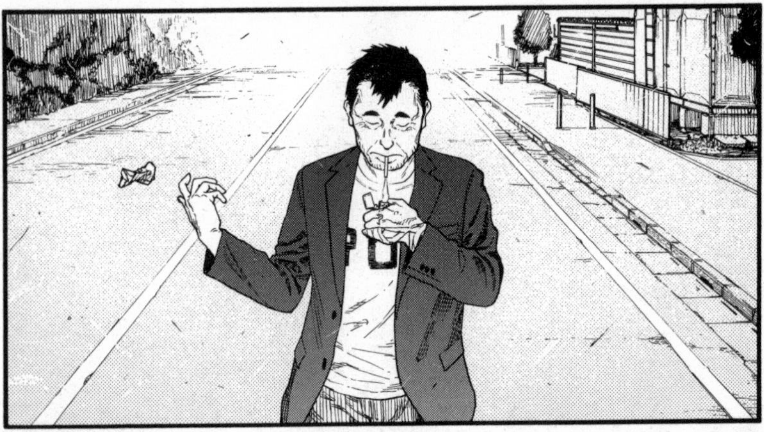

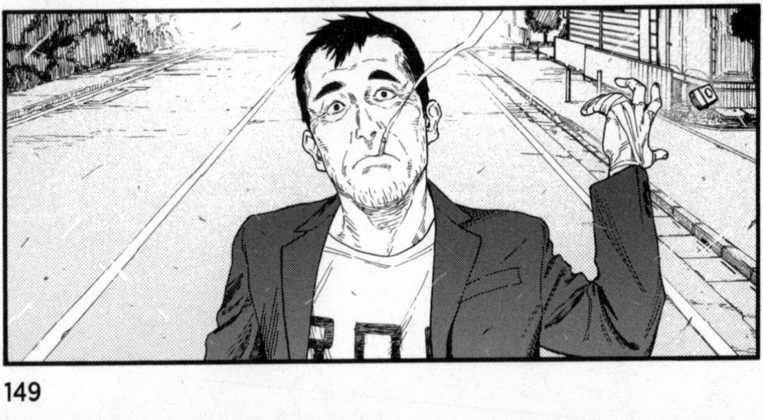

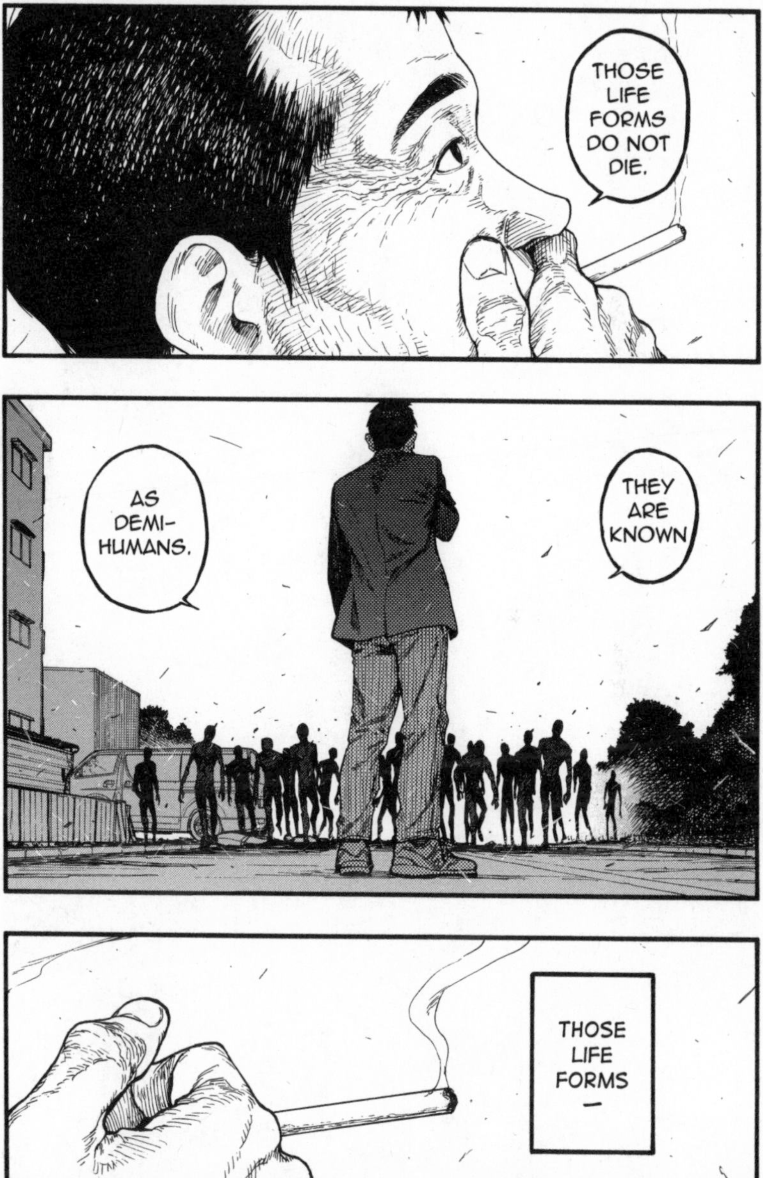
THOSE LIFE FORMS DO NOT DIE.
THEY ARE KNOWN
AS DEMI-HUMANS.
THOSE LIFE FORMS —

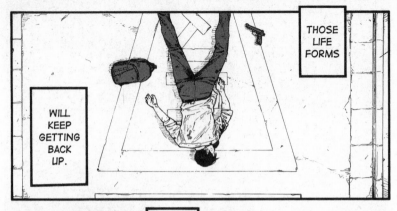

THOSE LIFE FORMS

WILL KEEP GETTING BACK UP.

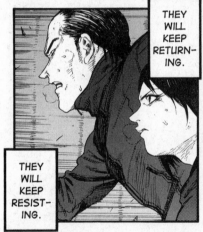

THEY WILL KEEP RETURNING.

THEY WILL KEEP RESISTING.

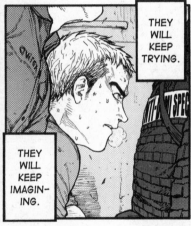

THEY WILL KEEP TRYING.

THEY WILL KEEP IMAGINING.

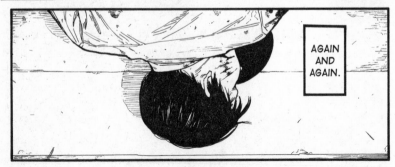

AGAIN AND AGAIN.

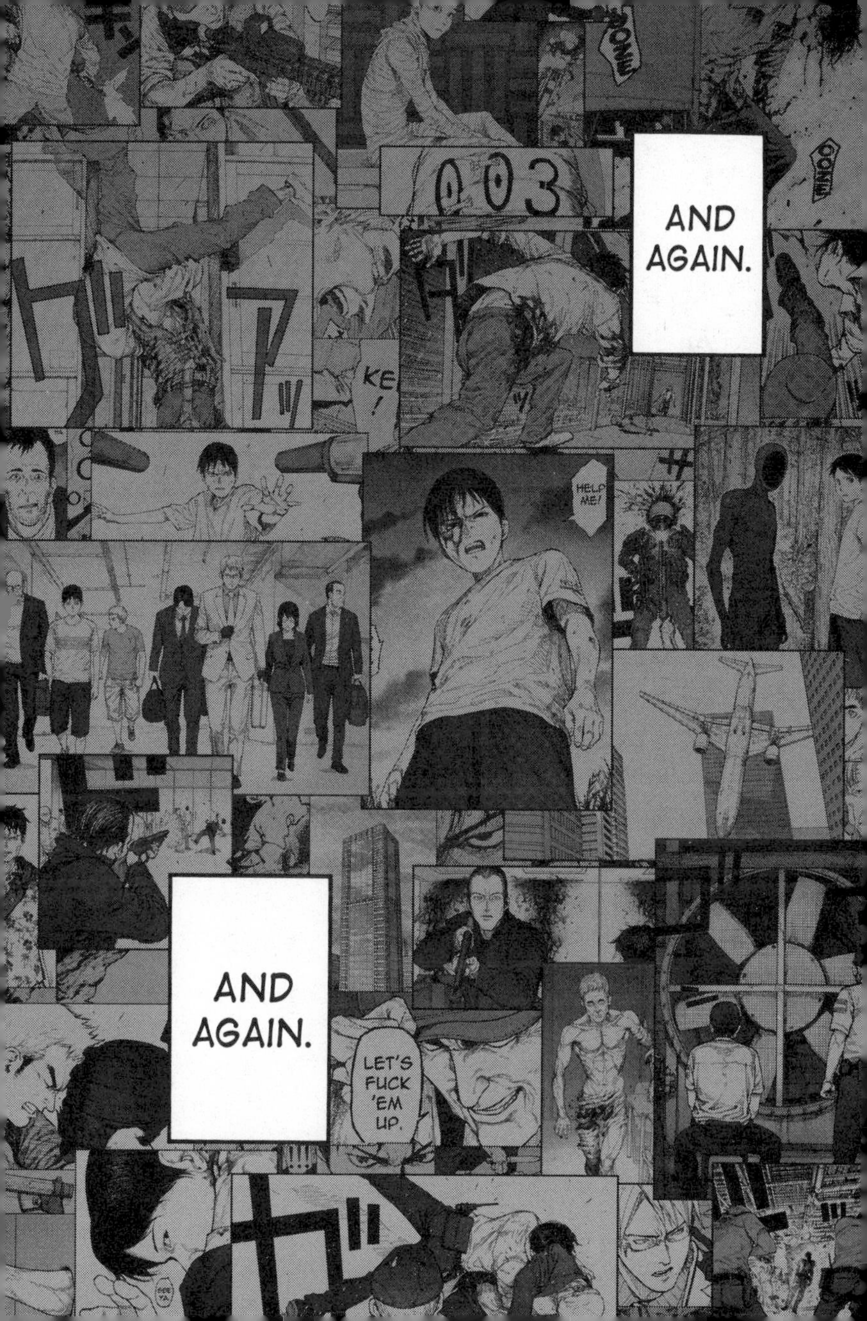
AND AGAIN.
003
KE!
HELP ME!
AND AGAIN.
LET'S FUCK 'EM UP.

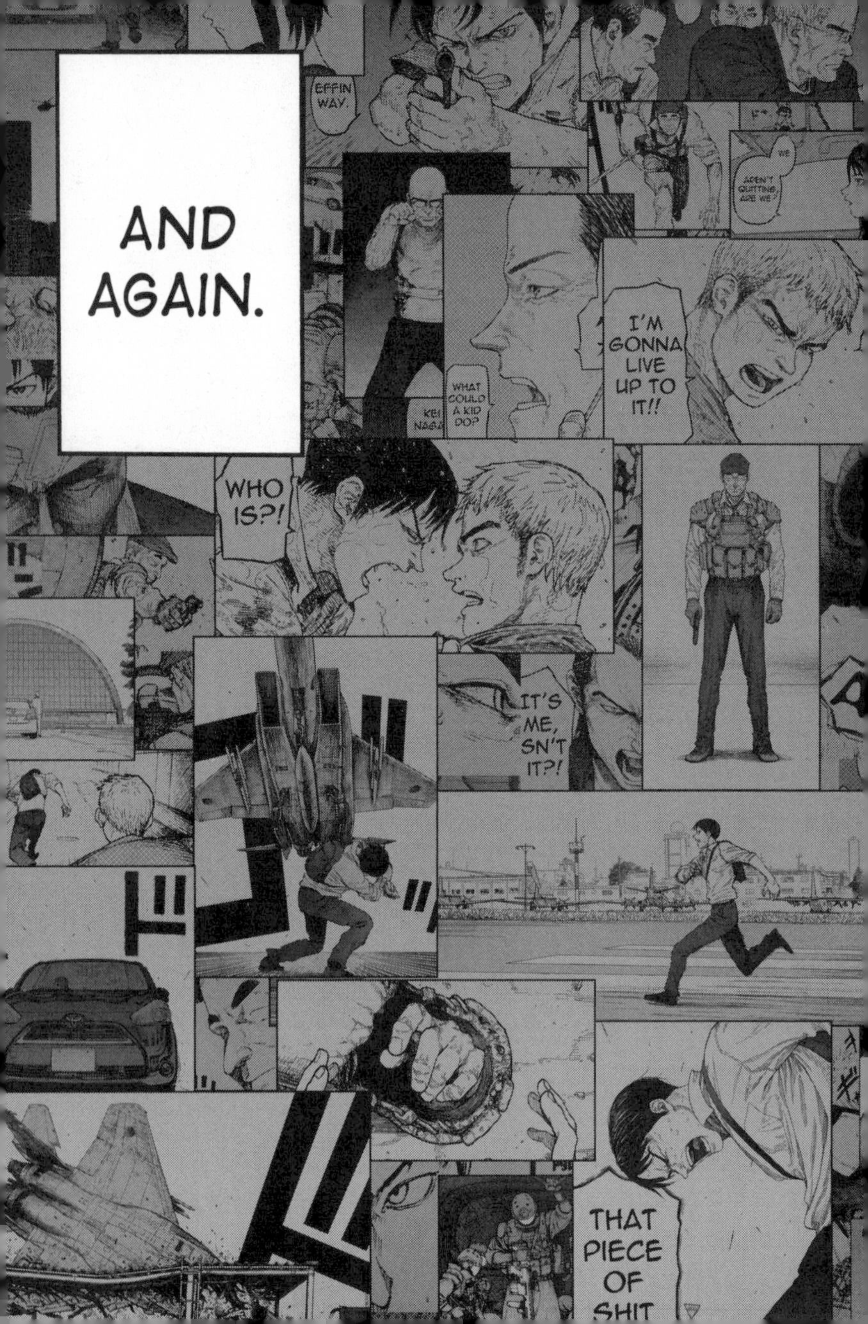
WE AREN'T QUITTING, ARE WE?
EFFIN WAY.
AND AGAIN.
I'M GONNA LIVE UP TO IT!!
WHAT COULD A KID DO?
WHO IS?!
IT'S ME, SN'T IT?!
THAT PIECE OF SHIT

GTUNK
YOU'RE RUNNING AWAY?!
DOESN'T THAT MAKE YOU ANGRY?

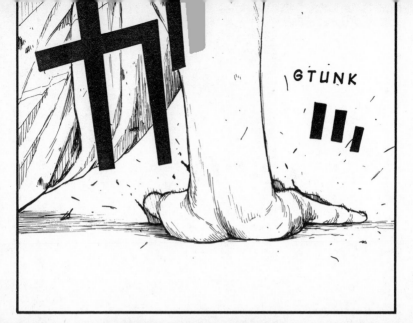

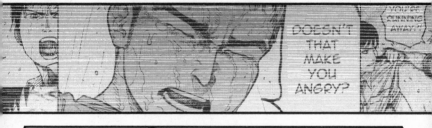

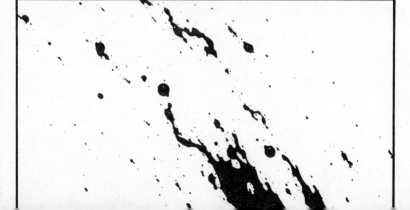

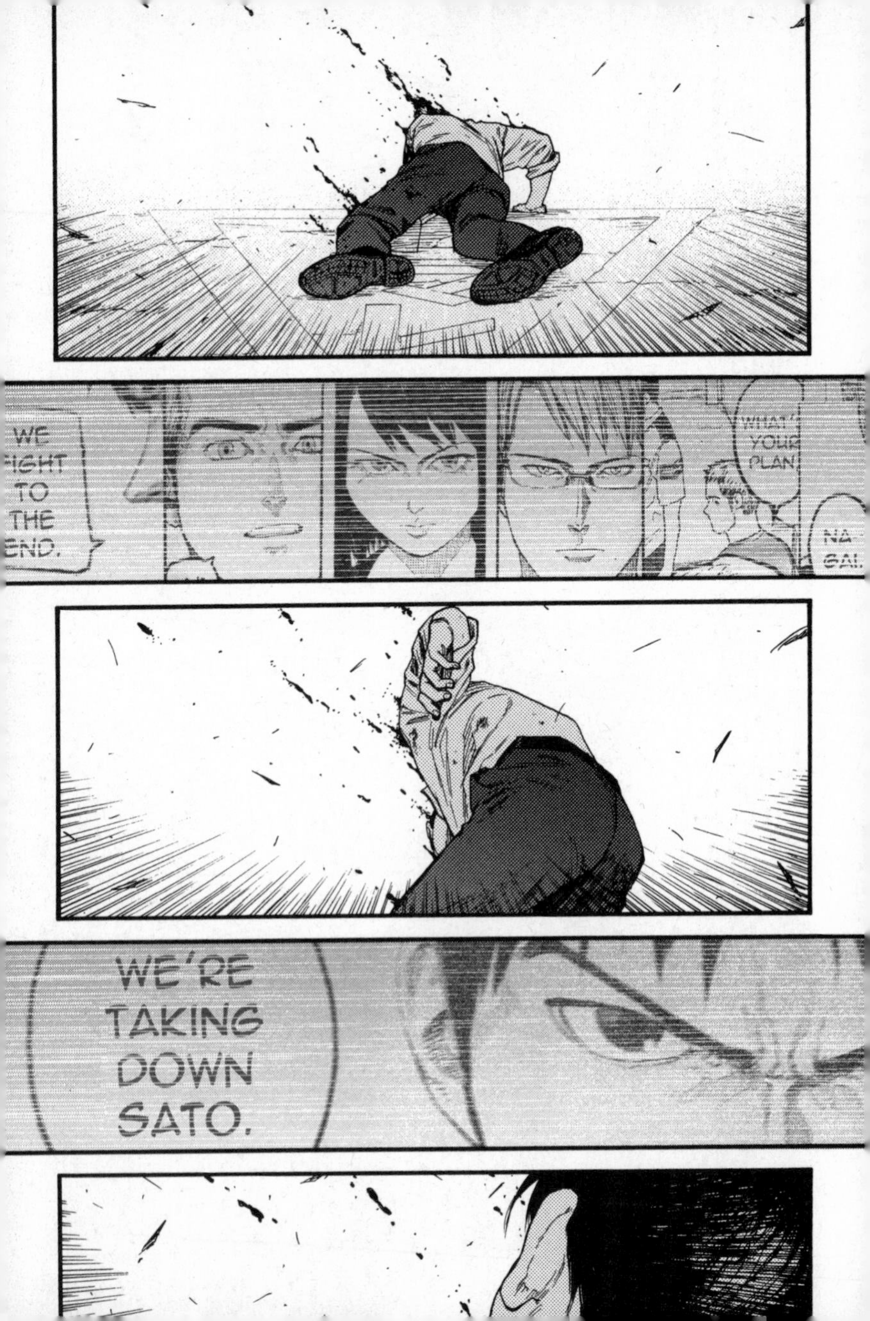
WHAT'S YOUR PLAN
NA-GAI.
WE FIGHT TO THE END.
WE'RE TAKING DOWN SATO.

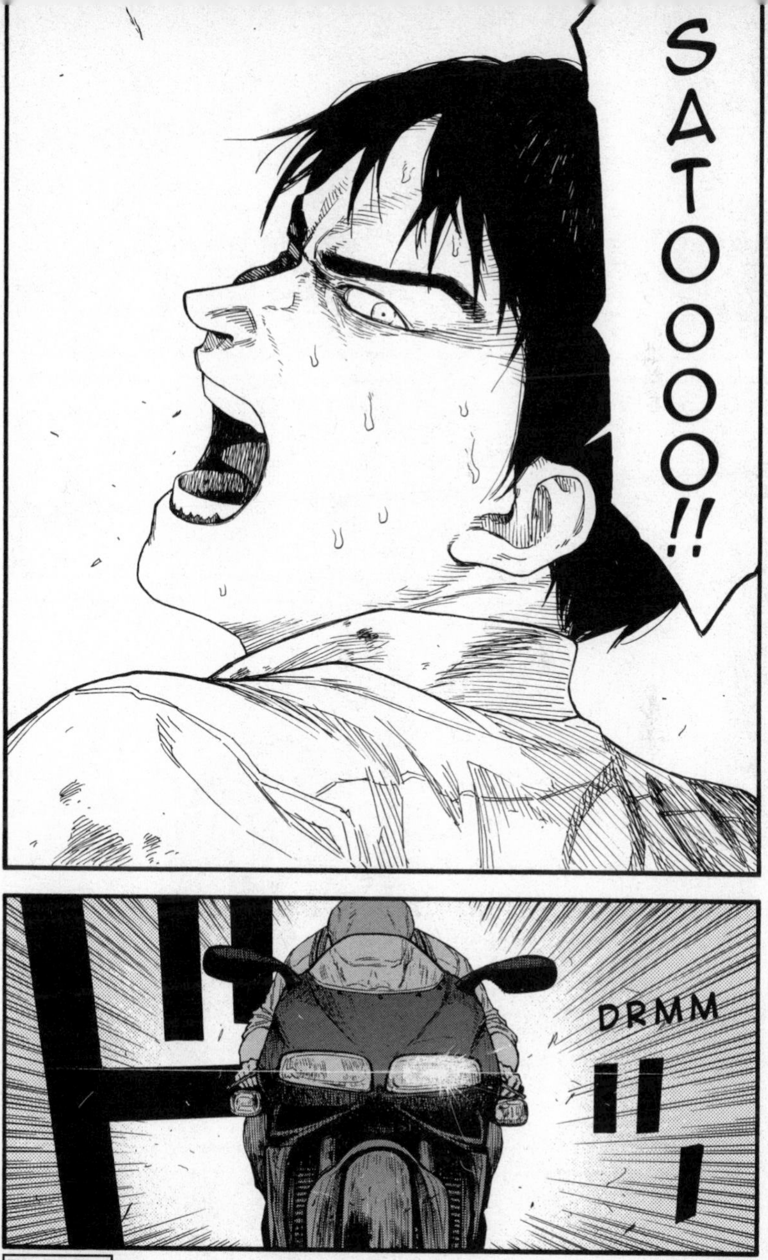
SATOOOO!!
DRMM

File:77 End

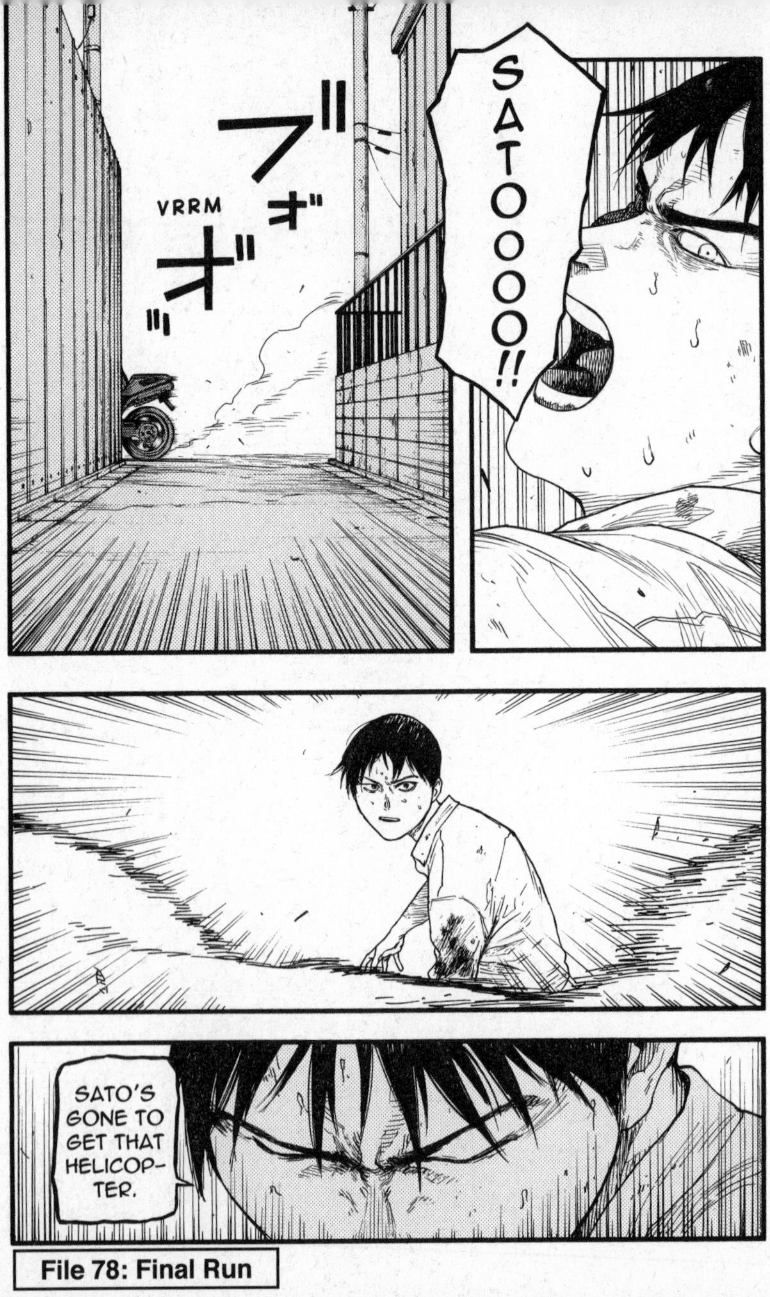
SATOOOO!!
VRRM
SATO'S GONE TO GET THAT HELICOPTER.

File 78: Final Run

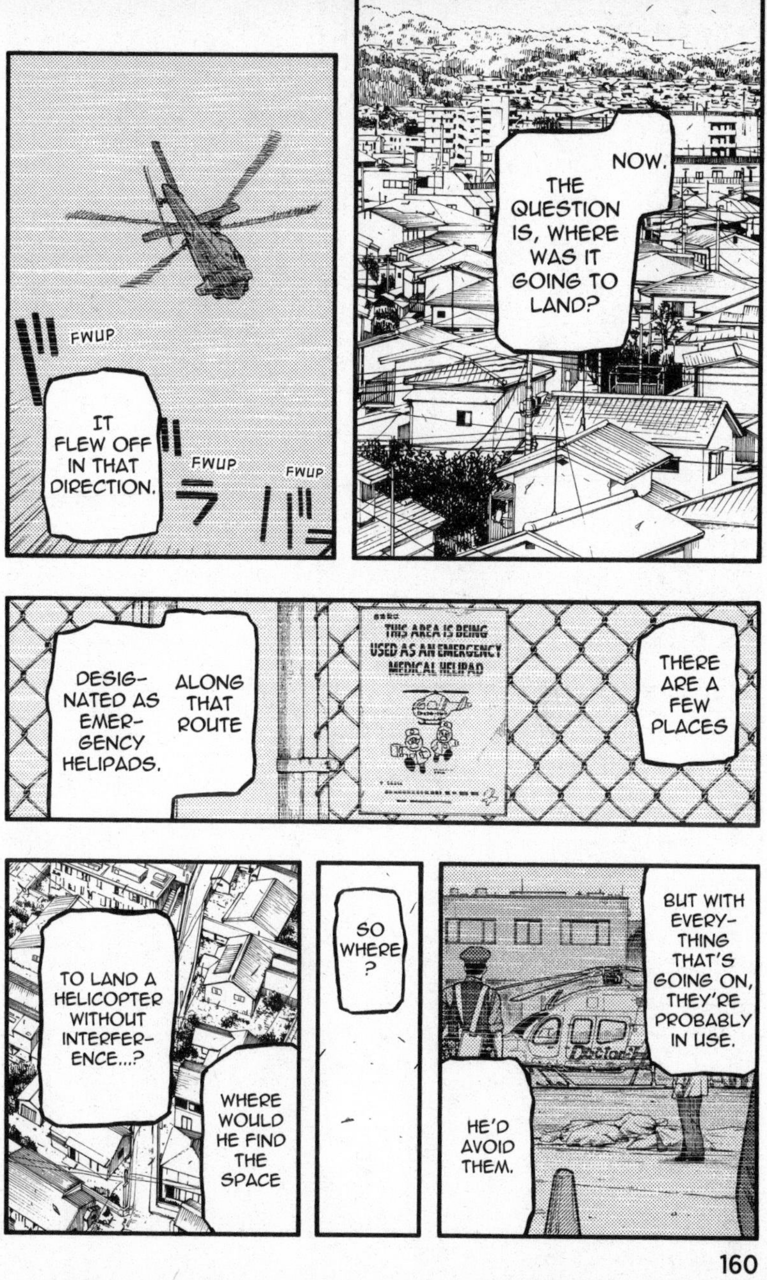

NOW.
THE QUESTION IS, WHERE WAS IT GOING TO LAND?
FWUP
IT FLEW OFF IN THAT DIRECTION.
FWUP
FWUP
THERE ARE A FEW PLACES
THIS AREA IS BEING USED AS AN EMERGENCY MEDICAL HELIPAD
ALONG THAT ROUTE
DESIGNATED AS EMERGENCY HELIPADS.
BUT WITH EVERYTHING THAT'S GOING ON, THEY'RE PROBABLY IN USE.
HE'D AVOID THEM.
SO WHERE?
WHERE WOULD HE FIND THE SPACE
TO LAND A HELICOPTER WITHOUT INTERFERENCE...?

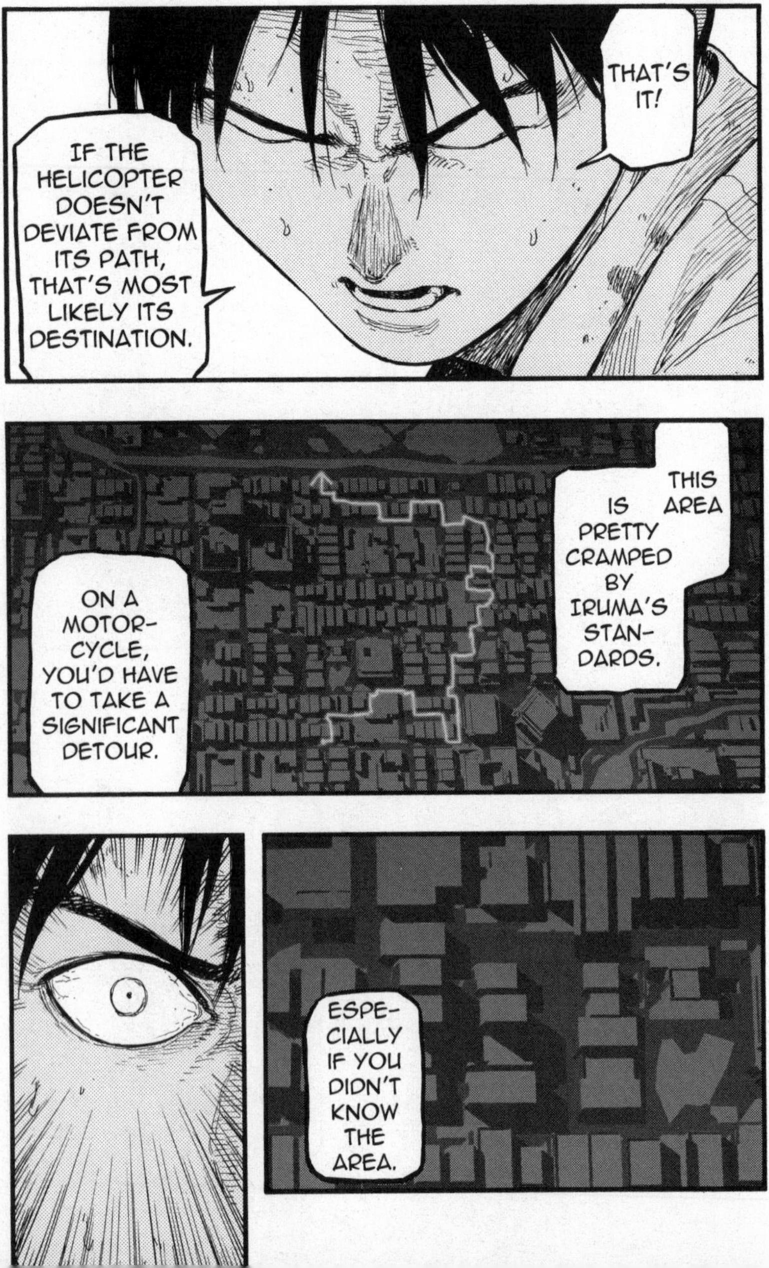
THAT'S IT!
IF THE HELICOPTER DOESN'T DEVIATE FROM ITS PATH, THAT'S MOST LIKELY ITS DESTINATION.
THIS AREA IS PRETTY CRAMPED BY IRUMA'S STANDARDS.
ON A MOTORCYCLE, YOU'D HAVE TO TAKE A SIGNIFICANT DETOUR.
ESPECIALLY IF YOU DIDN'T KNOW THE AREA.

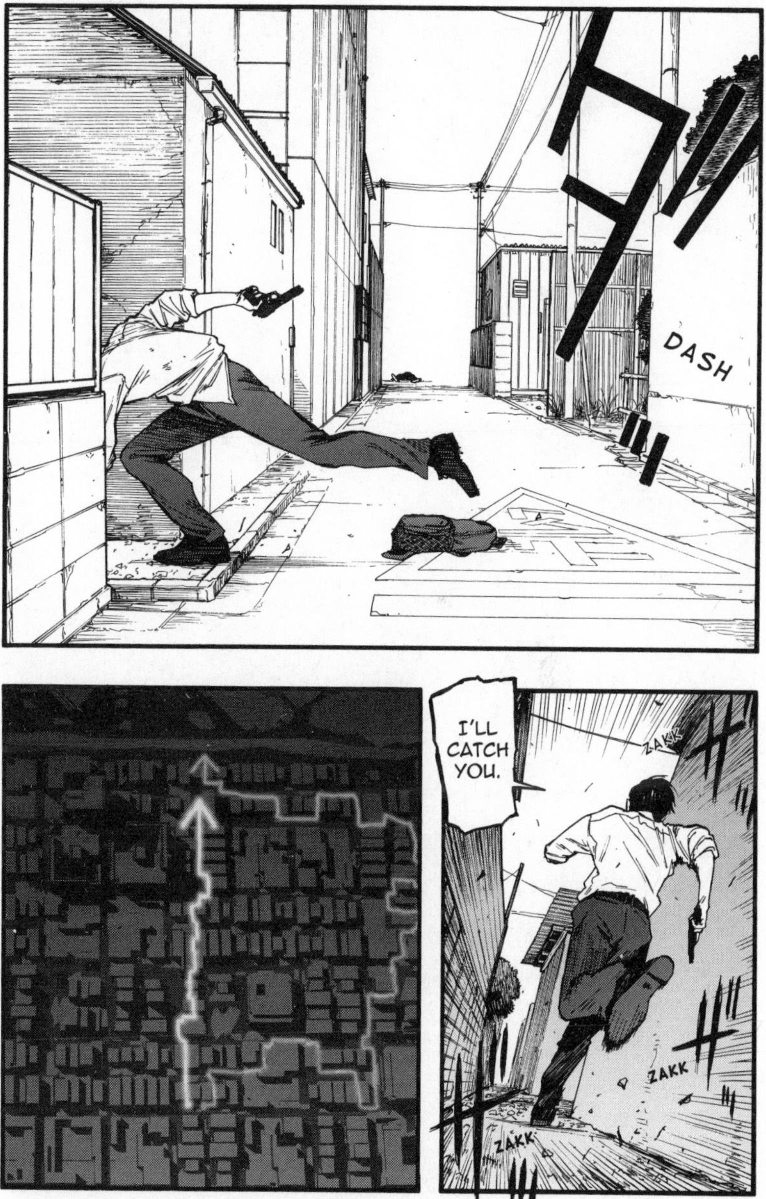
DASH
I'LL CATCH YOU.
ZAKK
ZAKK
ZAKK

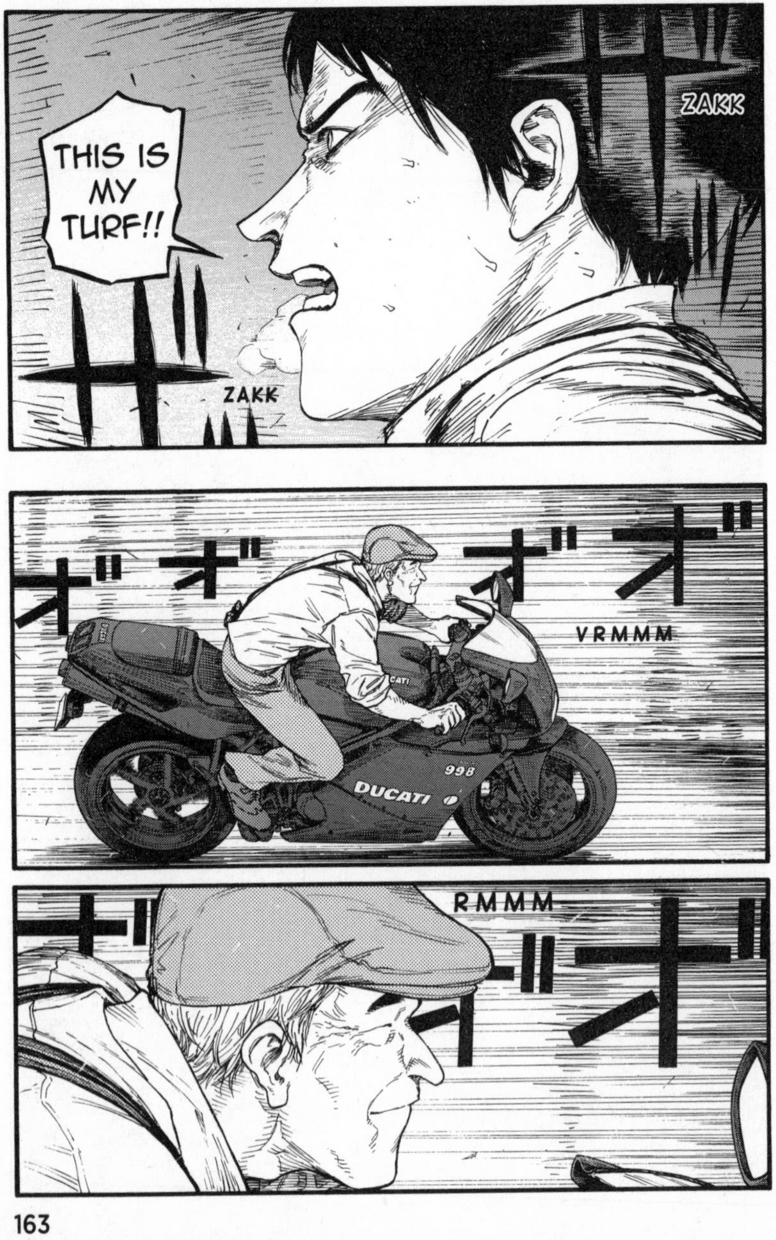
ZAKK
THIS IS MY TURF!!
ZAKK
VRMMM
RMMM

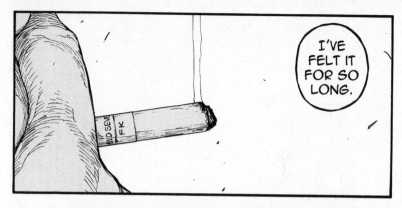

I'VE FELT IT FOR SO LONG.

THIS FATE.

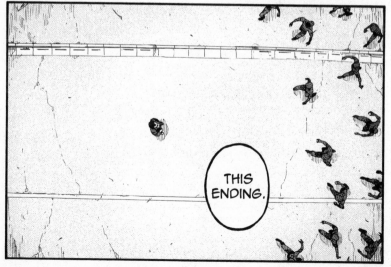

THIS ENDING.

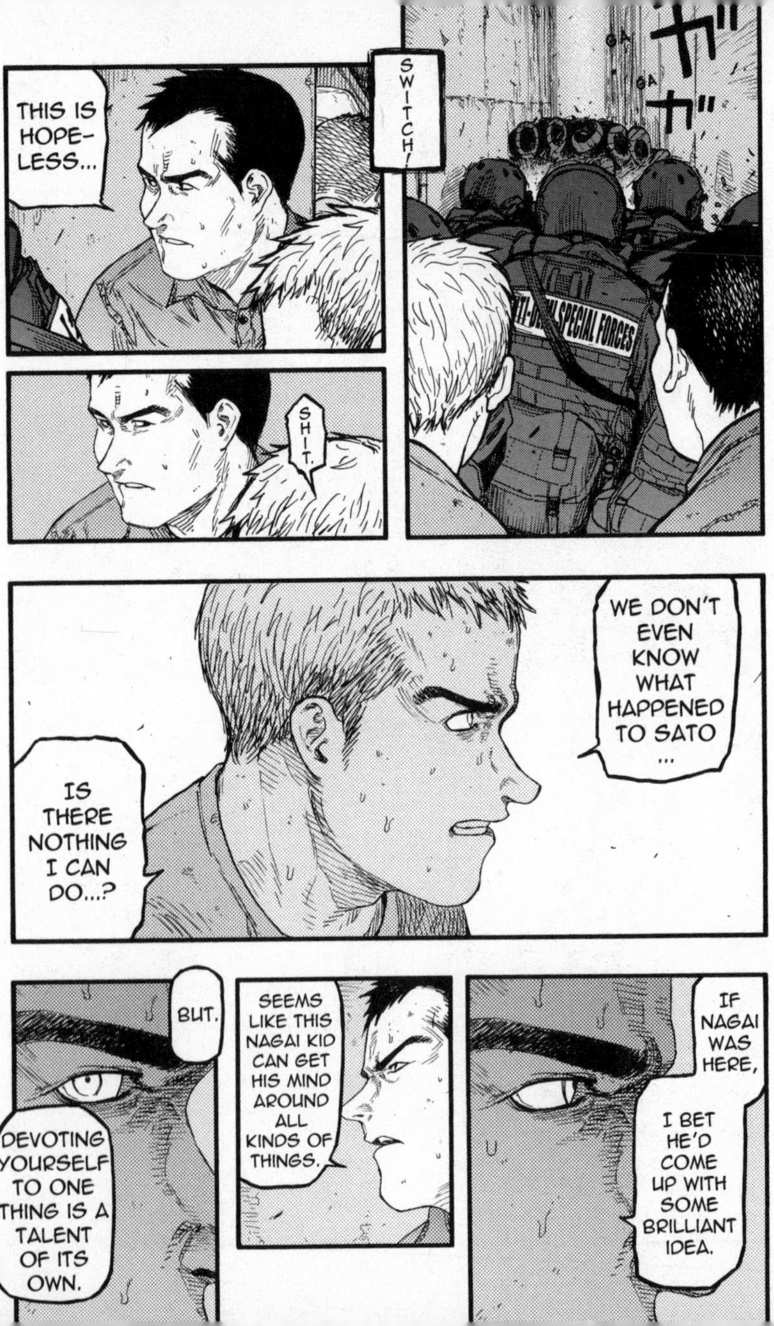
GA
GA
ガ
ガ
SPECIAL FORCES
SWITCH!
THIS IS HOPELESS...
SHIT.
WE DON'T EVEN KNOW WHAT HAPPENED TO SATO ...
IS THERE NOTHING I CAN DO...?
IF NAGAI WAS HERE,
I BET HE'D COME UP WITH SOME BRILLIANT IDEA.
SEEMS LIKE THIS NAGAI KID CAN GET HIS MIND AROUND ALL KINDS OF THINGS.
BUT.
DEVOTING YOURSELF TO ONE THING IS A TALENT OF ITS OWN.

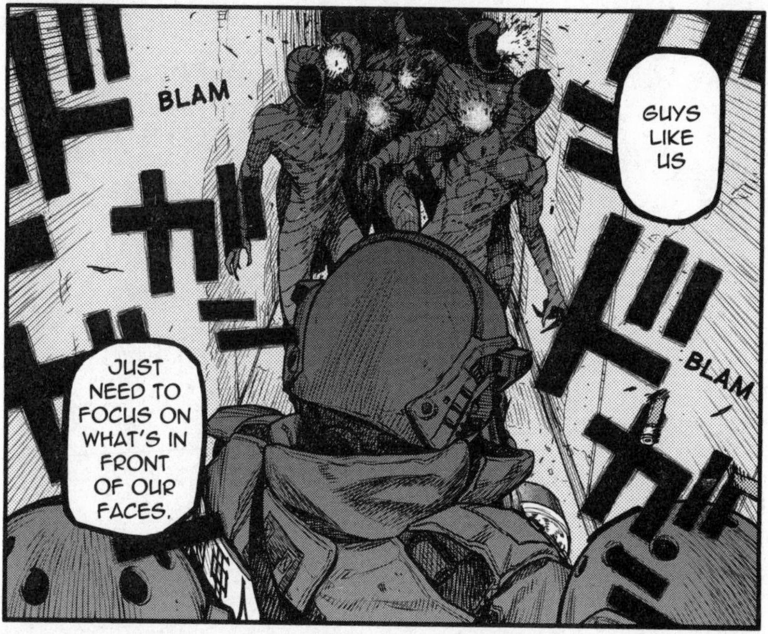
GUYS LIKE US
BLAM
BLAM
JUST NEED TO FOCUS ON WHAT'S IN FRONT OF OUR FACES.
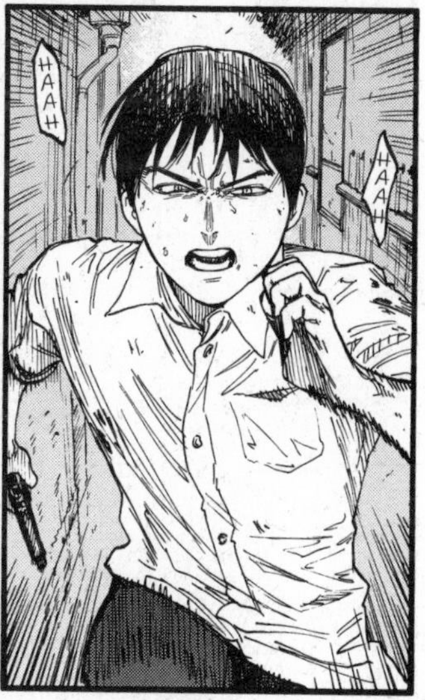
HAAAH
HAAAH
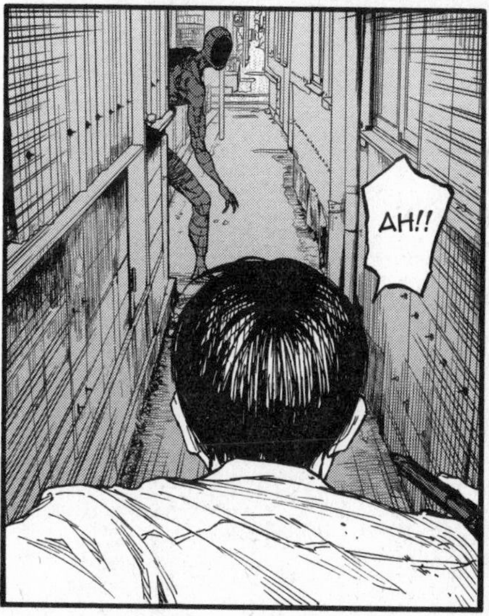
AH!!

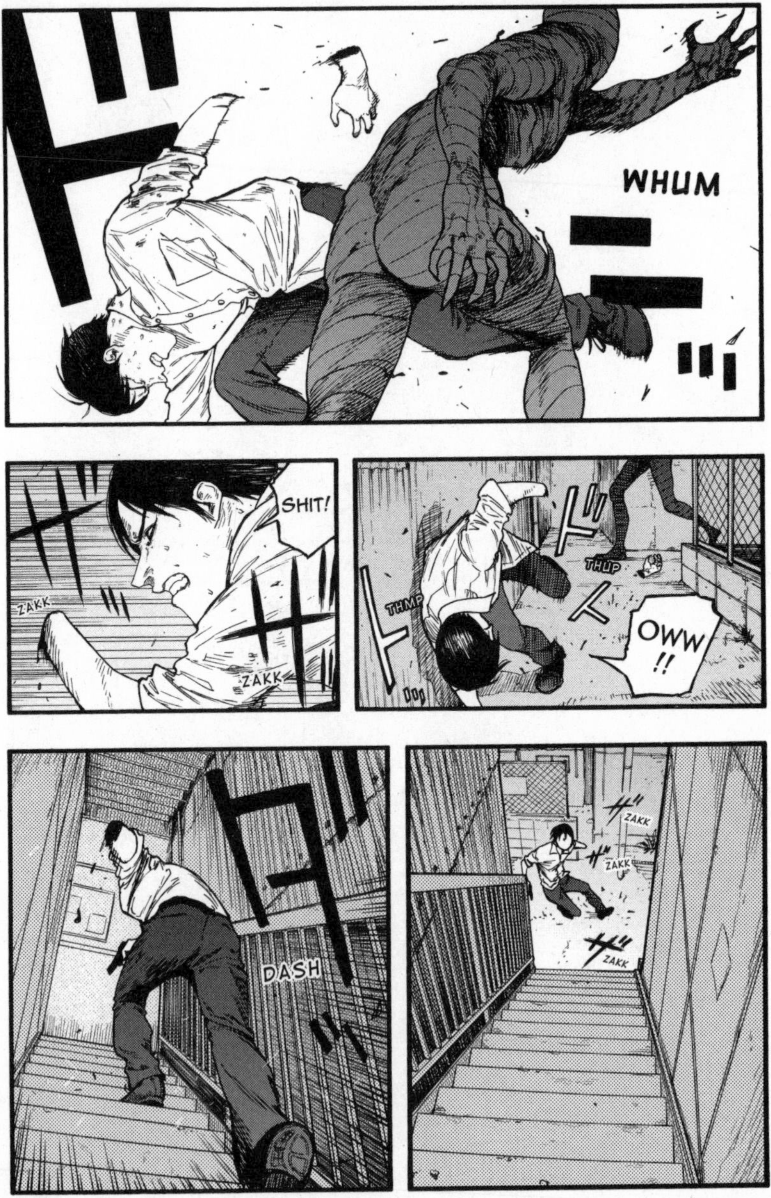
WHUM
THUP
THMP
OWW !!
SHIT!
ZAKK
ZAKK
ZAKK
ZAKK
ZAKK
DASH

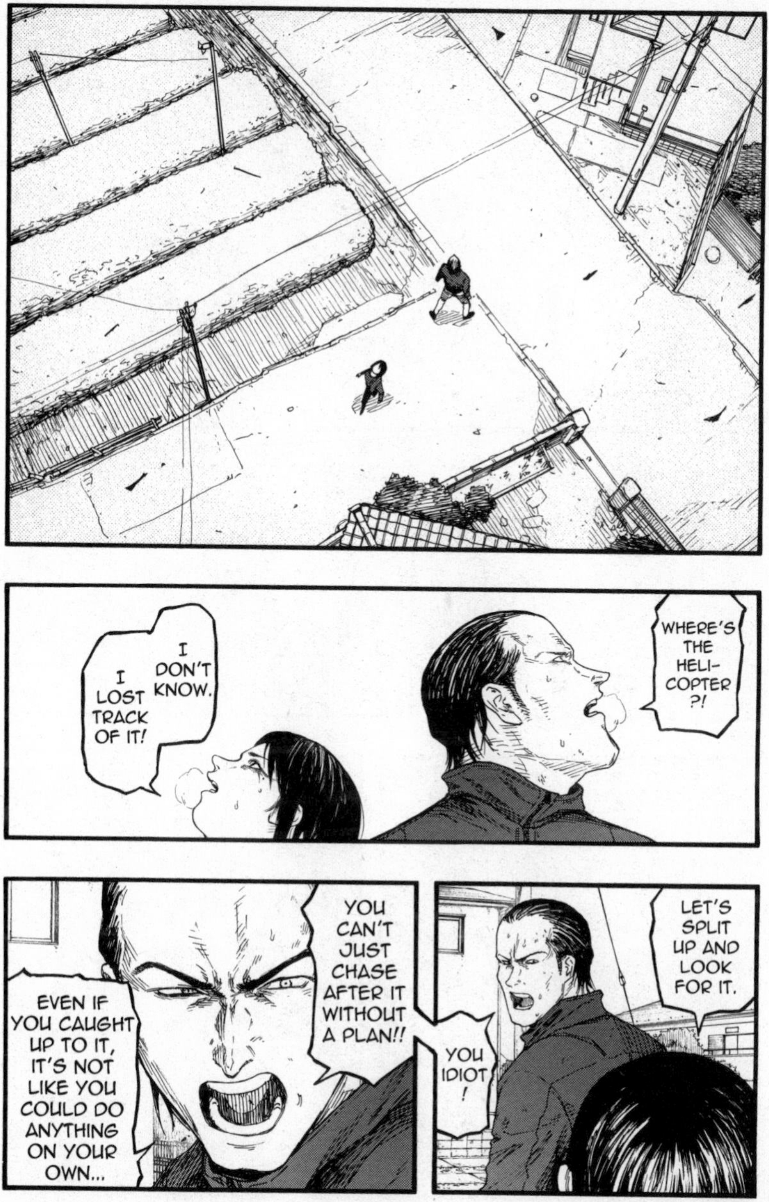
WHERE'S THE HELI-COPTER?!
I DON'T KNOW.
I LOST TRACK OF IT!
LET'S SPLIT UP AND LOOK FOR IT.
YOU IDIOT!
YOU CAN'T JUST CHASE AFTER IT WITHOUT A PLAN!!
EVEN IF YOU CAUGHT UP TO IT, IT'S NOT LIKE YOU COULD DO ANYTHING ON YOUR OWN...

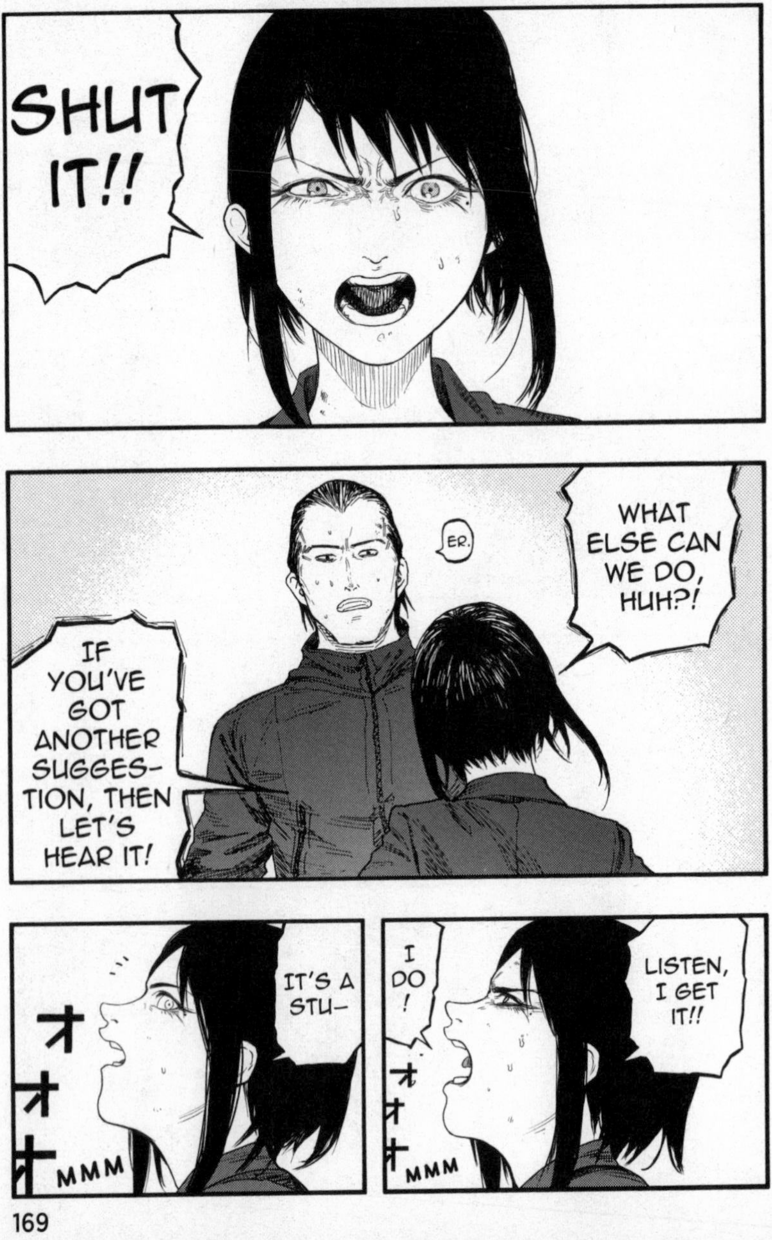
SHUT IT!!
WHAT ELSE CAN WE DO, HUH?!
ER.
IF YOU'VE GOT ANOTHER SUGGES- TION, THEN LET'S HEAR IT!
LISTEN, I GET IT!!
I DO!
オオオ MMM
IT'S A STU-
オオオ MMM

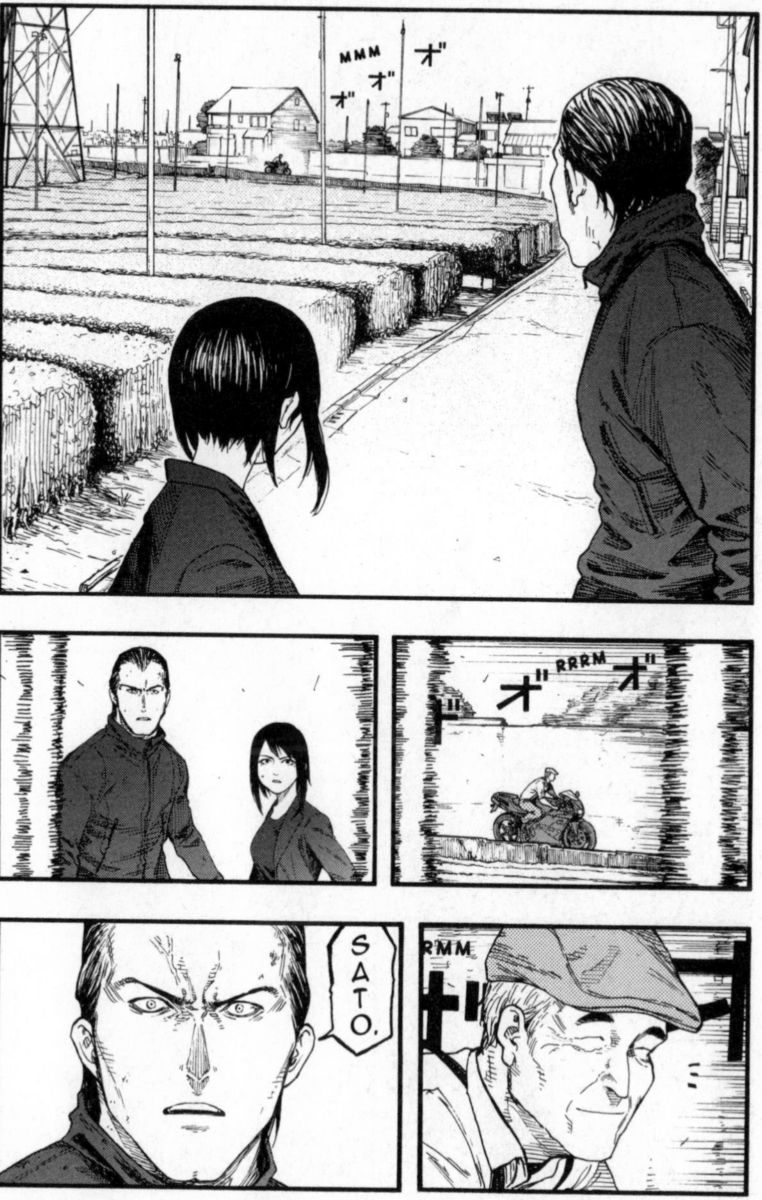
MMM
オ゛オ゛オ゛
RRRM
ドオ゛オ゛
RMM
SATO.

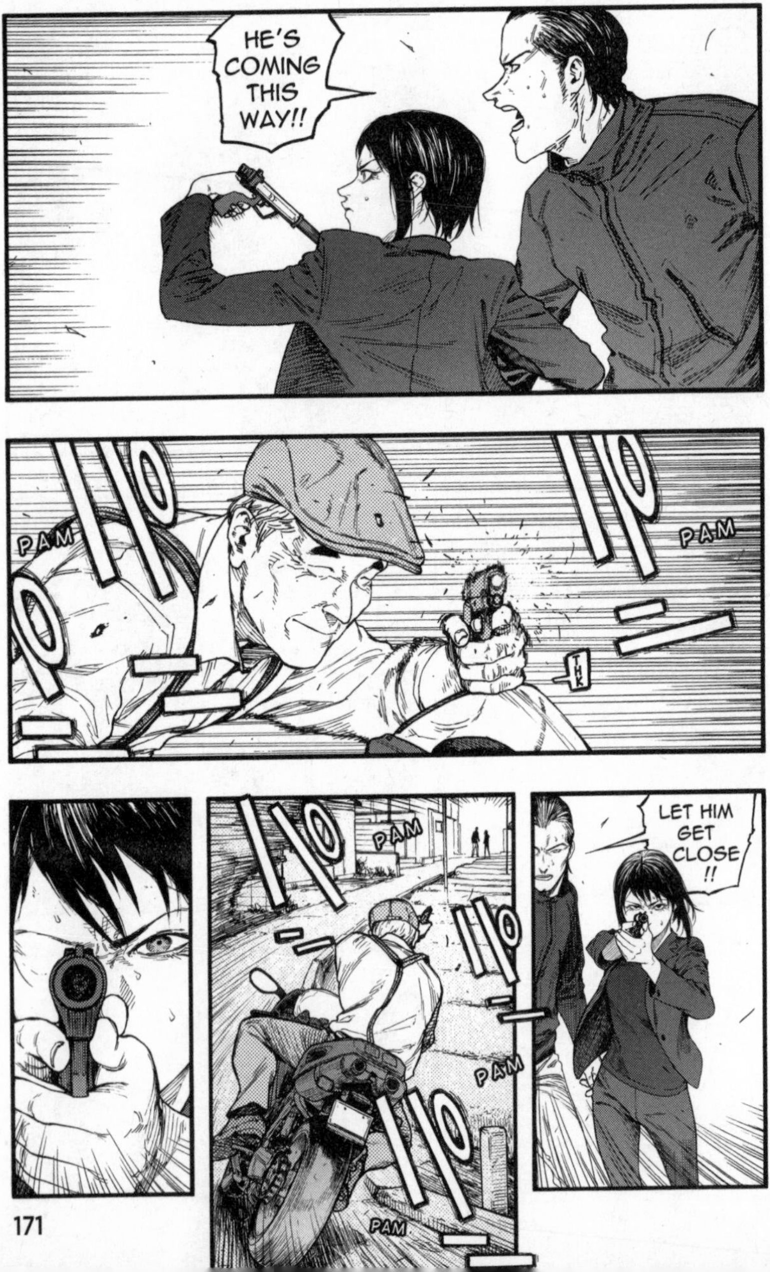
HE'S COMING THIS WAY!!
PAM
THK
PAM
LET HIM GET CLOSE !!
PAM
PAM
PAM

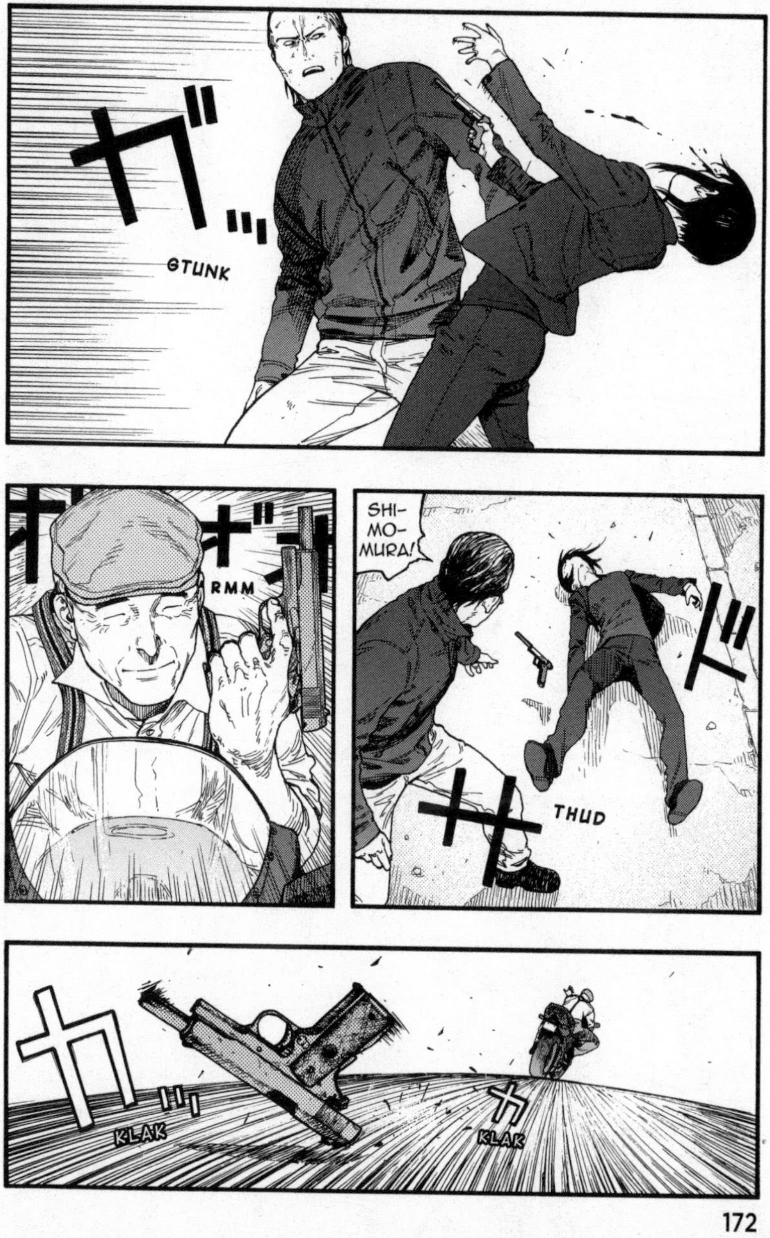
GTUNK
SHIMO-
MO-
MURA!
THUD
RMM
KLAK
KLAK

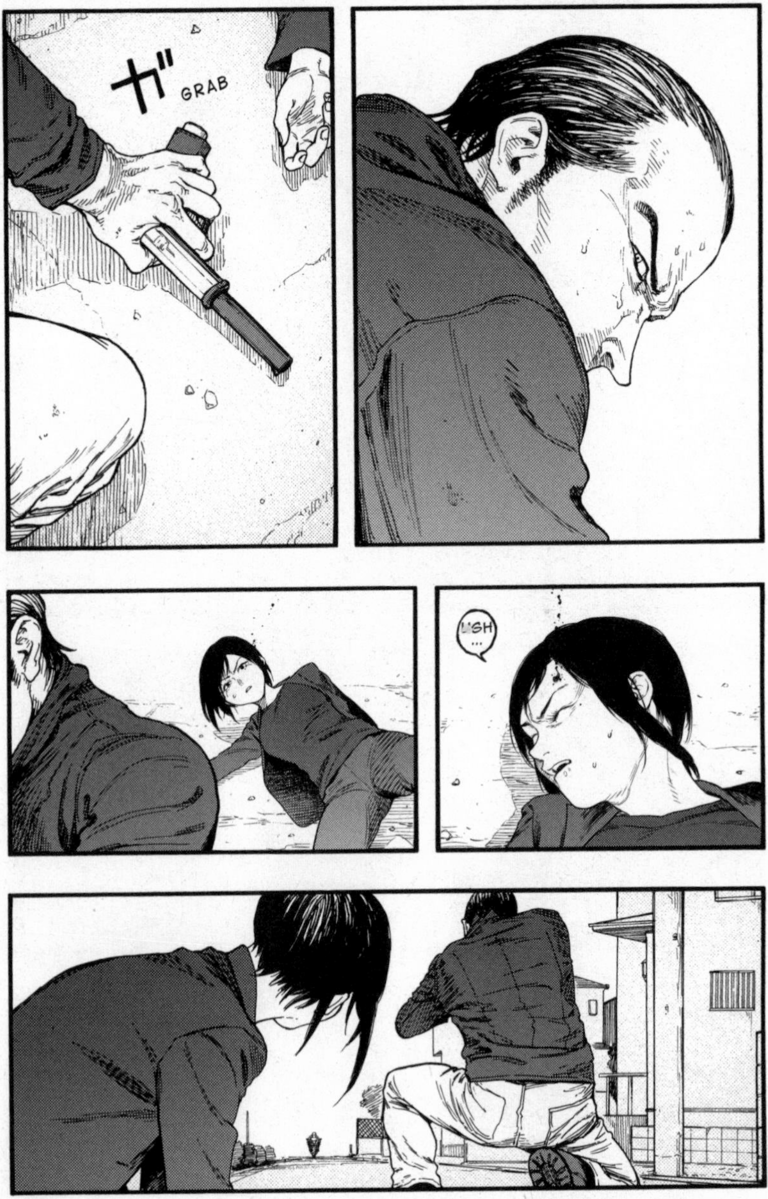
ガ
GRAB
USH
...

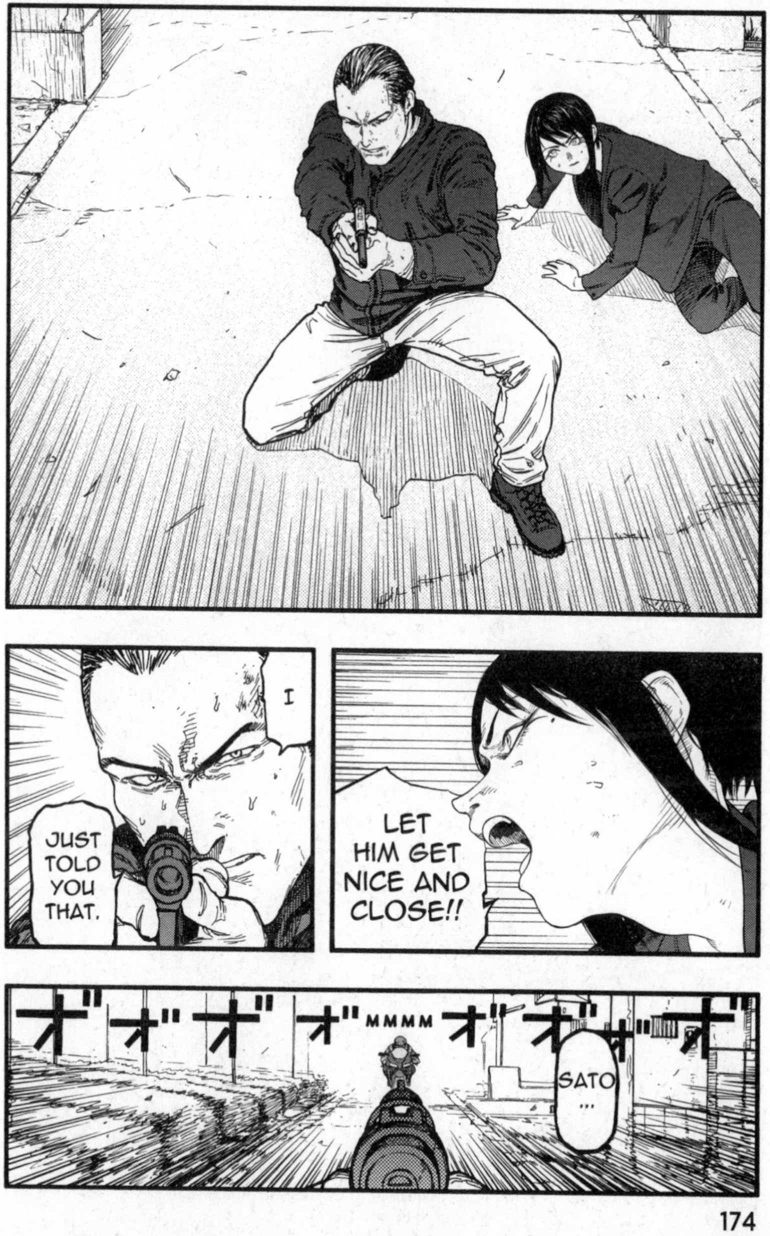
LET HIM GET NICE AND CLOSE!!
I
JUST TOLD YOU THAT.
オ゛オ゛オ゛オ゛MMMMオ゛オ゛オ゛オ゛
SATO ...

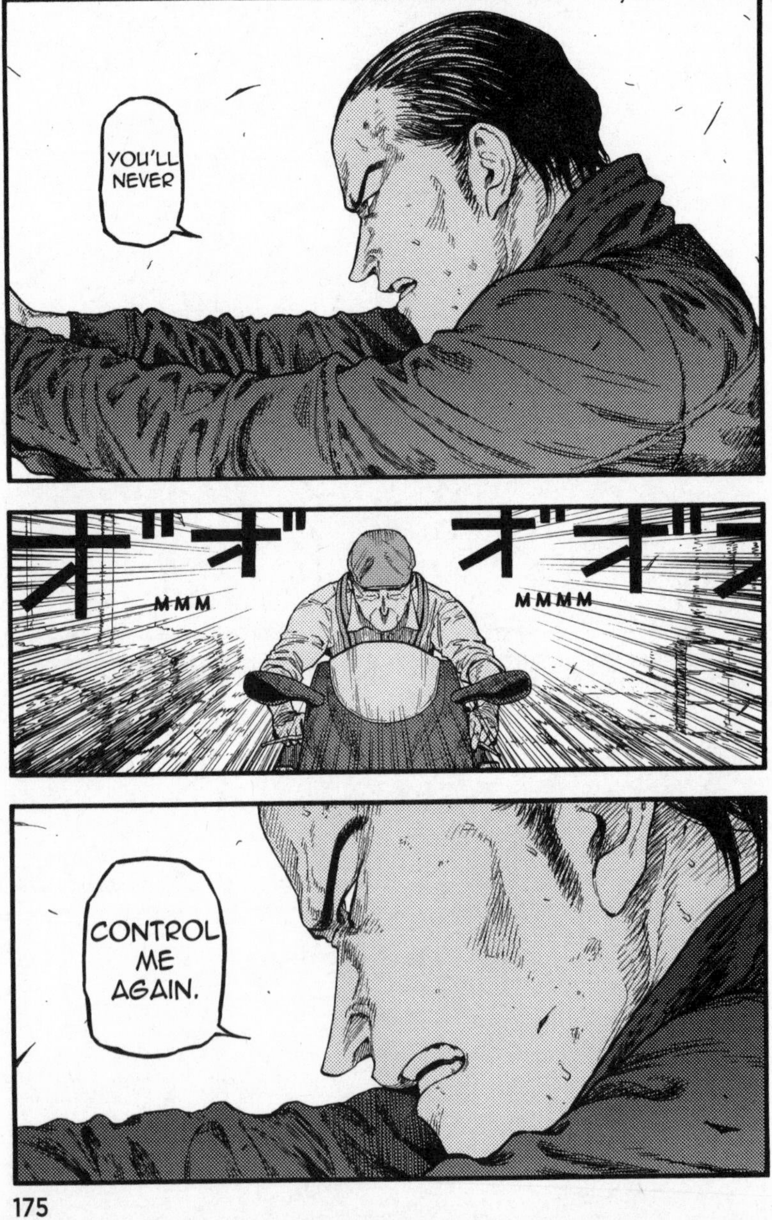
YOU'LL NEVER
MMMM
MMM
CONTROL ME AGAIN.

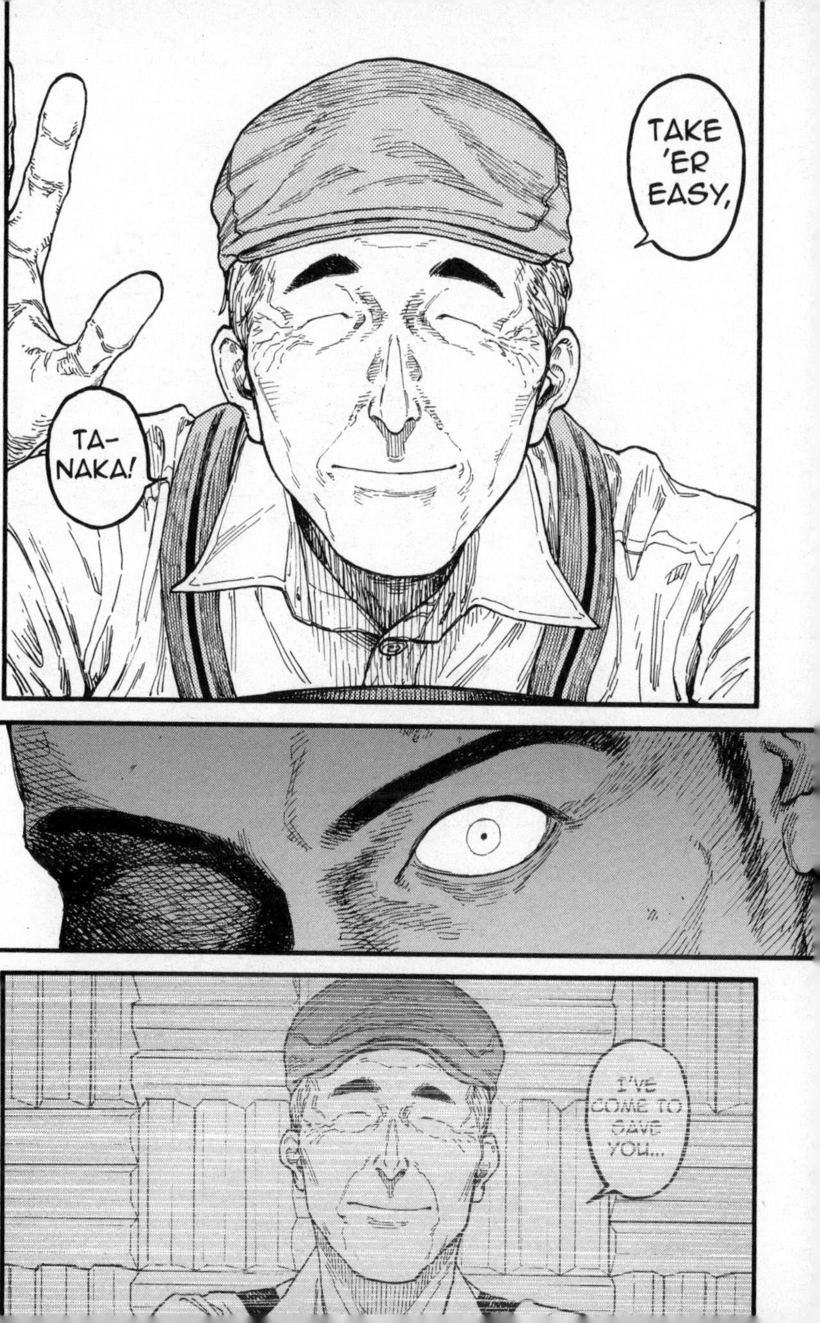
TAKE 'ER EASY,
TA-NAKA!
I'VE COME TO SAVE YOU...

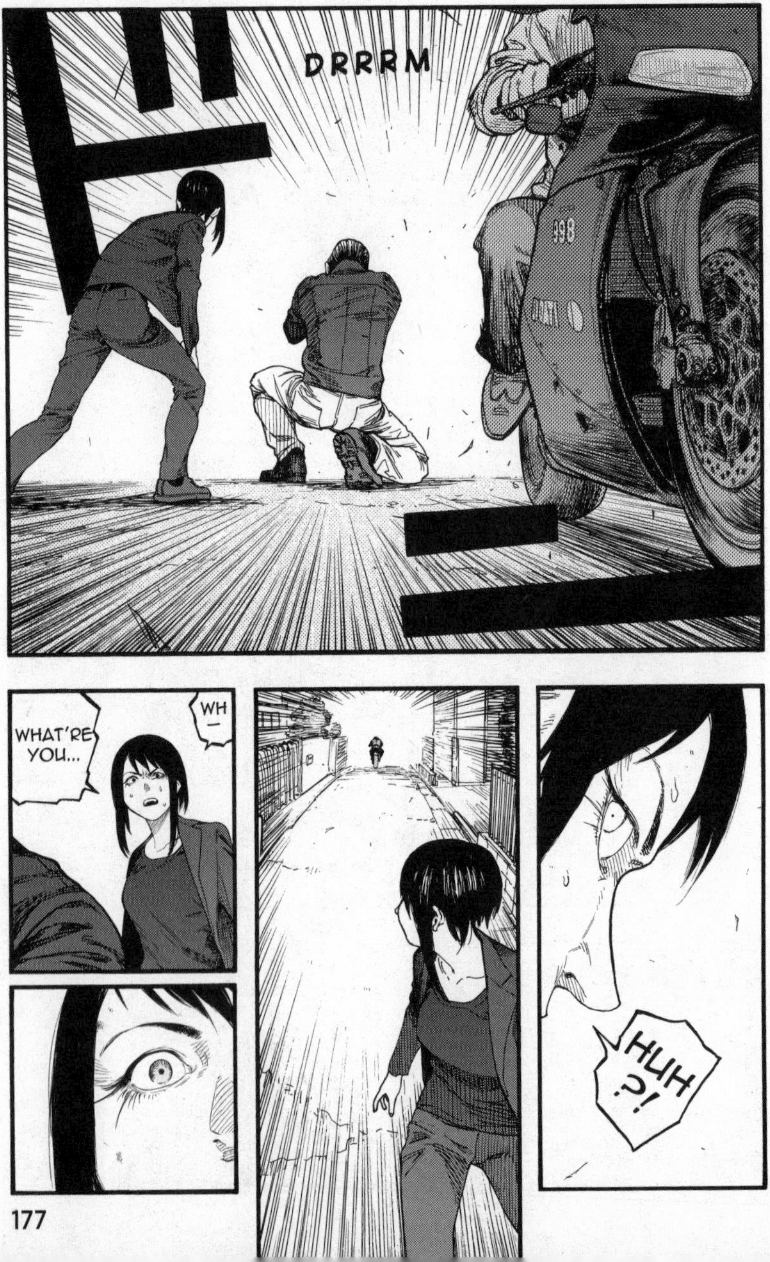
DRRRM
HUH ?!
WH—
WHAT'RE YOU...

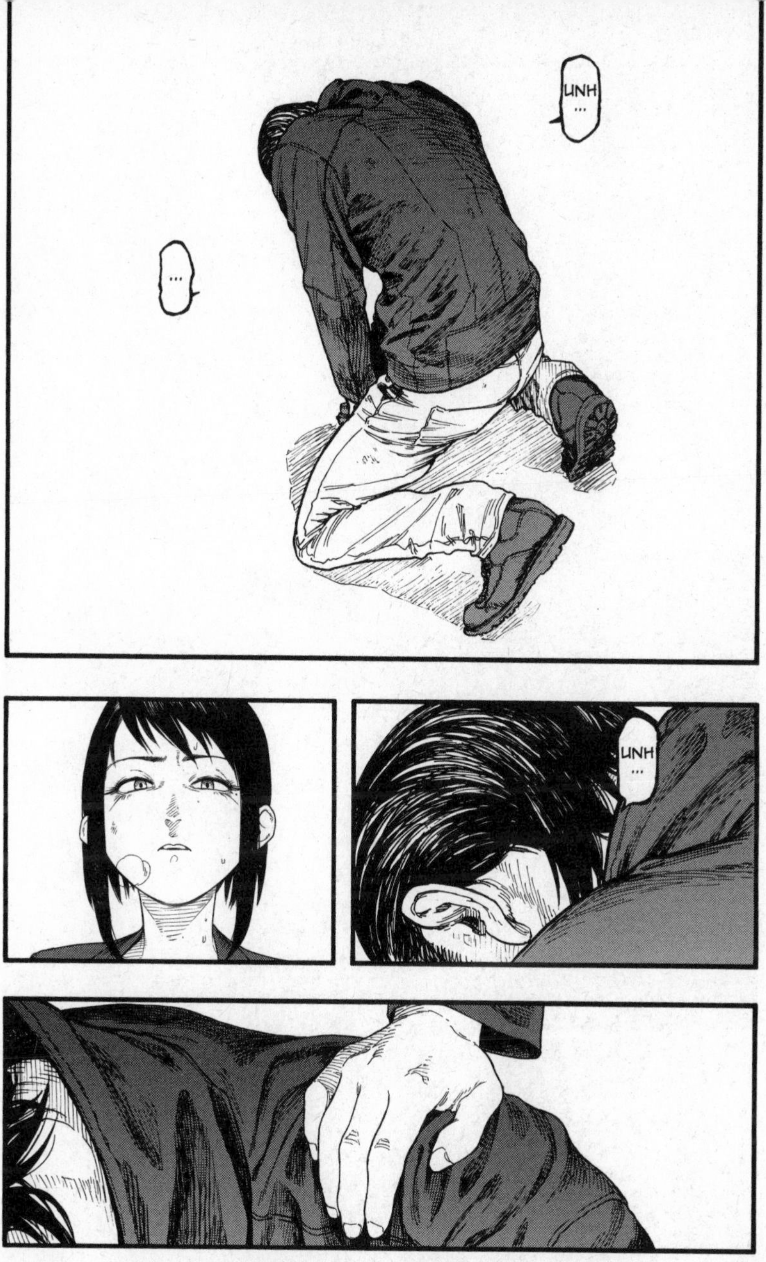
UNH ...
...
UNH ...

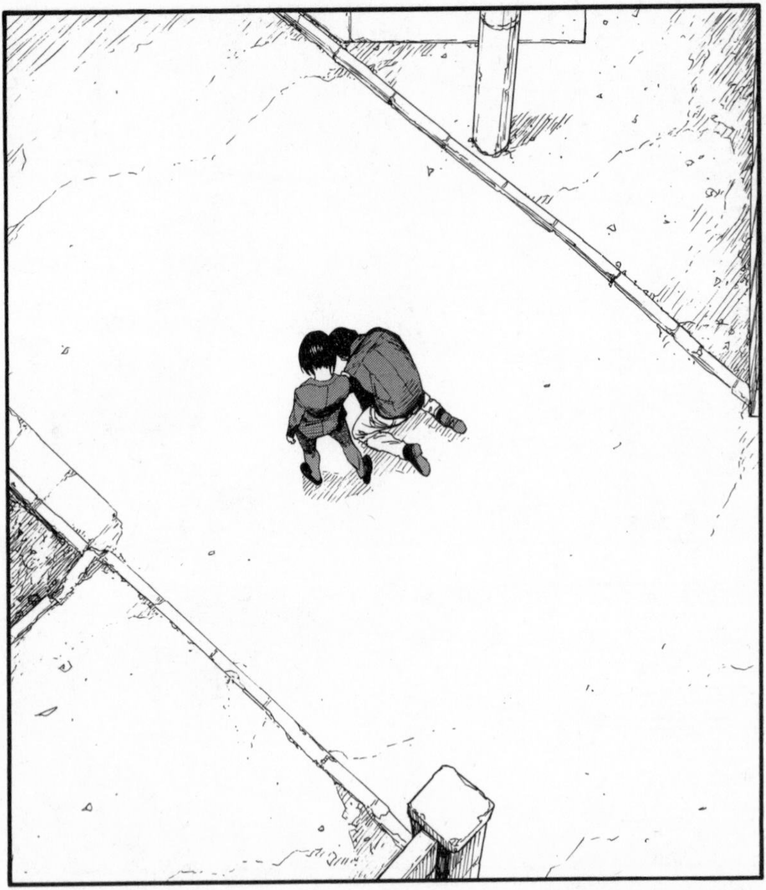
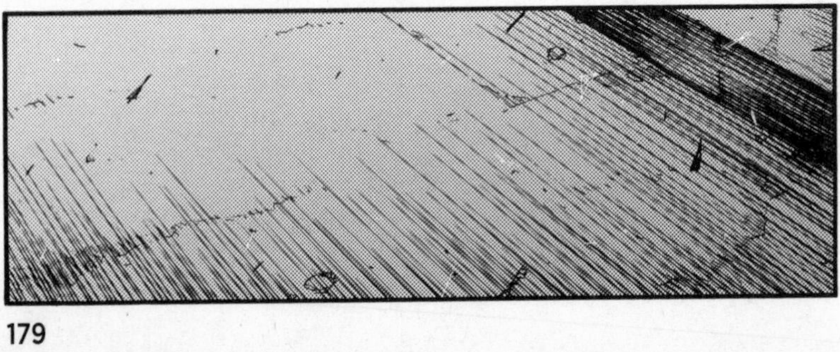

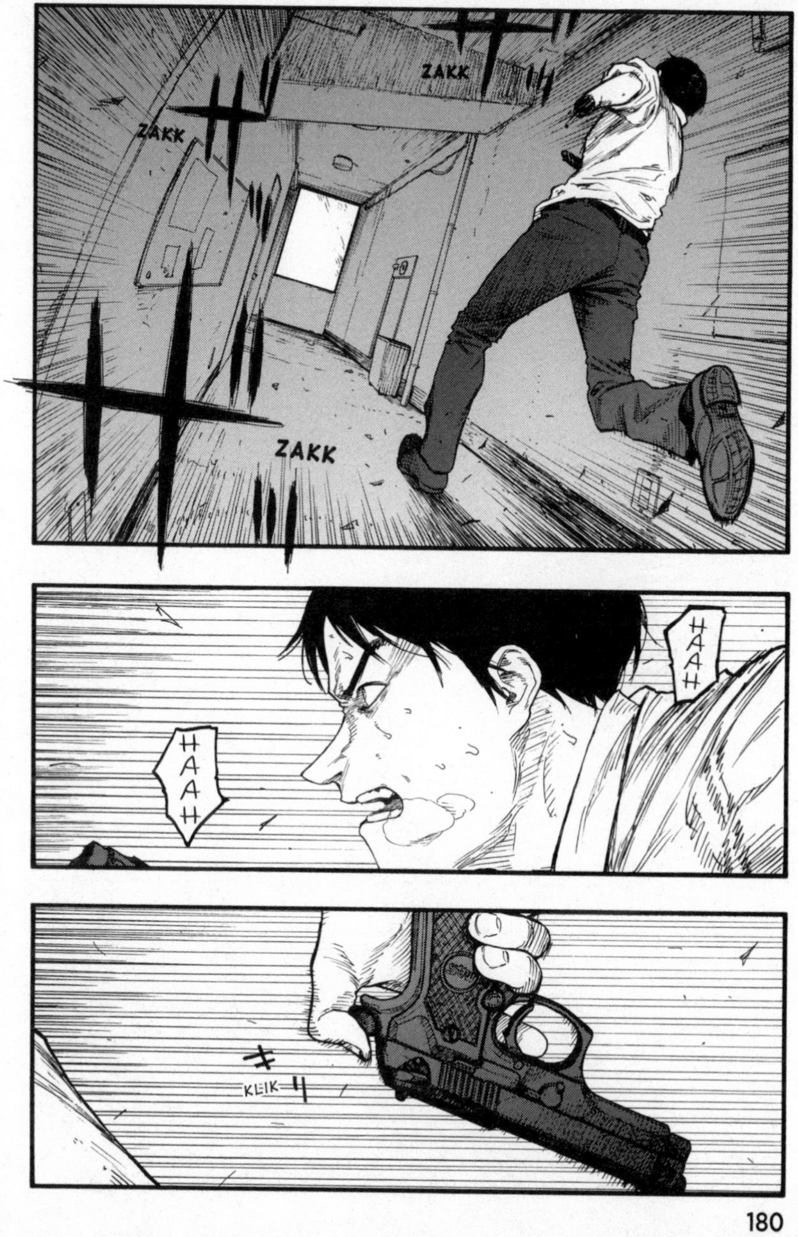
ZAKK
ZAKK
ZAKK
HAAH
HAAH
KLIK

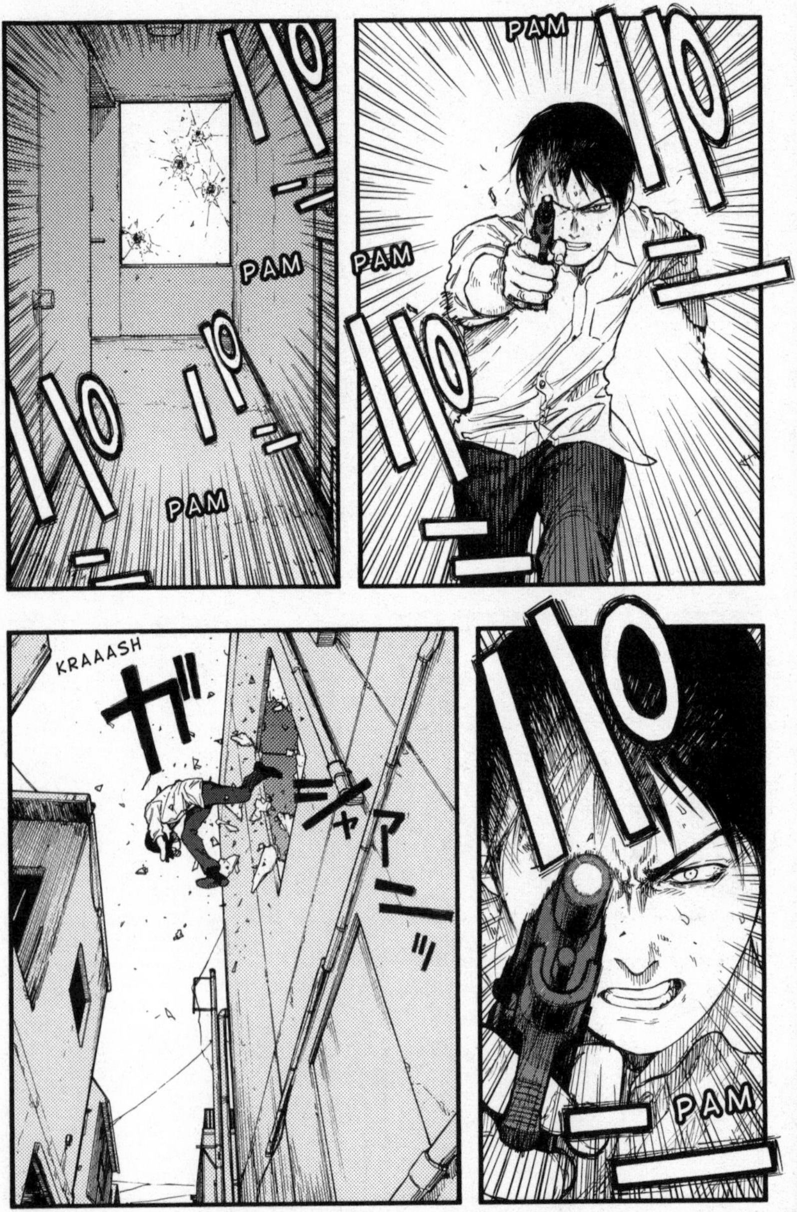
PAM
PAM
PAM
PAM
PAM
KRAAASH
ガシャアーンッ

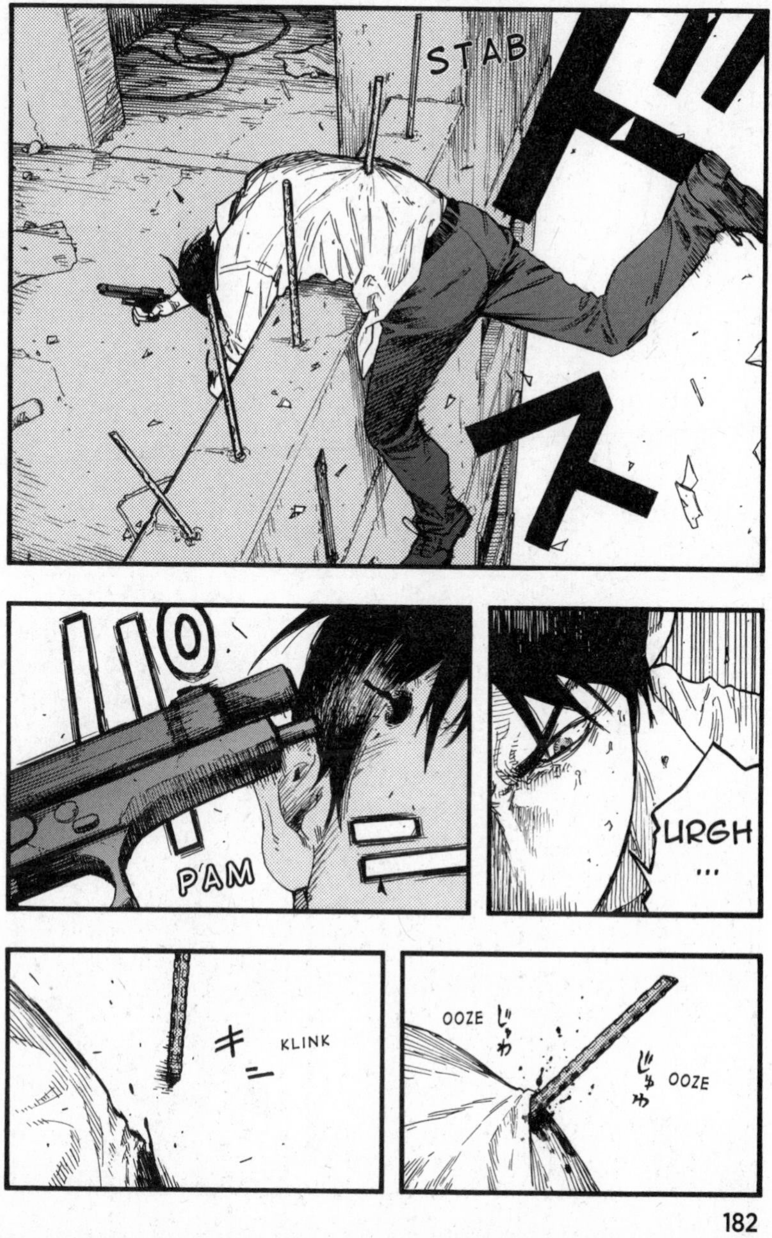
STAB
URGH
...
PAM
OOZE
OOZE
KLINK

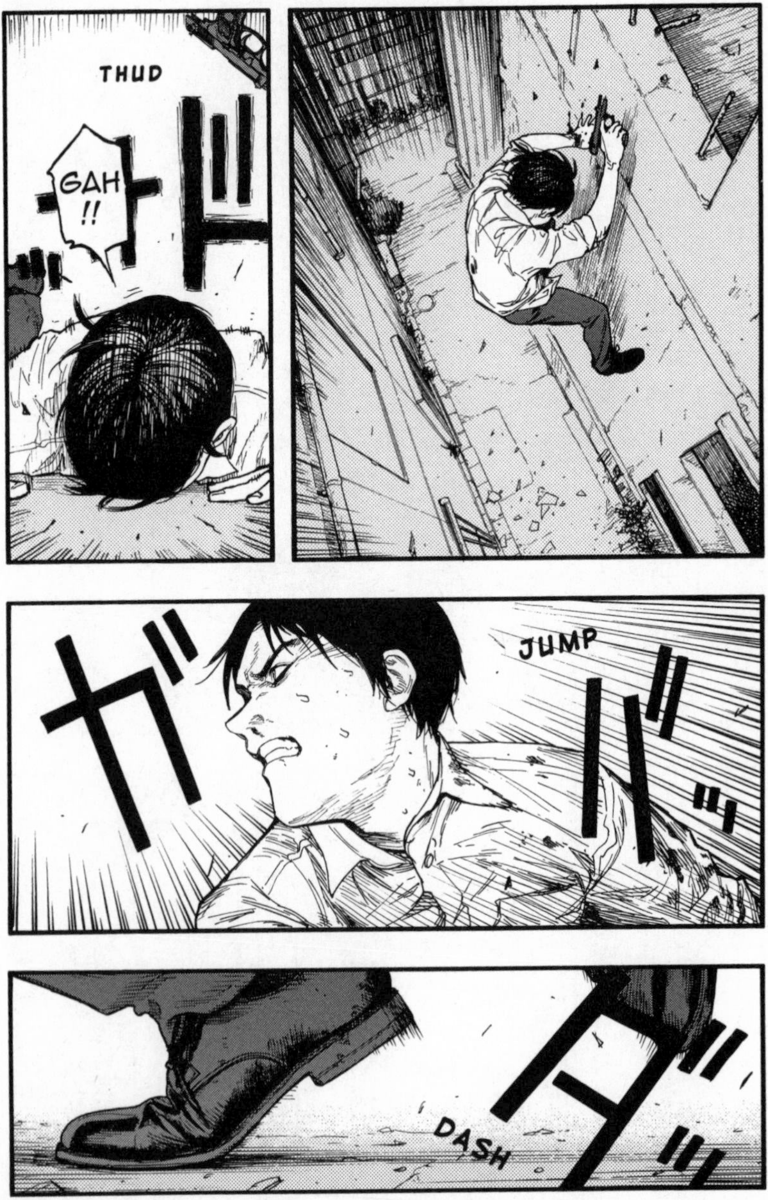
THUD
GAH!!
JUMP
DASH

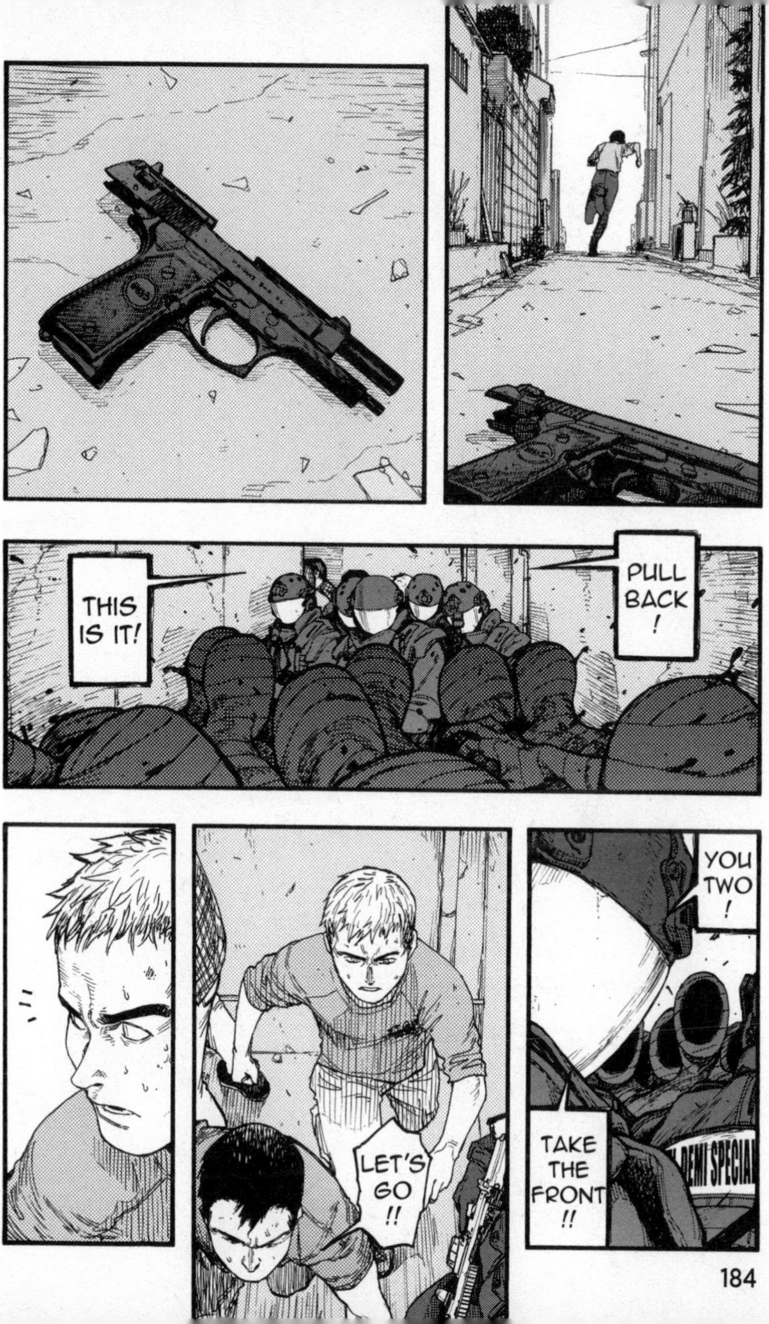
PULL BACK!
THIS IS IT!
YOU TWO!
TAKE THE FRONT!!
LET'S GO!!

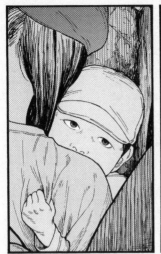
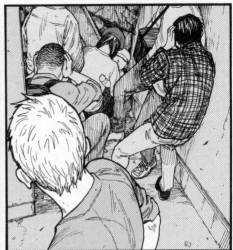
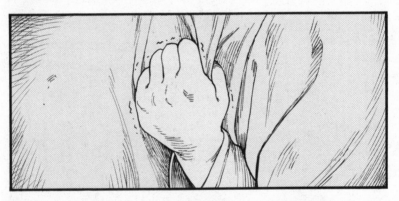
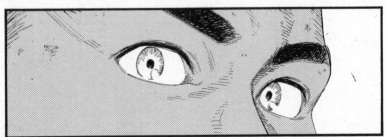

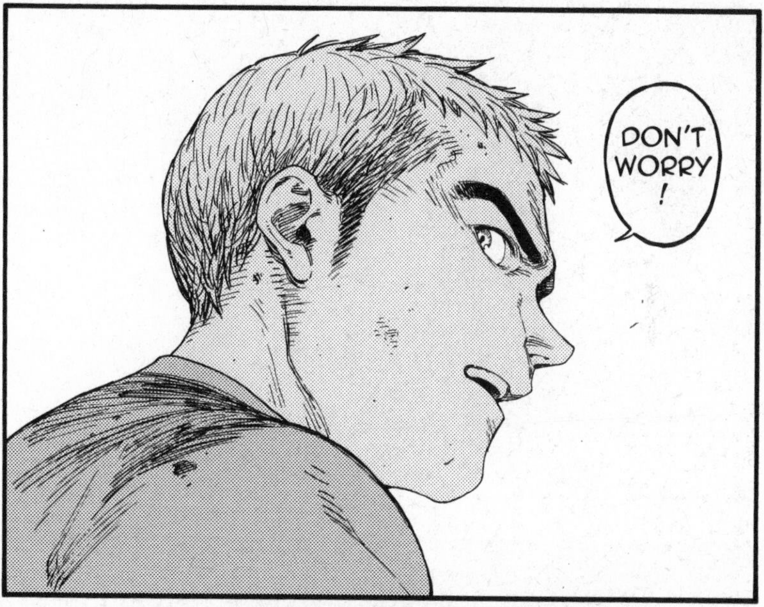
DON'T WORRY!

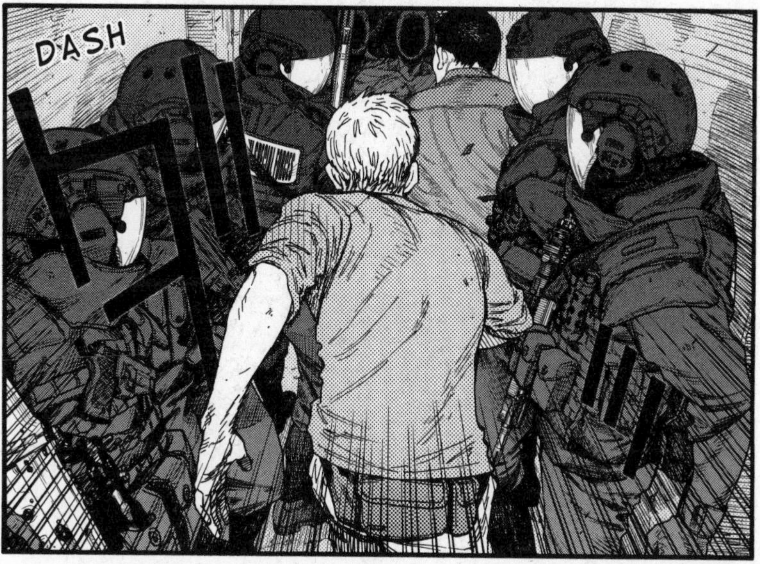
DASH

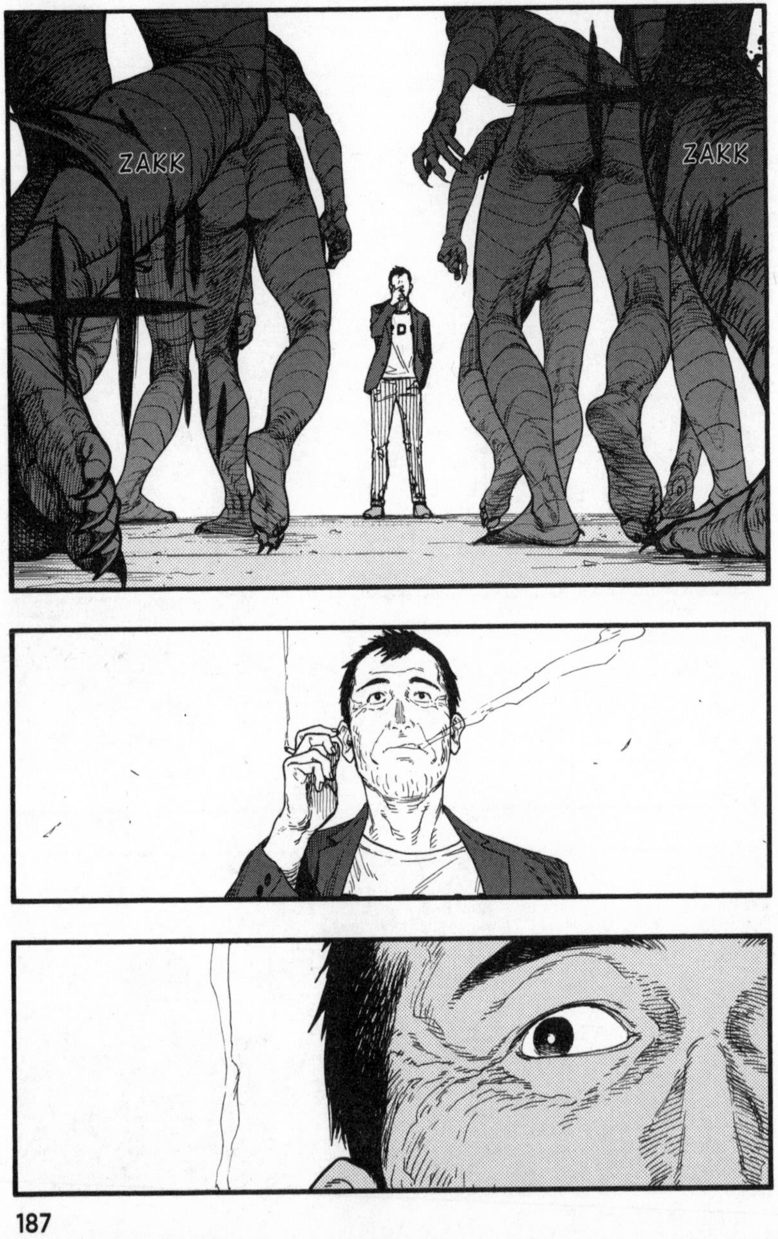
ZAKK
ZAKK

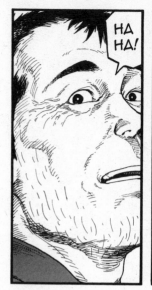

HA
HA!

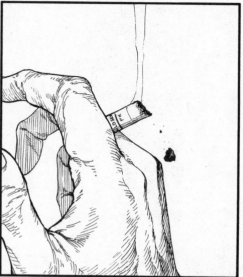

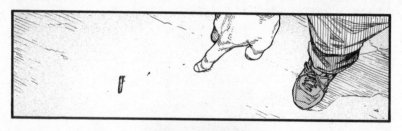

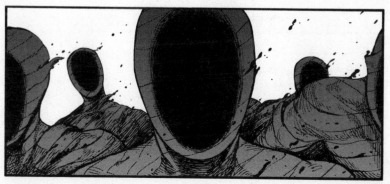

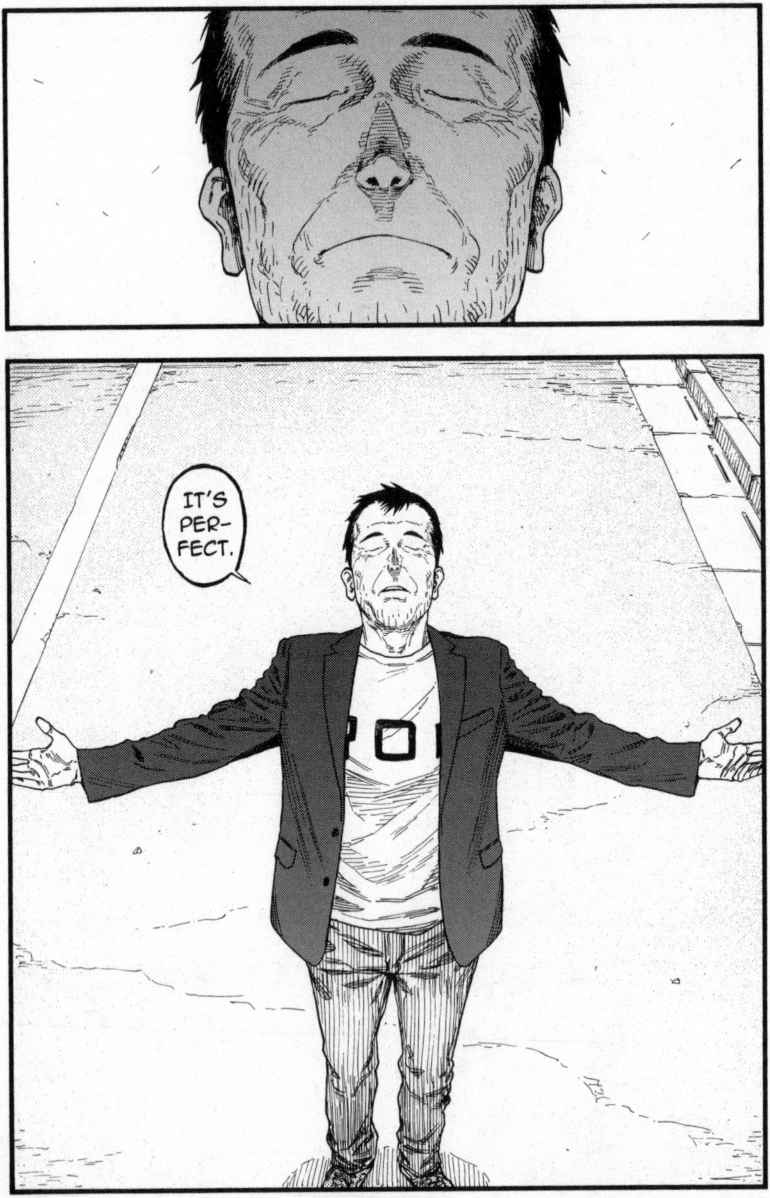
IT'S PER-FECT.

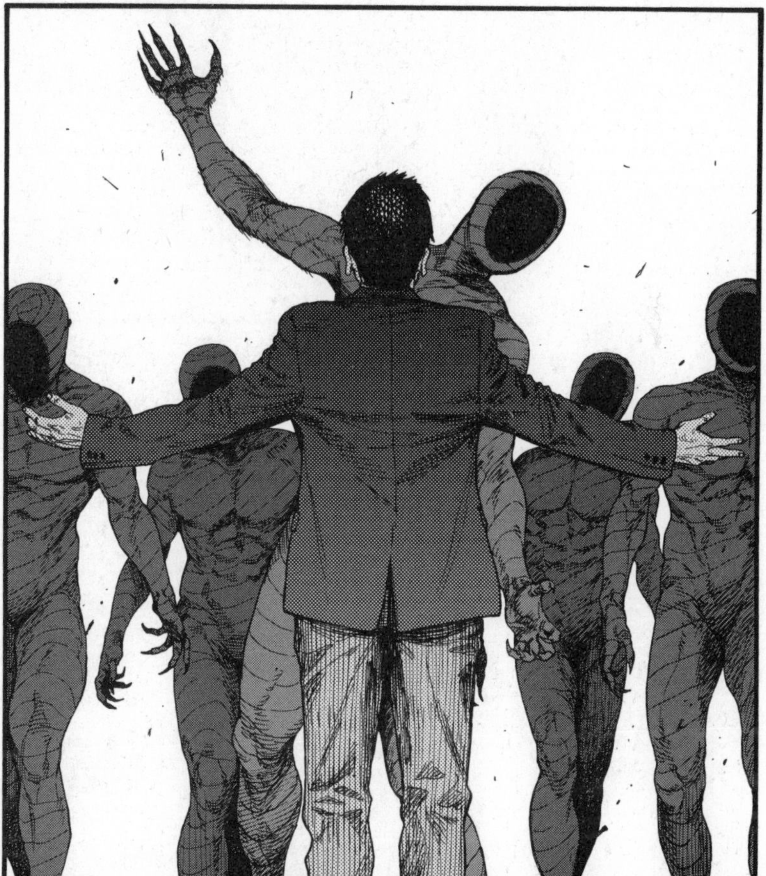

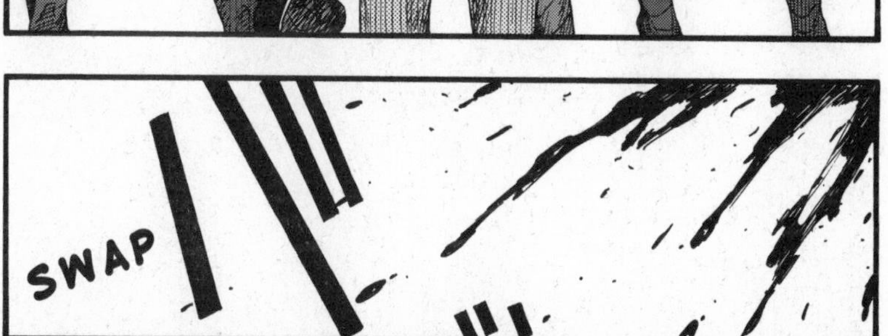
SWAP

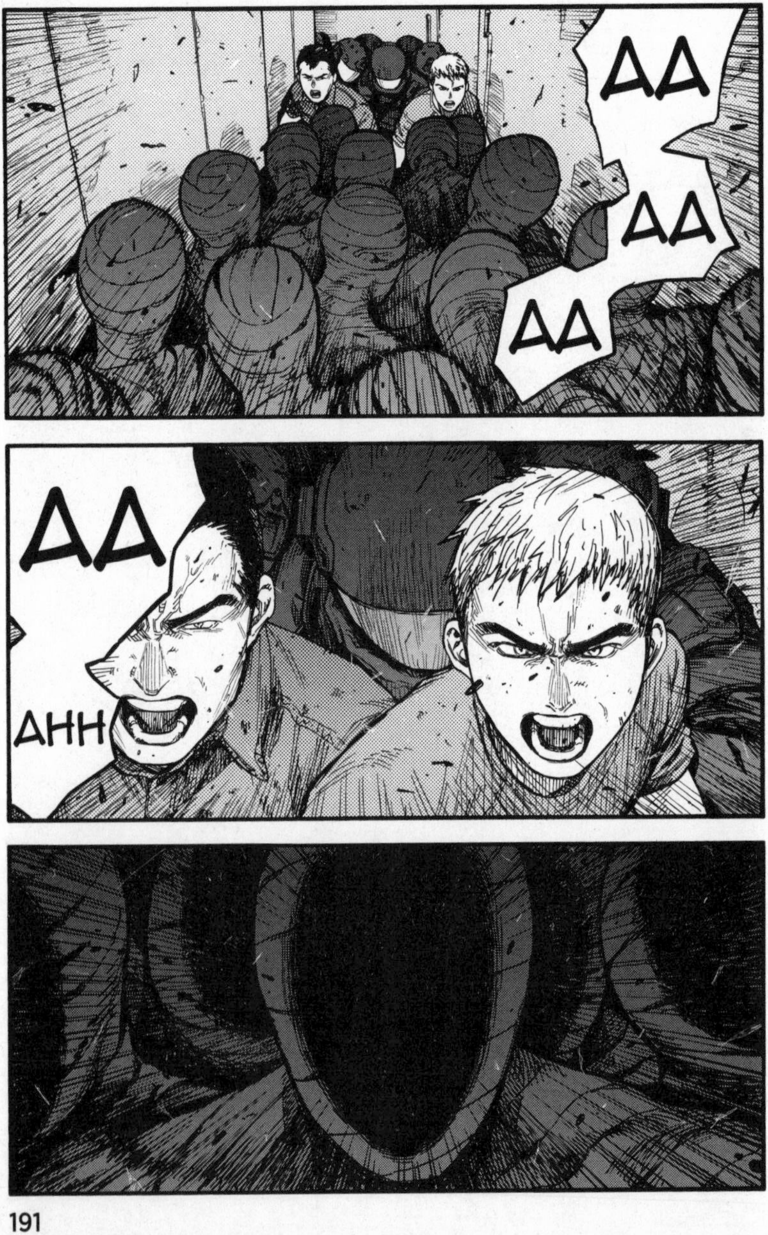
AA
AA
AA
AA
AHH

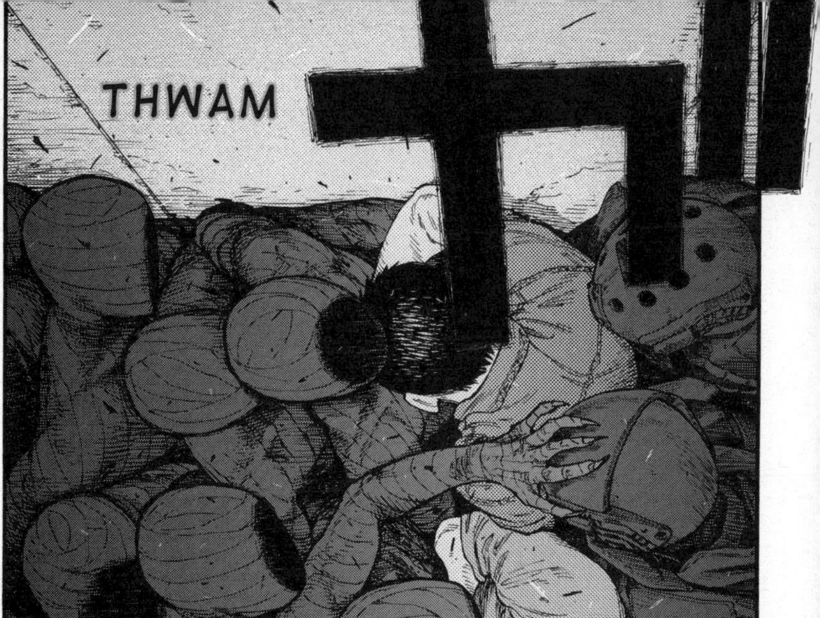
THWAM

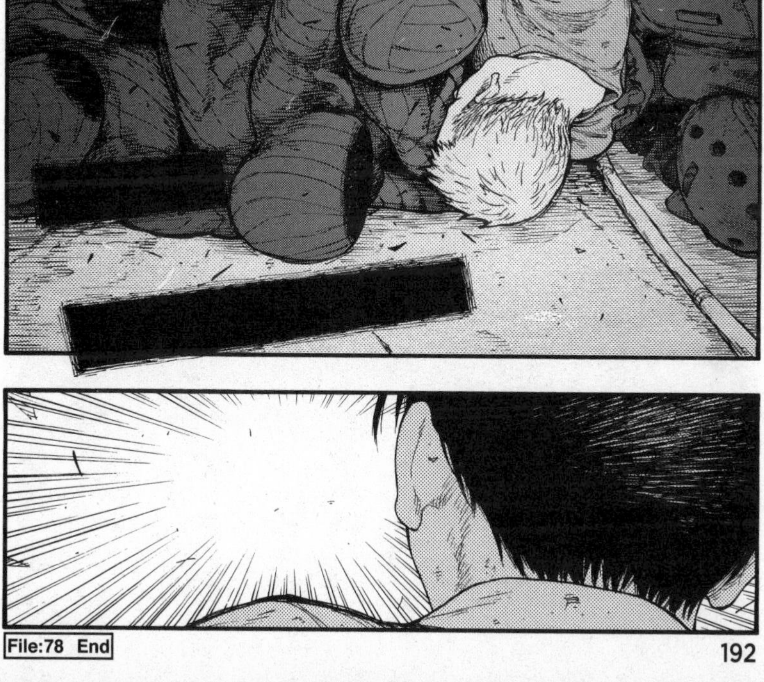

File:78 End

COMIC: GAMON SAKURAI

ASSISTANTS: CROUTON SANCHI (almost all tone range masking)

SAWANOSHOW (Line drawings

[Volume 16: throughout: Anti-Demi logo: 90%] [File 74: p. 6-7, panel 1: background: 75%] [File 74: p. 9, panel 3: guns: 92%] [File 74: p. 10, panel 1: cell: 90%]
[File 74: p. 10, panel 4: background: 75%] [File 74: p. 11, panel 4: background: 56%] [File 74: p. 11, panels 2, 3: car: 95%] [File 74: p. 16, panel 1: cars: 95%]
[File 74: p. 19, panels 1, 4: cars: 90%] [File 74: p. 20, panels 1, 2, 3: cars: 99%] [File 74: p. 23, panels 1, 2: cars: 95%] [File 74: p. 23, panel 2: background, extras, and announcer: 70%]
[File 74: p. 24, panels 2, 3: announcer: 90%] [File 74: p. 30, panels 1, 2: SCAR: 90%] [File 74: p. 33, panel 3: car: 95%] [File 74: p. 34, panel 3: car: 97%] [File 74: p. 35, panel 1: car: 99%]
[File 74: p. 36, panel 3: panel contents: 96%] [File 37: p. 37, panel 1: foot: 90%] [File 74: p. 37, panel 2: background: 96%] [File 74: p. 38, panels 1, 2, 3: background: 95%]
[File 74: p. 39, panel 2: background 96%] [File 74: p. 40, panel 3: car: 95%]

[File 75: p. 46, panels 2, 3, 4: car: 90%] [File 75: p. 49, panels 1, 2: car: 95%] [File 75: p. 50, panel 4: car: 99%] [File 75: p. 51, panels 1, 3, 5: car: 90%] [File 75: p. 54, panel 4: SCAR: 90%]
[File 75: p. 56, panels 1, 3, 4: SCARs: 90%] [File 75: p. 57, panels 1, 3, 6: car: 95%] [File 75: p. 58, panel 3: car: 98%] [File 75: p. 59, panels 5, 6: car: 97%] [File 75: p. 60, panel 2: car: 95%]
[File 75: p. 61, panels 1, 2, 3, 4, 5, 6: car: 90%] [File 75: p. 62, panels 1, 3: car: 90%] [File 75: p. 66, panels 2, 4, 5: car: 95%] [File 75: p. 67, panel 1: car: 99%]
[File 75: p. 68, panels 2, 4, 5: car: 85%] [File 75: p. 69, panels 3, 4: car: 92%] [File 75: p. 70, panel 2: periodic table: 99%]

[File 76: throughout: logo on Manabe's bag: 99%] [File 76: p. 93, panel 2: helicopter: 99%] [File 76: p. 94, panel 1: helicopter and background: 75%]
[File 76: p. 95, panels 1, 4: magazines and gun: 80%] [File 76: p. 96, panel 4: grenade: 82%] [File 76: p. 98, panel 1: car: 90%] [File 76: p. 101, panel 1: helicopter: 80%]
[File 76: p. 105, panel 2: background: 70%] [File 76: p. 105, panel 3: helicopter: 95%] [File 76: p. 108, panel 4: background: 90%] [File 76: p. 109, panel 1: background 90%]
[File 76: p. 109, panel 4: panel contents: 65%] [File 76: p. 110-111, panel 1: background and pistol: 85%] [File 76: p. 110-111, panel 2: rifle: 90%]
[File 76: p. 110-111, panel 3: helicopter: 90%] [File 76: p. 112, panel 2: background: 75%] [File 76: p. 114, panels 1, 2: guns: 89%] [File 76: p. 115, panel 2: motorcycle and rider: 70%]
[File 76: p. 116, panel 1: helicopter: 77%] [File 76: p. 116, panel 2: background: 95%] [File 76: p. 117, panel 3: helicopter: 95%]

[File 77: throughout: motorcycle: 90%] [File 77: p. 128, panel 1: gun and hand: 60%] [File 77: p. 129, panels 1, 2, 4: motorcyclist, car: 85%] [File 77: p. 130, panels 1, 5: cars: 82%]
[File 77: p. 131, panel 1: car: 35%] [File 77: p. 133, panel 4: car: 60%] [File 77: p. 134, panel 1: hand, cigarette, ashtray: 30%] [File 77: p. 135, panels 1, 2, 3, 5: car: 78%]
[File 77: p. 137, panels 3, 4: car: 88%] [File 77: p. 141, panel3: gun and hand: 90%] [File 77: p. 146, panel 1: gun and hands: 68%] [File 77: p. 147, panel 1: gun: 90%]
[File 77: p. 148, panel 1: hand and cigarette pack: 62%] [File 77: p. 150, panel 2: car: 90%] [File 77: p. 151, panel 1: gun: 99%] [File 78: throughout: motorcycle: 71%]

[File 78: p. 166, panel 3: background: 97%] [File 78: p. 167, panel 4, 5: background: 84%] [File 78: p. 172, panel 3: gun: 90%] [File 78: p. 180, panel 3: hand and gun: 70%]
[File 78: p. 183, panel 4: feet: 85%] [File 78: p. 184, panels 1, 2: gun: 90%] [File 78: p. 186, panel 2: SCAR and MP5: 97%])

KIMIYUKI MASAKI (Line drawings

[File 74: p. 5, panel 1: panel contents: 94%] [File 74: p. 6-7, panel 5: background: 96%] [File 74: p. 8, panel 1: panel contents: 97%] [File 74: p. 21, panels 1, 2: background: 95%]
[File 74: p. 23, panel 2: cameraman: 99%] [File 74: p. 23, panel 3: car: 90%] [File 74: p. 24, panels 1, 4: car: 96%]

[File 75: p. 50, panel 3: car: 90%] [File 75: p. 58, panels 2, 5: car, Ogura's hand and cigarettes: 83%] [File 75: p. 59, panel 3: panel contents: 95%]

[File 76: p. 98, panel 6: car and driver: 99%] [File 76: p. 99, panel 3: car: 90%] [File 76: p. 105, panel 3: background: 88%] [File 76: p. 109, panel 1: gun: 90%]
[File 76: p. 109, panels 2, 3: panel contents: 99%]

[File 77: p. 123, panel 4: truck: 93%] [File 77: p. 130, panel 4: Toyota Roomy: 98%] [File 77: p. 132, panels 3, 4: panel contents: 98%]

[File 78: p. 159, panel 2: background: 90%] [File 78: p. 160, panels 1, 3, 4, 6: panel contents: 95%] [File 78: p. 168, panels 3, 4: background: 100%] [File 78: p. 172, panel 4: gun: 90%]
[File 78: p. 183, panel 2: gun: 99%])

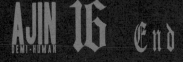

AJIN 16 End
DEMI-HUMAN

Ajin: Demi-Human, volume 16

Editor: Daniel Joseph
Translation: Ko Ransom
Production: Risa Cho
Lorina Mapa
Hiroko Mizuno

First published in Japan in 2020 by Kodansha, Ltd., Tokyo
Publication for this English edition arranged through Kodansha, Ltd., Tokyo

Published by Vertical, an imprint of Kodansha USA Publishing, LLC

Originally published in Japanese as *Ajin 16* by Kodansha, Ltd.
Ajin first serialized in *good! Afternoon*, Kodansha, Ltd., 2012-

This is a work of fiction.

ISBN: 978-1-949980-65-3

Manufactured in the United States of America

First Edition

Kodansha USA Publishing, LLC
451 Park Avenue South
7th Floor
New York, NY 10016
www.readvertical.com

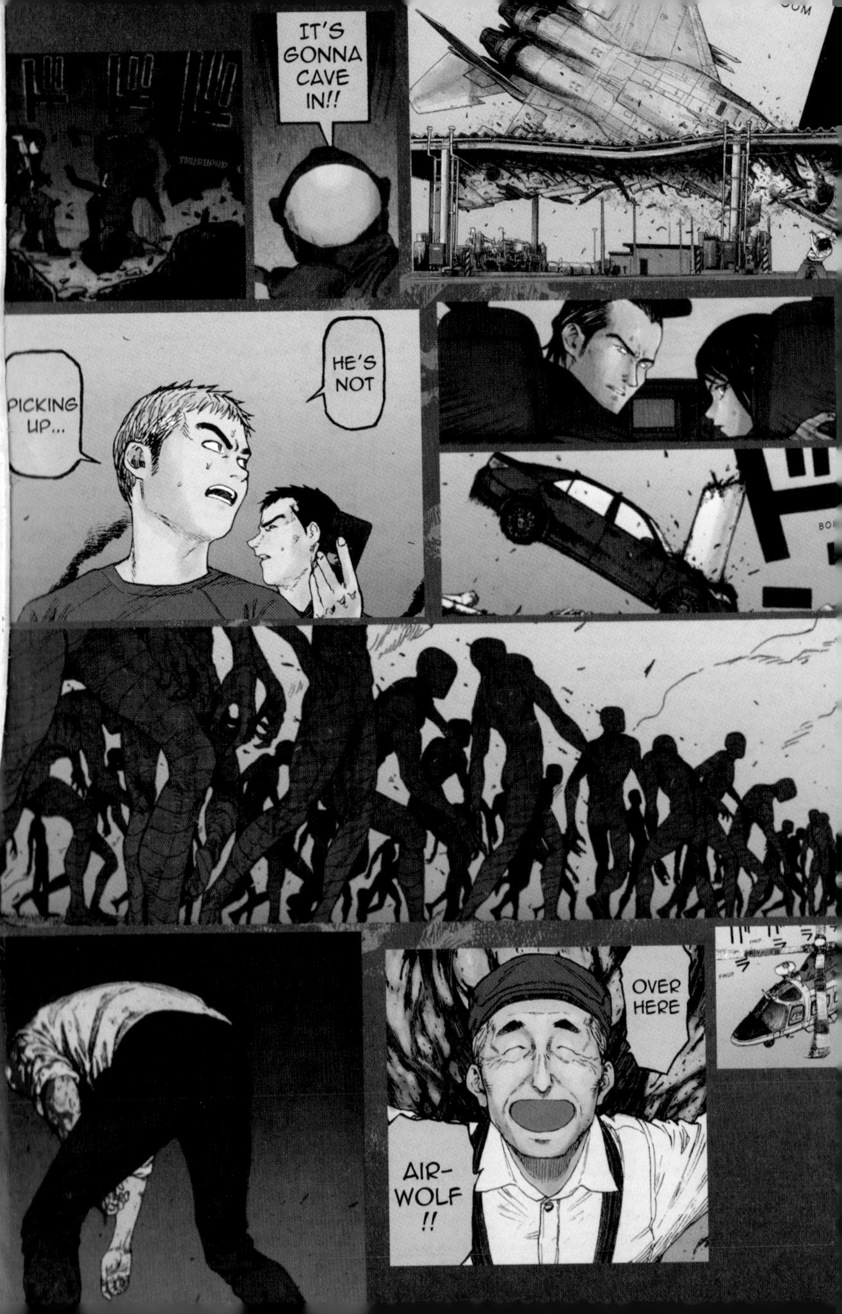
IT'S GONNA CAVE IN!!
HE'S NOT
PICKING UP...
FWUP
FWUP
OVER HERE
AIR-WOLF !!

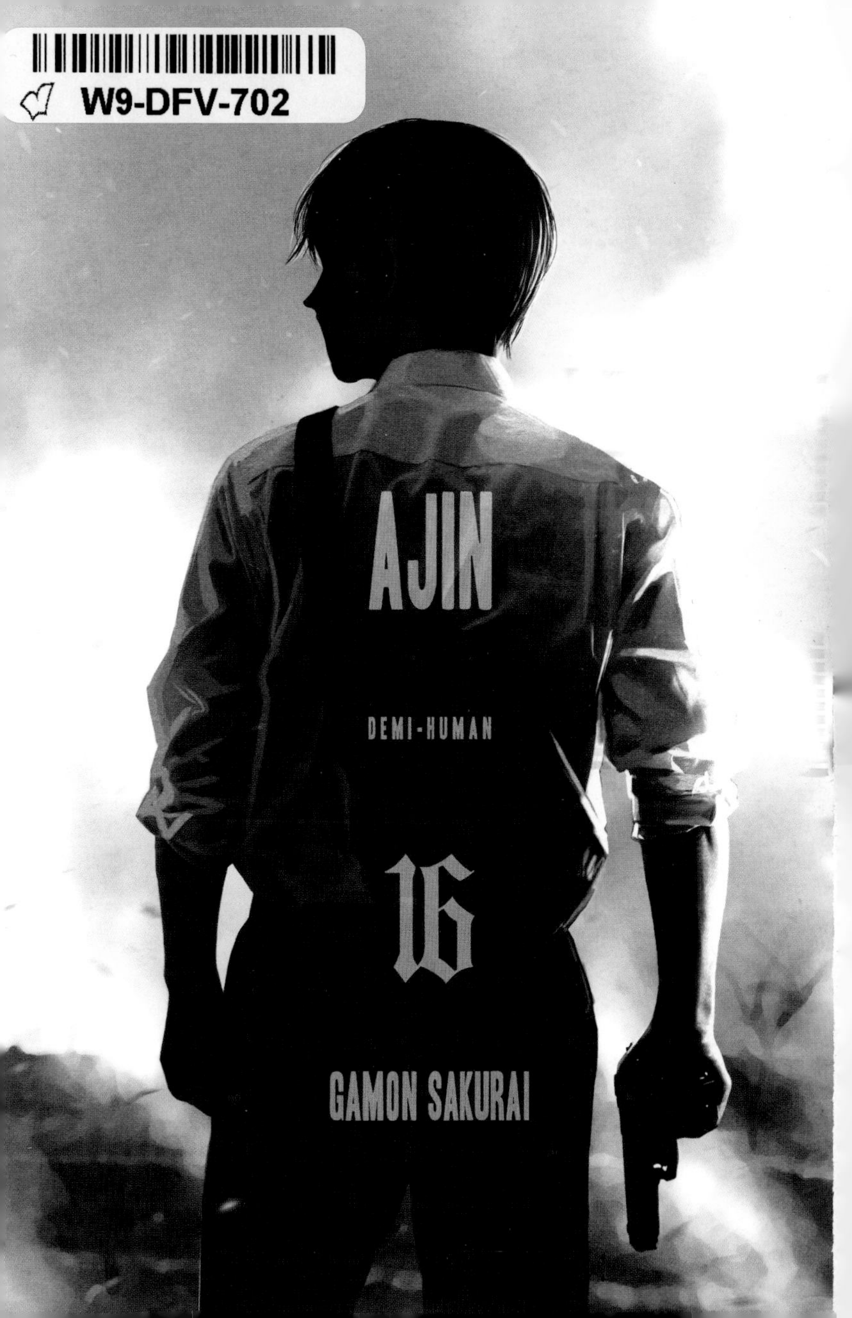
AJIN
DEMI-HUMAN
16
GAMON SAKURAI